JEFFERSONIAN AMERICA

Problems in American History

Series editor: Jack P. Greene

Each volume focuses on a central theme in American history and provides greater analytical depth and historiographic coverage than standard textbook discussions normally allow. The intent of the series is to present in highly interpretive texts the unresolved questions of American history that are central to current debates and concerns. The texts will be concise enough to be supplemented with primary readings or core textbooks and are intended to provide brief syntheses of large subjects.

In preparation

JEFFERSONIAN AMERICA

Peter S. Onuf and Leonard J. Sadosky

BLACKWELL
Publishers

Copyright © Peter S. Onuf and Leonard J. Sadosky 2002

The right of Peter S. Onuf and Leonard J. Sadosky to be identified as authors of this work has been asserted in accordance with the Copyright, Design and Patents Act 1988.

First published 2002

2 4 6 8 10 9 7 5 3 1

Blackwell Publishers Inc.
350 Main Street
Malden, Massachusetts 02148
USA

Blackwell Publishers Ltd
108 Cowley Road
Oxford OX4 1JF
UK

Library of Congress Cataloging-in-Publication Data has been applied for.

ISBN 1–55786–922–7 (hardback); 1–55786–923–5 (paperback)

British Library Cataloguing in Publication Data

A CIP catalogue record for this book is available from the British Library.

Typeset in 11 on 13 pt Sabon
by Ace Filmsetting Ltd, Frome, Somerset
Printed in Great Britain by T.J. International, Padstow, Cornwall

This book is printed on acid-free paper.

Dedicated to our
friends and colleagues
in the
Early American History Seminar
at the
University of Virginia

Contents

Acknowledgments

We are grateful to Brian Schoen for a meticulous reading of the entire manuscript. James E. Lewis, Jr., provided helpful comments on chapter 4.

Peter Onuf is primarily responsible for chapters 1 and 2, while Leonard Sadosky took the lead with chapter 4; the introduction and chapter 3 were collaborative efforts.

The maps accompanying the text were drawn by Leonard Sadosky using ArcView GIS version 3.2. The assistance of the staff of the University of Virginia Library's Geospatial and Statistical Data Center is greatly appreciated.

Onuf drafted his chapters while on sabbatical in Costa Rica. I am grateful to our good friends there, Daniel and Alejandra Masis, for their warm hospitality. As always, Kristin was a wonderful companion; while I was writing she produced some superb art. My indebtedness to Jan Lewis, another collaborator, will be apparent throughout the book, particularly in chapter 2. I have also learned much from past and current students, to whom Leonard and I dedicate this book, with gratitude.

Sadosky has to thank many in the University of Virginia community. Foremost among them is Peter – my advisor, mentor, and now collaborator – for inviting me to join him in this project, and then, as always, giving me the freedom to find my voice within it. Thanks also to Edward Ayers, Richard Drayton, Stephen Innes, Joseph Kett, Maurie McInnis, H. C. Erik Midelfort, Sophie Rosenfeld, John C. A. Stagg, Olivier Zunz, as well as Andrew R. L. Cayton, my advisor at Miami University. Special thanks go to the staff of the Papers of James Madison, especially David Mattern, for pointing me in the right direction during research for this book.

Many friends proved most supportive during this manuscript's gestation, especially Carl Bon Tempo, Kristin Celello, Jennifer Creger, Kristina Howard, Ann Marie Macdonald, Johann Neem, Kate Neem Destler, Ann Paggioli, Brian Schoen, David Young, and the dearly missed Hedda Lautenschlager. Thanks to my family, especially my grandparents, Samuel J. and Genevieve Robb, Marie Therese Duchaine, and the late Leonard J. Sadosky, Sr., as well as my sister Jennifer E. Sadosky, my niece Shaylee Sadosky, my father, Leonard J. Sadosky, Jr., and my mother, Jo-Ann Robb Sadosky.

Charlottesville,
August 2000

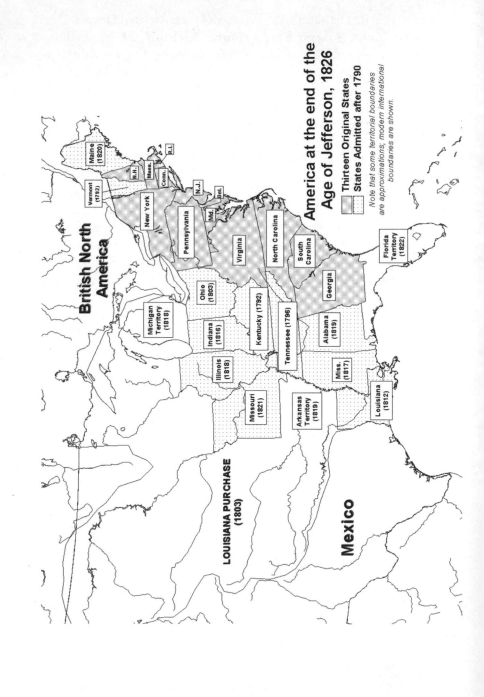

America at the end of the Age of Jefferson, 1826

Thirteen Original States
States Admitted after 1790

Note that some territorial boundaries are approximations; modern international boundaries are shown.

British North America

Maine (1820)
Vermont (1792)
N.H.
Mass.
R.I.
Conn.
New York
N.J.
Pennsylvania
Md.
Del.
Virginia
North Carolina
South Carolina
Georgia

Michigan Territory (1818)
Ohio (1803)
Indiana (1816)
Illinois (1818)
Kentucky (1792)
Tennessee (1796)
Alabama (1819)
Miss. (1817)
Louisiana (1812)
Missouri (1821)
Arkansas Territory (1819)

Florida Territory (1822)

LOUISIANA PURCHASE (1803)

Mexico

Introduction

"If our country, when pressed with wrongs at the point of the bayonet, had been governed by it's heads instead of it's hearts, where should we have been now?"

         Thomas Jefferson to Maria Cosway, 12 October 1786.[1]

Throughout the course of his public life, Thomas Jefferson endeavored to articulate a vision of a republican America. Jefferson's vision was shaped both by his "head," enlightened reason, and his "heart," a sensitive and earnest sensibility. It was a vision he expressed in his copious writings and sought to make real through his statecraft. The creation of a perfect republic, a community whose politics, economy, and social life were governed, within and without, solely by republican principles, was the central project of Jefferson's life. This project proved to be an enormous challenge; to accomplish it, Jefferson enlisted many allies and made more than a few enemies. The story of Jefferson's struggles – from his first efforts to discover and articulate how a republic worked to his attempts to remake his native Virginia, and then the entire American union, in this republican image – illuminates the history of the crucial first fifty years of the United States of America. Our goal in this book is thus to show that "America" in this period is in some meaningful sense "Jeffersonian." We recognize, of course, that this history can be characterized in many other ways and that Jefferson himself is only one of many actors in a complicated narrative. But for contemporaries, and for subsequent generations as well, Jefferson's impact on his times, for better or worse, was definitive: this was the "Age of Jefferson."

Jefferson's vision of republican America and its prospects

has always been controversial. Historians argue endlessly both about what they think he believed and about the continuing relevance of his ideals. What exactly did Jefferson have to say – and to say to us – about the proper role of government, the organization of society and economy, gender and race relations? There have been as many answers to these questions as there have been writers on them. This contention has many sources. The vast corpus of Jefferson's writings form a treasure, to be sure, but his complex and often contradictory stands on so many issues defeat straightforward interpretations. The interpretative challenge is further complicated by the enormous knowledge which historians have gathered in recent decades about the period's social, cultural and economic history, the history of politics beyond Washington and Monticello, as well as the histories of groups that had been traditionally considered peripheral: women, African Americans, and American Indians. As historians have learned more about the world in which Thomas Jefferson lived, the man himself becomes harder to understand, and his status as an iconic figure harder to sustain. To the modern mind, Jefferson's rhetoric seems utterly disconnected from the reality of Jeffersonian America. For many scholars, the disconnection between "Jefferson" and "America" has either turned the benevolent author of the Declaration of Independence into a locus of evil or simply made him an irrelevant figure.

Yet, even in the harsh light of modern criticism, Jefferson remains a compelling figure. The republican vision that Jefferson and his collaborators formulated addressed the broad range of concerns that animate his modern critics, though his prescriptions often seem anachronistic or morally abhorrent. Why then is it useful to reconstruct and reconsider Jefferson's republican vision? When we reexamine Jeffersonian republicanism in the light of our new understanding of the period's history, an extraordinarily textured account of the intersection of political thought and lived reality emerges. Jefferson's vision was much more than a blueprint for organizing government or mobilizing a political opposition. It was, at bottom, a vision for the reordering of the world in order to make men free. In exploring the basic elements as well as the nuances of Jeffersonian thought, we can take a fresh look at the distinctive but interdependent histories of different groups of Americans – both those who benefited and those who were victimized, marginalized, or displaced under the new republican dispensation.

Our overarching argument is that republicanism, as Jeffersonians conceived and elaborated it, constituted a coherent vision of the future of America and the world. It offered a prescription for creating republican polities that would reorder the American union and the world beyond it for the betterment of all mankind. The republican order began with the organization of the family, the building block of republican society, and extended through local and state governments to the new nation's diplomatic interaction with foreign powers. It was a bold and dynamic vision, born in the heat of battles over the American future. Agriculture, commerce, family life, cultural relations, and of course politics, were all to be recast by the emerging Jeffersonian worldview. Yet, as the Jeffersonians sought to reorder American life in accordance with their ideals, the real world resisted. The making of America in the Age of Jefferson was never a neat process of the scientific application of republican principles to American society, of turning human beings into automatons, or what Benjamin Rush called "republican machines."[2] Jeffersonian America was ultimately the product of hundreds of thousands of ordinary men and women pursuing happiness in their own ways as Jefferson and other political leaders struggled to understand and impose order on – or discover order in – these myriad pursuits. This process of interaction and contestation was the crucible in which Jeffersonian Republicanism took form.

Jeffersonian America is a set of interpretative essays that explore selected themes in the history of the early republic. Our goal is to introduce some of the main areas of recent and ongoing research that have transformed our understanding of this formative period in American history: the relevant historiography is cited and discussed in a bibliographical essay at the end of the volume. Though our debts to fellow historians will certainly be apparent, our effort to reconstruct and contextualize the Jeffersonian vision sometimes leads us beyond conventional interpretations. Jeffersonian republicanism meant many different things to different groups and individuals; at the same time, we suggest, Jefferson's contemporaries grasped underlying symmetries and connections between domains of experience that often elude historians. Our essays thus juxtapose and combine apparently discrete topics of inquiry: family structure and the structure of local government; political economy and race; federalism and diplomacy. We invite readers to join us in trying to make sense of the early history of the new American nation, of a self-proclaimed, self-constituted "people" we will find both strangely different and somehow familiar.

The Age of Jefferson was not Jefferson's work alone. Jefferson himself modestly disclaimed responsibility for his greatest achievement, the Declaration of Independence. "Neither aiming at originality of principle or sentiment, nor yet copied from any particular and previous writing," he told a correspondent near the end of his life, the Declaration "was intended to be an expression of the American mind, and to give to that expression the proper tone and spirit called for by the occasion."[3] The modesty of this statement should not be exaggerated: its remarkable premise is that there *was* an "American mind" and that Jefferson was capable of both expressing that mind and giving it "tone." But Jefferson could have done nothing without devoted political "friends," most notably his lifelong collaborator James Madison, and receptive audiences. Moreover, it was the sustained struggle against sinister foes – British counter-revolutionaries and Tory fellow-travelers, "merciless savages" and insurgent slaves, and, most insidiously, Anglophiliac Federalists who supposedly plotted the establishment of an aristocratic, even monarchical, regime on the ruins of republicanism – that gave Jeffersonian republicanism its sometimes hysterical tone and its widespread popular appeal. There was no authoritative or comprehensive "Republican

Manifesto." The Republican vision was instead elaborated in state papers, such as Jefferson's First Inaugural Address, or in more sustained works of natural philosophy and political science such as his *Notes on the State of Virginia*, Madison's *Federalist* essays, and John Taylor's many pamphlets and books, or in the partisan effusions of myriad polemicists. The Republican vision also informed all these men's personal correspondence, as well as their actions. In thought and in deed, Republicans embraced a shared worldview, perhaps not coherent enough to be called an "ideology" and certainly too broad to be seen simply as a political program. The system of ideas that motivated Jeffersonians both served as the lens through which they saw the world and provided the tools with which, for better or worse, they reshaped it.

The most important tenets of Jeffersonian republicanism were articulated and developed in the years between the Philadelphia convention and the election of 1800, when the Republicans did not hold the reins of national political power. As Republican oppositionists sought to build a national coalition against the Federalist administrations of George Washington and John Adams, prominent leaders from other states and regions joined the Virginians in promoting and defining the Republican cause. Our first chapter describes the story of this process: how the Jeffersonians emerged as the opposition to the Federalists, how Republicanism came to power in Virginia, the South, the West, and became a contender for political power in the Northeast, and how these regionally diverse Republican movements both differed and worked in concert with one another. Republicanism took shape within a political realm defined by intense partisan conflict, as states engaged in the acrimonious task of constitution-making, debated the structure of the American union, and struggled to adapt to, and counter, the centralizing initiatives of the Federalist presidential administrations.

The Republicans' rise to national power was made possible by the mobilization of political factions in the various states. The party's diverse constituencies and agendas – and the virtual absence of anything we might now recognize as party organization – stand in sharp contrast to the homogeneity and the shared principles and interests that Jefferson imputed to the American people in his Inaugural Address. In our second chapter, we explore the broad appeal of the Jeffersonian Republican vision for so many Americans, notwithstanding their diverse origins and contentious histories. The anti-partisan Jefferson did not understand his party's success *as a party* and thus could overlook its heterogeneity – indeed, he preferred to think that "the republicans are the *nation*" and not a party at all.[4] Jefferson's followers were happy to hear that they were a "people" with an important role to play in world history, that their revolutionary opposition to the despotic authority of a corrupt British ministry – or of its Federalist successors – made them the benefactors of mankind, and that their respective "pursuits of happiness" would bring them ever closer together in an affectionate union of harmonious interests. The Jeffersonian conception of unity in diversity, of a new republican empire without a powerful metropolis or an aristocratic ruling class, valorized what Alexis de Tocqueville later called "individualism." The triumph of Republicanism thus offered Americans a flattering image of themselves, a national identity to counter the sense of inferiority so prevalent among provincial Anglo-Americans before independence – and since.

The family was central to the political discourse of the Age of Jefferson. We suggest that Republicanism resonated most profoundly with American fathers and their sons – future fathers – as they sought both to make their households into autonomous "little republics" and to participate freely and consensually in the business of the world. The fantasy of household independence was crucial to the conceptions of minimal government so eloquently articulated by Jefferson and his Republican colleagues. Republican politics presupposed a natural social order, with the family as its basic building block. Where citizens governed themselves, government by a privileged ruling class was banished: all men were "created equal"; at the same time, these republican patriarchs could now see themselves exercising unfettered dominion in their own households, free from the interference of any ostensibly superior authority. Republicanism thus expressed widely shared social aspirations of a growing class of newly politicized white men. The Republican appeal was powerful precisely because its horizons were so modest, apparently within the reach of so many Americans.

Yet early national households were never truly independent or self-sufficient. In chapter 3 we examine ways in which Americans – even, perhaps especially, anti-statist, strict constructionist Jeffersonians – called on government to facilitate their various pursuits of happiness. The involvement of government at every level, in encouraging foreign and domestic trade, in improving transportation facilities, and in promoting economic development generally is a familiar theme in the literature on the "commonwealth" era. The role of the state looms even larger when we focus on the acquisition of Indian land through war and diplomacy, or on the institution of racial slavery, the foundation of prosperity in the most dynamic sector of the national economy, the staple-producing plantations of the south and west. The myth of the spontaneous, irresistible expansion of westward settlement, or what a later generation would call "manifest destiny," obscured the importance of state-sponsored violence in displacing Indians from their ancestral lands; in similar fashion, the maintenance of racial order in plantation society would have been impossible without the pervasive exercise of coercive power by American governments. Not surprisingly, when slaveowners sought to justify slavery, they identified their peculiar, "domestic" institution with family values, insisting that racial hierarchy was grounded in "nature," not in force and fear.

The contrast between myths of self-sufficiency, spontaneous union, and a natural harmony of interest – in which the state disappeared from view (if it did not wither away altogether) – and the routine recurrence to government to facilitate the myriad pursuits of enterprising Americans illuminates the central theme of this book. The genius of Republicanism, its widening appeal to a newly self-conscious American "people," was in its extraordinary ability to reconcile apparent opposites, to resolve the dialectic between liberty and power that defined the political world of the founding generation.

The dialectic was most conspicuous in the new nation's relations with the larger world, for the very existence of an independent nation depended on the massive exercise of force. Republicans might be able to overlook the manifold uses of state power in their everyday lives – like the economists' marketplace, the rule of law was so ubiquitous and diffuse as to seem almost "natural" – but they could not ignore governments that taxed their property and sent their young men into battle. The history of the early American republic was marked by periodic warfare and the chronic threat of war. During the entire revolutionary period, from the first shots at Lexington and Concord in 1775 to the end of the War of 1812, the United States found themselves in the anarchic conditions that theorists described as a "state of nature." Revolutionaries knew that self-preservation – securing their independence against hostile powers – was the first law of American politics as it was the first law of nature. The juxtaposition of republican dreams of peace, prosperity, and the progress of civilization with the harsh realities of a world that was, with few intervals, constantly at war frames our concluding chapter. The hopes of Jeffersonians for their union, a model world order of peaceful republican states, are themselves the most eloquent testimony to inescapable, omnipresent conflict and war in the Age of Democratic Revolution. The collapse of the European balance of power during the French Revolutionary and Napoleonic wars seemed to underscore the distinctiveness of America's multilayered federal system. But the union itself was constantly at risk, both from internal stresses and external threats. And Jeffersonians did not hesitate to make war, the ultimate exercise of state power, to preserve the union, even at the expense of constitutional principles. As they did so, Federalist and dissident Republicans alike wondered whether the "Revolution of 1800" made any difference after all. Would dangerous concentrations of power in the federal government subvert cherished republican principles and destroy the union, regardless of the ideological tenor of the administration?

Jefferson and his followers thought that question had been

resolved, once and for all, when he ascended to the presidency in 1801. *Jeffersonian America* offers a more complex, ambiguous assessment. The surge of nationalist sentiment that Jefferson celebrated in his Inaugural Address – "we are all federalists, we are all republicans" – left an indelible imprint on American history. Americans increasingly thought of themselves as a single people, "a rising nation, spread over a wide and fruitful land, traversing all the seas with the rich productions of their industry, engaged in commerce with nations who feel power and forget right, advancing rapidly to destinies beyond the reach of mortal eye." With Jefferson, many Americans believed – and continue to believe – that the consensual, uncoerced union of liberty-loving states and citizens made the United States "the strongest Government on earth," that expanding commerce would forge a reciprocally beneficial harmony of interests that would cement the union.[5] The Civil War may be taken as the definitive refutation of the Jeffersonian vision, or at least as a powerful reminder that the exercise of state power had always been its inevitable, necessary concomitant. But if Jeffersonians could confuse "nature" and "power," imagining that republican principles conformed with nature's design, they also captured the political imagination of Americans across the continent, giving them a sense of their collective identity that would survive the destruction of Jefferson's union.

When Jefferson wrote the Declaration of Independence, Americans were anything but a united people. They never had been. The thirteen North American colonies had been founded at different times in the seventeenth and eighteenth centuries. Diverse groups of English, and later British, subjects, as well as lesser numbers of Dutch, German, French, and Scandinavians populated the first settlements. By the end of the seventeenth century, many of these settlers had begun to exploit enslaved African labor, thus precipitating the largest transatlantic population movement of them all. As importations increased, the slave population mushroomed, particularly in the Chesapeake tidewater and in the Carolina low country;

by the time of the American Revolution, Africans outnumbered whites throughout the most prosperous export staple-producing regions. The Atlantic economy provided the dynamic force behind all these folk movements, voluntary or coerced, with different economic activities playing a major role in determining the distribution of races and ethnic groups. All of the colonies cultivated agricultural products or harvested timber, furs, fish, or other natural commodities for export: rice, indigo, and tobacco dominated in the southern colonies; in the middle colonies, wheat and other grains (usually produced by free or indentured labor) led the way, while fishing and timber were the major export sectors in New England.

Each colony had its own capital, and its own legislative and judicial institutions. Despite a few precocious and abortive efforts such as the short-lived Dominion of New England (1685–9), no sustained effort to reform the empire and curb the colonies' autonomy had been made before the imperial crisis of the 1760s. (The Plan of Union that Benjamin Franklin presented to an intercolonial conference at Albany in 1754 received a chilly reception on both sides of the Atlantic, notwithstanding the obvious need to rationalize and coordinate frontier defense measures.) The colonies had relatively little to do with each other: for the ambitious provincial politician, the pathway of preferment ran toward the transatlantic metropolis. Economic interest also pointed eastward. A Massachusetts merchant or a Virginia planter would be much more interested in what was happening in London than in the capital "cities" of neighboring provinces.

American colonists defined their place in the world in relation to the British metropolis. Colonial political institutions were at least in theory subordinate to those of the King in Parliament. Though there was always some smuggling in violation of Parliament's Navigation Acts, most colonists shipped their products to British ports or ports elsewhere in the empire. Americans purchased vast quantities of British manufactures from British merchants (usually on credit) and imported them in British ships. Few Anglo-Americans saw any injustice or oppression in these customary commercial relations. They were more likely to congratulate themselves on their good fortune in being British subjects. We emphasize this point because it is so difficult for contemporary Americans to grasp. British North Americans were not "Americans on the inside, just waiting to get out." Nor was it easy for them to shed their British identity or their allegiance to their sovereign, King George III.

Patriot leaders of the resistance movement had to overcome enormous resistance – their own, as much as that of their fellow colonists—in order to start the revolution and *then* finally declare their independence. The break with Britain came only after a decade of ferocious debate about the governance of Britain's transatlantic empire; beginning with the Stamp Act crisis of 1765, protests greeted each of Parliament's inept and ill-timed attempts to reform imperial government – and to get the Americans to shoulder a (small) portion of its costs. The ideological origins of the resistance movement remain controversial. Were tax-averse patriots simply motivated by self-interest, narrowly defined? Were they paranoid about nonexistent conspiracies against their liberties (and, of course, their property)? Or, as some of the most persuasive recent scholarship suggests, was resistance to British policy innovations warranted by a customary understanding of the British constitution, widely shared on both sides of the Atlantic? Broad new assertions of Parliamentary supremacy (such as the Declaratory Act of 1766) were hard to reconcile with any notion of constitutional limitations. Most Britons and Americans acknowledged the existence of some kind of "imperial constitution" – "unwritten," like the British constitution itself – but were hard-pressed to define the jurisdictional lines between imperial and provincial authorities or, to change the metaphor, to prescribe the proper distribution and balance of powers between metropolitan center and colonial periphery. While they fretted about "conspiracies" to "enslave" them, Americans accurately discerned a shifting constitutional framework that threatened to compromise their interests and subvert their traditional corporate "rights." If, for instance, they failed to resist the "Coercive Acts" of 1774 (especially the

Massachusetts Government Act, which reconstituted local government in the colony), no colony would be safe in the empire. If the colony constitutions were destroyed, individual Americans would no longer be protected against the arbitrary and despotic rule of a distant, irresponsible imperial government.

The danger of unlimited, unconstitutional power was clear enough to Anglo-American patriots. But it was less clear, once independence had been declared, how Americans should reconstitute *their* "empire." Economic prosperity, political stability, and a transcendent national identity (as Britons) had all developed under the aegis of the British connection. Foreign commentators generally, and British commentators particularly, were convinced that centrifugal forces pulling the self-constituted state-republics in different directions would make any durable union impossible. In the light of such dire predictions, the very survival of the United States was itself something of a surprise. But the revolutionary leadership had few illusions about their future prospects. The Articles of Confederation were more of a treaty of alliance than a frame of government; they gave Congress few powers and even fewer sanctions to compel the obedience of the recalcitrant among the several states. As a consequence, frustrated "nationalists" – many of whom would attend the Constitutional Convention in 1787 – began to agitate for a thoroughgoing reform of the Confederation. The states barely sustained enough unity to keep Congress afloat for the duration of the war and it seemed doubtful that it could survive the peace. Congress's powerlessness was felt most keenly by the officer corps of the Continental Army. As they overcame inefficient logistics, chronic manpower shortages, and often inept subordinates to prosecute the war against Great Britain, men such as General Henry Knox and Colonel Alexander Hamilton, and of course, the commander-in-chief, General George Washington, increasingly called for a more vigorous, centralized government for the union. Even before the United States' decisive victory at the Battle of Yorktown (October 1781), Hamilton published *The Continentalist*, a precocious series of essays arguing for constitutional reform.

The patriot leadership knew that the happy outcome of the revolution was as much the result of developments in the international arena as it was of American battlefield successes – and this was probably an excessively generous estimate. Following early successes at Lexington and Concord and the British evacuation of Boston in March 1776, American forces rarely tasted victory. Washington lost New York City in the campaigns of 1776, and Philadelphia the next year; Charleston, South Carolina, was occupied by the British in 1780. The notable exception to this sorry trend was Horatio Gates's defeat of John Burgoyne at the Battle of Saratoga in the autumn of 1777. Victory at Saratoga kept the strategic Hudson Valley in American hands, while finally making it possible for Benjamin Franklin and his fellow diplomats in Europe to make a plausible case for increased foreign support. France, which had already been providing clandestine assistance to the rebels, now embraced the United States openly, concluding treaties of alliance and commerce in February 1778 that constituted the first formal international recognition of the new nation's existence. This confirmation of the Declaration gave a boost to flagging patriot morale. More importantly, French men and materiel made success on the battlefield possible. In 1781 the French navy under the Comte de Grasse defeated the British navy in the Battle of the Capes, preventing the resupply of Lord Cornwallis's troops at Yorktown, held under siege there by Washington's Continentals and the Comte de Rochambeau's expeditionary force.

The Franco-American Alliance transformed the American Revolution from a civil conflict within Britain's recognized dominions into a world war. Still smarting from the humiliation of France's defeat in the Seven Years' War, Louis XVI's foreign minister, the Comte de Vergennes, eagerly grasped any opportunity to weaken Britain. With the United States now enjoying the status of a recognized belligerent, Vergennes could build an anti-British alliance. By 1781, France had allied with the Dutch and the Spanish; the combined navies of the three countries constituted a formidable challenge to the British Royal Navy, keeping the Admiralty from focusing all of its efforts on North America and paving the way for Grasse's – and, therefore, Washington's – triumph. General Nathanael Greene's unprecedentedly successful campaign in the Carolinas in 1780–1 set the stage for Yorktown, enabling Americans to share some of the glory. But France's role was critical: French diplomacy isolated Britain and escalated the costs – and risks – of a war that was increasingly unpopular at home; without French financial support, the Americans' Continental Army would have long since abandoned the field.

American leaders were acutely aware of the international context of their revolution and of the vital importance of a credible diplomatic presence for the new nation's future security and prosperity. The American diplomatic team at the Paris peace talks – Franklin, John Adams, John Jay, and Henry Laurens – broke with Vergennes in 1783 to conclude a separate peace with Britain on unexpectedly favorable terms (most notably in recognizing American territorial pretensions west to the Mississippi). But the international arena remained perilous for the Americans. As Laurens returned home, Jay became Secretary for Foreign Affairs and Adams moved on to Britain; in 1784 Jefferson arrived in France to replace Franklin. The great goal of these revolutionary diplomats was to secure treaties of commerce with the three great Atlantic powers and thus to open European ports to American produce. But their ability to accomplish anything was severely constrained by the fragility of the American union and the notorious weakness of the Confederation Congress.

The years following the Treaty of Paris were difficult for many Americans. Six years of warfare had done considerable damage to important sectors of the American economy. In the south, for instance, advancing and retreating armies had destroyed many of the most productive prewar plantations; large numbers of slaves, the most productive laborers, escaped to freedom. Everywhere, the war spawned runaway public debt as states were forced to contract loan after loan. Many states raised taxes to unprecedented levels to fund their debts, thus draining specie (hard currency) from cash-starved economies. Debt-saddled farmers clamored for relief. Their pleas were heard in several states, including Virginia and Pennsylvania, where legislatures offered various forms of tax relief or postponed payments to creditors. Other states simply raised taxes. New taxes in Massachusetts led to Shays's Rebellion, the most widespread and effective agrarian uprising of the period: already burdened by the highest taxes in the United States, outraged farmers took up arms to prevent tax collection and close down county courts.

The spectacle of an armed uprising against a republican government, elected by and supposedly responsive to the people, shocked contemporary observers. Popular resistance to legitimate authority seemed contagious, as court closings were reported in other states – including even Virginia, where the legislature had pursued a more indulgent fiscal policy. Disorder in the states reinforced the determination of constitutional reformers to overhaul the government of the union as a whole. The Confederation Congress was evidently too weak to contain centrifugal tendencies that threatened to unleash conflict within as well as among the state-republics. Without the unifying force of the struggle against Britain, the increasingly disunited states began a slow descent into anarchy. States enacted tariffs to regulate foreign commerce and tax their neighbors, thus subverting the promise of a harmonious and prosperous free trade regime that would bind the states together. As Jefferson and his fellow diplomats discovered, European powers refused to sign commercial treaties with a confederacy whose commercial regulations were both diverse and unstable and whose future was uncertain.

Congress and the states competed with each other over who had the proper right to treat with the various Indian nations. And states argued with one another over conflicting claims to the vast western region that was recognized as falling within American boundaries at the Treaty of Paris. Cessions by Virginia (1784) and large, "landed" states defused this crisis, clearing the way for the orderly disposal and government of the new national domain under Congress's Land Ordinance of 1785 and the Northwest Ordinance of 1787. But, as Hamilton warned in *The Federalist*, "the dismemberment of the confederacy . . . would revive this dispute, and create others on the same subject."[6] Meanwhile other jurisdictional disputes simmered, including a longstanding controversy between Maryland and Virginia over the Potomac River and Chesapeake Bay. Representatives from the two states worked out an accord at the Mount Vernon Conference in 1785; building on their success they called for a broader discussion of commercial issues involving all the states. The failure of the poorly-attended Annapolis Convention in 1786 set the stage for the Constitutional Convention at Philadelphia in May 1787. Reformers agreed that a stronger federal framework was necessary if the union were to survive. Otherwise, the "imbecilic" Confederation would surely collapse, perhaps giving way to three or four smaller confederacies.

Called to revise the Articles of Confederation, the Philadelphia Convention quickly scrapped them, and spent the summer of 1787 drawing an entirely new frame of government. In place of a weak legislative body, the United States would now have a strong bicameral Congress with broad new powers to regulate national and interstate commerce, collect taxes, support an army and navy, and coin money. Members of the lower house, the House of Representatives, would be elected by the people, while senators would be chosen by the state legislatures. Executive power was vested in a single man, the President, who, with the advice of his cabinet, would carry the laws into operation, handle most diplomatic activity, and serve as commander-in-chief during time of war. A third branch of government, a federal judiciary led by a Supreme Court, was also established, though its precise role in the Constitutional system remained unclear. The convention spent more than half of its time calibrating the delicate balance between state and national interests, as well as between small and large states. The delegates had to make so many compromises over controversial issues that there seemed to be something in the Constitution to displease practically everyone. Even its most ardent supporters wondered if the complicated new federal machinery would prove workable. New York's Alexander Hamilton had hoped for a much stronger executive (thus fostering the

suspicion that he favored a return to monarchy); both Hamilton and Virginia's James Madison regretted that the national
legislature had not been granted more extensive powers. Madison had argued for a congressional veto over state legislation:
"without such a check in the whole over the parts, our system
involves the evil of imperia in imperio," the logical absurdity
of a sovereignty within a sovereignty.[7]

Yet Madison also began to grasp the revolutionary nature
of the new federal government. The diffusion of sovereign
powers between its three branches as well as between the federal and state governments might enable the Americans to
reconcile liberty and power in an "extended republic." Conventional wisdom, embodied in the writings of Enlightenment
thinkers such as the Baron de Montesquieu, held that republican government was possible only in small states, where
elected representatives could remain close to the people. But
Madison and fellow advocates of the Constitution now insisted that the new federal government would enable Americans to have it both ways: a "more perfect union" would
guarantee the new nation's interests abroad while securing
the rights of individuals *and* of their state-republics at home.

The new dispensation was nonetheless a tough sell. Ratifying conventions in relatively small, dependent or vulnerable
states – Delaware, Connecticut, New Jersey, and Georgia – endorsed the Constitution quickly. But ratification was bitterly
contested in Pennsylvania, Massachusetts, Virginia, and New
York, larger states with more diverse populations and interests. To placate skeptical voters who wanted the powers of the
new central government to be more carefully circumscribed,
Federalists in Massachusetts and states that subsequently ratified promised to work for amendments after the new system
was in operation. Making good on this pledge, Madison personally shepherded the first twelve amendments through the
First Congress; within two years, the states ratified the ten
amendments that became known as the Bill of Rights.

The First Congress would face several issues that proved
far more controversial than Constitutional amendments. An
overwhelming number of presidential electors had chosen

George Washington to be the first president, while the man with the second highest number of votes, John Adams, became vice-president. Washington filled his cabinet with talented men, naming Hamilton as secretary of the treasury, Jefferson as secretary of state, and Henry Knox secretary of war. Hamilton quickly became the dominant figure in the administration, drafting successive reports on public credit, banking, and manufactures that defined the administration's financial program. The treasury secretary urged Congress to create a national bank, assume and pay the outstanding debts of the states, and pass legislation to promote manufacturing. The proposed assumption of state debts was by far the most controversial measure. Hamilton wanted the federal government to redeem badly inflated state securities at face value, a potential bonanza for speculators. Jefferson opposed the program on principle, and Madison led the opposition in the Congress, emphasizing the injustice to the original debt-holders – ordinary soldiers and farmers, widows and orphans – who had received so little compensation for their formerly worthless paper. The impasse threatened to bring the new government to a standstill until the "dinner-table bargain" of the summer of 1790, in which Jefferson and Madison agreed to support Hamilton on assumption, if he would get pro-administration congressmen to back their efforts to locate the new national capital on the Potomac.

The assumption controversy was only the opening salvo in a contest between two emerging factions: "Federalist" supporters of the administration's policies and "Republican" oppositionists. With some important exceptions, the Federalists of the 1790s had been Federalist supporters of the Constitution in 1787–8; the Republicans (or "Jeffersonian Republicans") included disenchanted Federalists as well as Antifederalists. While some Republicans rejected Hamilton's entire program, many saw his constitutional justification of the legislation – the implied powers of the "necessary and proper" clause – as pregnant with untold future dangers. For his most fearful, strict constructionist critics, Hamilton's loose interpretation of the Constitution pointed toward the ultimate consolidation of all power at the federal level and the destruction of republican government in the states.

Party divisions on foreign policy issues in 1793–5 seemed to confirm these fears. When the French Revolution began in 1789, most Americans were gratified by this apparent sequel to their own struggle for liberty. But enthusiasm cooled and opinion polarized after successive efforts to reform the monarchy failed and the French Revolution entered its most radical phase. Threatened interference on behalf of beleaguered King Louis XVI led France to declare war on Austria and Prussia in April 1792; after insurrections in the summer of 1792 overthrew the Paris Commune and the National Assembly, the newly elected National Convention abolished the monarchy in September and promptly tried the king for treason. Louis XVI's execution in January 1793 was a shock to most of the world, including many in America who had supported the French Revolution. Austria and Prussia were soon joined by Great Britain, Holland, and Spain in their war against France. As this "conspiracy of kings" aligned against France, the new republican government dispatched Edmond Genêt as its minister to the United States. The administration awaited Genêt's arrival with mounting trepidation, wondering what the minister would demand. While many Republicans remained sympathetic to the French cause, virtually no one wanted the United States embroiled in the emerging world war. Controversy over what the United States owed to France under the terms of the 1778 Treaty of Alliance sparked debate in the increasingly partisan press and divided Washington's cabinet. President Washington's Proclamation of Neutrality on 22 April 1793 guaranteed that Genêt would receive a chilly official reception, particularly after he had arrived in Charleston, South Carolina, and begun commissioning privateers to prey on British shipping in the West Indies. As he traveled northward to the capital of Philadelphia, Genêt continued to flout American neutrality – and thus to embarrass Jefferson and other Republicans who had enthusiastically supported the French Revolution. The revolution's image was further tarnished the next year, as word of the Reign of Terror arrived in America.

The American posture toward Britain was equally controversial in these years. France opened trade with its colonies in the West Indies when war was declared, and American merchants rushed to fill the commercial vacuum. In response, the British government invoked the "Rule of 1756," a formerly moribund Admiralty court ruling that a trade not open to neutral nations in peacetime could not be opened to them in time of war. British naval superiority made it possible to enforce this somewhat dubious interpretation of the law of nations. The immediate consequence was that British warships began to seize large numbers of American merchantmen in the Caribbean. Washington dispatched veteran diplomat John Jay to London in April 1794 to put an end to these maritime depredations and negotiate a commercial treaty. As its terms gradually became known, the Jay Treaty generated extraordinary controversy. Jay had been able to secure the evacuation of British troops from forts on American soil in the Northwest Territory, and commercial reciprocity was established in the direct trade between Britain and the United States. But Jay failed to gain concessions on American trade with the British West Indies and other issues, such as compensation for slaves taken by the British during the revolutionary war and the ongoing impressment of American sailors, were ignored. Throughout 1795, angry public meetings across the country condemned the treaty. Republicans saw it as a bald attempt to use the power of the federal government to favor the interests of a few – Federalist-aligned mercantile interests – at the expense of a larger majority – including farmers and planters who exported foodstuffs to the West Indies. Although the Jay Treaty was eventually ratified, the debate it unleashed constituted a defining moment for the Republican movement. Republicans were convinced that Washington's Neutrality Proclamation had been tilted toward Britain; the administration's Anglophile tendencies – and its hostility to republican France – were now unmistakably revealed in an accord that critics thought made the new nation a virtual satellite of the old mother country.

The partisan battle between the Federalists and Republicans grew more acrimonious in the next few years. John Adams was elected president in 1796, narrowly beating Jefferson by an electoral vote of 71 to 68. (A series of maps following this chapter chart the declining fortunes of the Federalist party from Adams's election to the election of 1820.) During Adams's administration, the United States came perilously close to war with France. In response to the Jay Treaty, which they saw as tying the United States to the British interest, the French Directory authorized assaults on American shipping. Adams dispatched a special mission, including Elbridge Gerry of Massachusetts, a former Antifederalist who at this point was not aligned with either party, and Federalists John Marshall of Virginia and Charles Cotesworth Pinckney of South Carolina, to negotiate an end to the crisis. When agents of the French foreign minister, Charles Maurice de Talleyrand-Périgord, demanded a bribe before opening talks, the insulted negotiators refused. An outraged American public supported the administration's refusal to pay a "tribute," and in the congressional elections of 1798, the Federalists received solid majorities in both houses. During the so-called "Quasi-War," a series of naval battles between the two nations, Hamilton's wing of the Federalist party relentlessly pressed for a wider conflict, spurring Congress to mobilize men and resources and to suppress internal dissent through the controversial Alien and Sedition Acts. Adams's determination to pursue a more moderate course, keeping open the possibility of a negotiated peace, led to a fateful rupture in the Federalist ranks. A second peace mission appointed by Adams, led by William Vans Murray, concluded the Convention of Môrtefontaine and ended the Quasi-War in September 1800. But it was too late for Adams and the badly divided Federalists. In the 1800 presidential election, Jefferson and New York Republican Aaron Burr each received 73 electoral votes, while Federalists Adams and Pinckney received 65 and 64 votes respectively. The deadlock in the electoral college pushed the election into the House of Representatives, where a few Federalist votes eventually made Jefferson, not Burr, the third president of the United States.

The election of 1800 was the turning point in the history of the early republic. The triumphant Republicans now sought to arrest and reverse the tendency to concentrate power in the central government that had characterized the previous decade of Federalist rule. Jefferson liked to think of the "Revolution of 1800" as a reenactment of the revolution of 1776, the spontaneous act of an enlightened people, not as a hard-fought, barely successful, partisan political campaign. The people's collective wisdom seemed to be confirmed by a prosperous American economy, though this prosperity was more the result of events abroad than of administration policy. The ongoing French revolutionary wars offered new commercial opportunities in the Caribbean, the Mediterranean, and Europe that enterprising American merchants and producers rushed to exploit. In 1803, as a brief period of peace drew to a close, the exigencies of warfare prompted France's First Consul, Napoleon Bonaparte, to sell the immense territory of Louisiana to the United States. The Louisiana Purchase, Jefferson's greatest diplomatic triumph, thus was also the result of fortuitous international circumstances, not of design or policy. Yet contemporaries were willing to credit Jefferson's administration for their good fortune. In the election of 1804 Jefferson won a landslide victory, and New York Republican stalwart George Clinton was elected vice-president. (Aaron Burr, having killed Alexander Hamilton in a duel earlier that year, was not on the ticket.) The key figures in Jefferson's administration were secretary of state James Madison and secretary of treasury Albert Gallatin. Under Madison's guidance, the administration pursued its opportunistic diplomacy, and Gallatin began an aggressive program to streamline the federal budget and retire the national debt that Hamilton had so lovingly cultivated. The navy was dry-docked and the army decreased, all in the name of fiscal conservatism.

As Jefferson's second term drew to a close, the administration's efforts to shrink the federal government were disrupted by the widening war in Europe. By 1807, Britain and France were the only belligerents left standing in the ongoing Napoleonic War. As the combatants struggled to survive, they ignored conventional limitations on war prescribed in the law of nations, proclaiming comprehensive, unenforceable blockades on each other's ports and launching indiscriminate assaults on neutral shipping that they claimed sustained their enemy's war effort. American merchantmen touching in Britain were liable to seizure at continental ports by French authorities, and those not bound directly for Britain stood a good chance of being intercepted and seized by the ever aggressive Royal Navy. In response, Jefferson ordered the American merchant marine to stay in port. This controversial embargo, presumably a temporary expedient, dragged on for the rest of his presidential term.

Despite the economic disruption caused by Jeffersonian commercial policy – especially in New England – Jefferson's longtime political ally James Madison was elected president by a sizable majority in 1808. Although Congress repealed the Embargo as he took office, Madison was unable to chart an alternative course that would enable the United States to remain neutral in a world at war. When France apparently relented on its commercial restrictions in 1811, and the British did not immediately follow suit, Madison asked Congress to declare war on Great Britain. The ensuing "War of 1812" actually lasted from June 1812 until the early days of 1815. Distracted by the serious business of finishing off Napoleon, Britain was only able to fight a defensive war as the Americans' ineffectual campaigns against Canada were bogged down by poor internal transportation, inefficient logistics, and an insufficiently trained army. But after Napoleon's abdication in 1814 the British could finally concentrate on the American war, launching offensives in the Hudson Valley, the Gulf Coast, and Chesapeake Bay. American victories at Plattsburgh and New Orleans turned back the British offensive, and the occupation and burning of the capital city of Washington, DC, while humiliating, proved strategically inconsequential. After nearly two years of talks at three different sites, British and American negotiators finally ended the war with the Treaty of Ghent on 24 December 1814.

The United States had enjoyed only limited and belated

success in the War of 1812. Given the federal government's incompetence and the growing strength of antiwar and disunionist sentiment, however, the new nation's very survival justified patriotic rejoicing. This "Second War for Independence" was, after all, not so different from the first: nearly disastrous in fact, but increasingly glorious in retrospect. But those who had struggled to lead the war effort knew that such happy endings were not inevitable. President Madison and his administration, with secretary of state James Monroe and treasury secretary Alexander Dallas leading the way, hoped to ensure that the United States would not encounter the difficulties it faced during the War of 1812 in any future conflict. Led by the Congressmen who had supported the war, notably Kentucky's Henry Clay and South Carolina's John C. Calhoun, these young "National Republicans" chartered a new Bank of the United States and made ambitious plans for internal improvements that would aid national defense. But Madison threw a constitutional roadblock in the way of his own preparedness program, vetoing one of Calhoun's measures for federally-funded internal improvements on his last day in office. The split in Republican ranks that the Bonus Bill Veto revealed and exacerbated provided an ironic counterpoint to the postwar "Era of Good Feelings" when James Monroe, the last of the Virginia presidential dynasty, held office. The "feelings" of Republicans were increasingly frazzled as the rift between Old Republicans of Monroe's generation and the rising National Republicans deepened. Recalling the dangers of Hamiltonian loose construction, Madison and Monroe insisted on the need for new constitutional amendments to sanction federal sponsorship of internal improvements and economic development.

During the Missouri Crisis of 1819–21, when the federal government threatened to "interfere" with the spread of slavery, former National Republicans such as Calhoun began to share Old Republican misgivings about federal power. Congress divided along sectional lines, as northern "restrictionists" attempted to prevent the admission of Missouri as a slave state. The eventual compromise saw Missouri admitted as a slave state and Maine as a free state, but the damage had been done. Jefferson himself was especially pessimistic. The Missouri controversy threatened to subvert everything he and his fellow patriots had accomplished in the American Revolution; it was, he wrote, "a fire bell in the night" that "awakened and filled me with terror. I considered it at once as the knell of the Union."[8] As the Age of Jefferson drew to a close, the dream of a political system that would secure republican government and individual liberty seemed as fragile and tenuous as it had been fifty years before.

NOTES

1   TJ to Maria Cosway, 12 Oct. 1786, Julian Boyd et al., eds., *The Papers of Thomas Jefferson*, 27 vols. to date (Princeton, NJ, 1950–), 10:451.

2   Benjamin Rush, *A Plan for the Establishment of Public Schools and the Diffusion of Knowledge in Pennsylvania* (Philadelphia, 1786), in Frederick Rudolph, ed., *Essays on Education in the Early Republic* (Cambridge, Mass., 1965), 17.

3   TJ to Henry Lee, 8 May 1825, Merrill D. Peterson, ed., *Thomas Jefferson Writings* (New York, 1984), 1501.

4   TJ to Col. William Duane, 28 Mar. 1811, Andrew A. Lipscomb and Albert Ellery Bergh, eds., *The Writings of Thomas Jefferson*, 20 vols. (Washington, DC, 1903–4), 13:28–9.

5   First Inaugural Address, 4 Mar. 1801, Peterson, ed., *Jefferson Writings*, 494, 492, 493.

6   Jacob E. Cooke, ed., *The Federalist* (Middletown, Conn., 1961), no. 7 (Hamilton), 37.

7   James Madison to TJ, 24 Oct. 1787, J. C. A. Stagg et al., eds., *The Papers of James Madison: Congressional Series*, 17 vols. (Chicago and Charlottesville, 1959–91), 10:209.

8   TJ to John Holmes, 22 Apr. 1820, Lipscomb and Baugh, eds., *Writings of Thomas Jefferson*, 15:249.

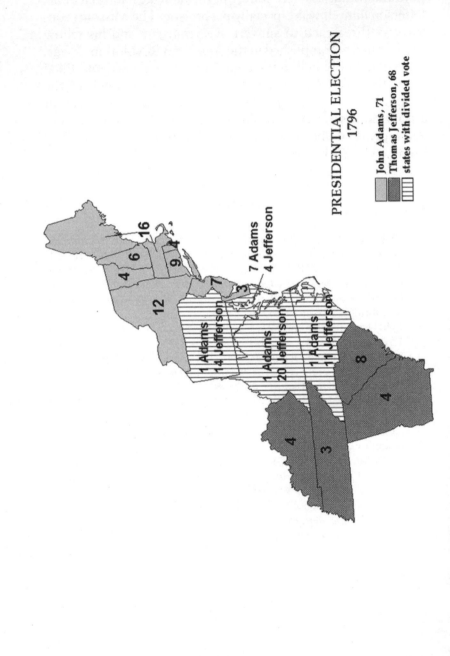

PRESIDENTIAL ELECTION
1796

John Adams, 71
Thomas Jefferson, 68
states with divided vote

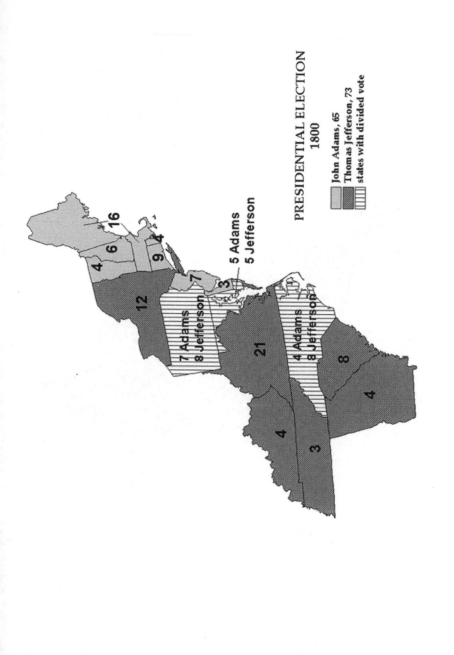

16

6

4

9 4

7

12

3

5 Adams
5 Jefferson

7 Adams
8 Jefferson

21

4 Adams
8 Jefferson

8

4

4

3

PRESIDENTIAL ELECTION
1800

John Adams, 65
Thomas Jefferson, 73
states with divided vote

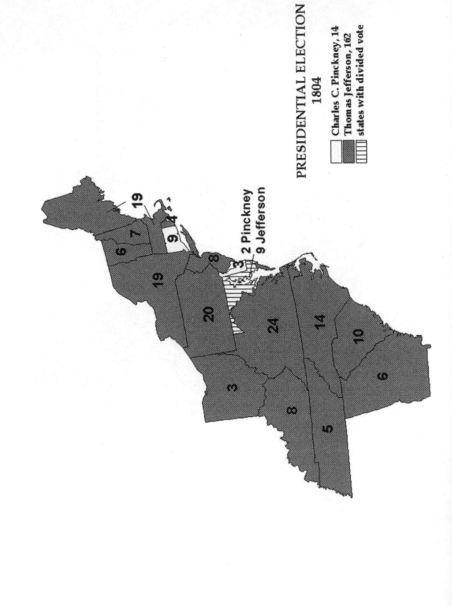

PRESIDENTIAL ELECTION
1804

Charles C. Pinckney, 14
Thomas Jefferson, 162
states with divided vote

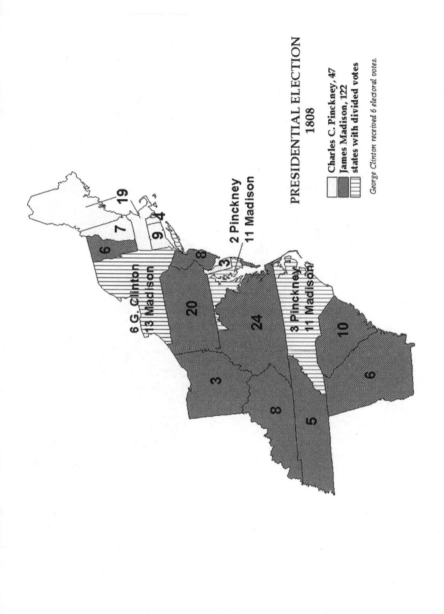

PRESIDENTIAL ELECTION
1808

Charles C. Pinckney, 47
James Madison, 122
states with divided votes

George Clinton received 6 electoral votes.

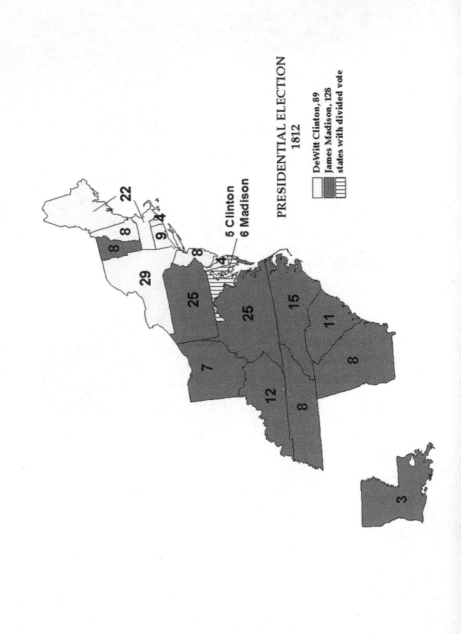

PRESIDENTIAL ELECTION
1812

DeWitt Clinton, 89
James Madison, 128
states with divided vote

5 Clinton
6 Madison

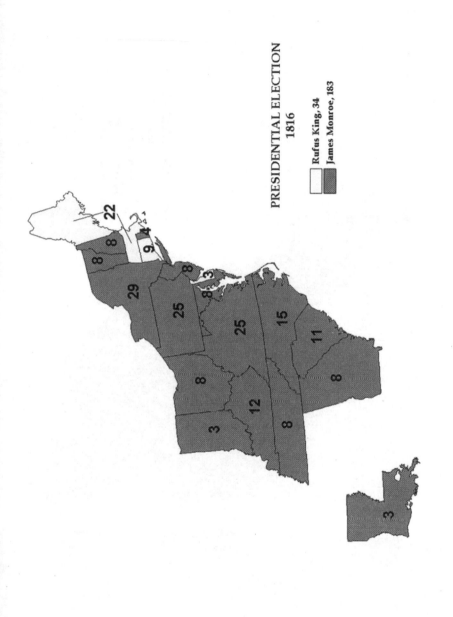

PRESIDENTIAL ELECTION
1816

Rufus King, 34
James Monroe, 183

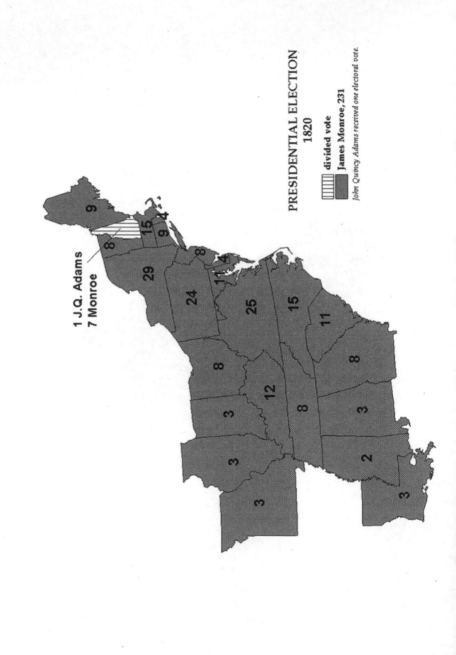

PRESIDENTIAL ELECTION
1820

divided vote

James Monroe, 231

John Quincy Adams received one electoral vote.

1 J.Q. Adams
7 Monroe

1

The Republican Revolution

"Let us, fellow-citizens, unite with one heart and one mind . . . We have called by different names brethren of the same principle. We are all republicans, we are all federalists."
Jefferson's Inaugural Address, 4 March 1801.[1]

On March 4, 1801, Thomas Jefferson delivered his first inaugural address in a crowded and chilly senate chamber in the new national capital at Washington, DC. One of the great state papers in American history, Jefferson's address was widely hailed for its conciliatory tone as well as for its bold statement of "federal and republican principles" that defined the American Revolution. "We are all federalists, we are all republicans," Jefferson told his fellow Americans, urging them to move beyond the vicious party conflicts of the 1790s.

Jefferson's inauguration marked the cresting of "a mighty wave of public opinion" that had swept over the United States in the previous three years.[2] In 1798, when the new nation had stood on the brink of war with France, belligerent Federalists commanded unprecedented electoral support; exploiting their partisan advantage, they sought to demolish the opposition by curtailing free speech and revising naturalization laws to keep immigrants from claiming the rights of citizenship – and augmenting Republican voting strength. But when the war scare passed and President Adams's ultimately successful peace initiative left his party disastrously divided, Republican hopes revived. Without an imminent war, the administration's repressive legislation seemed worse than pointless; new taxes, as Jefferson had predicted, had a sobering, "sedative" effect, soon cooling the people's "ardor."[3]

The growing discrepancy between the belligerent, Federalist-dominated Sixth Congress (1799–1801) and an increasingly peace-minded and Republican electorate set the stage for the "Revolution of 1800," for Jefferson a triumphant reaffirmation of the principles of 1776. The revolution proceeded in two stages. First, in the elections of 1800 Republicans gained their first workable majorities in the Senate (18–14) and the House of Representatives (69–36). The presidential canvass also gave the Republican candidates Jefferson and Aaron Burr (73 votes each) a narrow edge over Federalists Adams (65 votes) and Charles C. Pinckney (64 votes). But because of an oversight in the constitution of the Electoral College, votes for president and vice-president were not distinguished: the recipient of the greatest number of votes was named president, and the runner-up (Jefferson himself in 1796) served as vice-president. The resulting electoral impasse – and constitutional crisis – constituted the second, and in many ways most crucial phase of the Revolution of 1800.

With Jefferson and Aaron Burr deadlocked at 73 votes each, the election was referred to the House of Representatives that had been elected in 1798 and was still dominated by Federalists. The opportunity to bargain for concessions, or even to elevate a compliant and unscrupulous Burr over Jefferson, was hard for Federalists to resist. For nearly a week, from 11 to 17 February 1801, the outcome hung in suspense, with Federalists unable to muster a majority of state delegations for Burr, but unwilling to capitulate to Republican delegations that would not waver from their support for Jefferson. Finally, on the thirty-sixth ballot, the Federalists capitulated, with abstentions in two divided delegations (Vermont and Maryland) shifting their votes to Jefferson's column and giving him a winning majority.

The constitutional crisis of 1801 was crucial because it enabled Jefferson and his allies to translate a closely contested election into a resounding reaffirmation of American nationhood. For Jefferson the crisis was a virtual plebiscite, a moment in which the American people became fully conscious of itself. "Accounts received from individuals at a distance" combined with "the feelings of citizens on the spot" to produce an extraordinary sense of simultaneous presence, an awareness of national identity.[4] Federalist usurpers now stood revealed before their countrymen – including the credulous and misguided voters who had elected them – for what they had always been: enemies of their country, foreigners in principle and in practice.

Jefferson was confident that the American people would not allow the Federalists to steal the election. Republican governors Thomas McKean of Pennsylvania and James Monroe of Virginia had both put their states in a state of military preparedness should Jefferson's enemies attempt to seize the government. Yet, as Jefferson assured Joseph Priestley, the great British scientist and theologian, "there was no idea of force, nor any occasion for it." Had the election failed, and the constitutional "clock . . . run down," the sovereign people would have soon set it in motion once again: "a convention, invited by the republican members of Congress, with the virtual President and Vice-President, would have been on the ground in eight weeks, would have repaired the Constitution where it was defective, and wound it up again."[5]

The impasse over the presidential election in Congress provided a climactic chapter in the Republican narrative of the republic's redemption. The fiction of a sovereign people proclaiming its will was brought into dramatic focus by the Federalists' fumbling efforts to block Jefferson's path to the presidency. Republicans now could juxtapose "the will of faction" to "the will of the people," unanimous in the Virginian's support. The Federalist House, elected in 1798 when Americans were caught up in the delirium of the Quasi-War, "is not the Representative of the people at this time." The people would not be denied: the "unanimous and firm decision of the people throughout the U.S. in favour of Mr. Jefferson will be irresistible."[6]

Jefferson believed he made his greatest contributions to his country by articulating the widely shared principles, grounded in nature and self-evident to the common understanding, on which its republican government was founded. There were times, of course, when the people lost sight of these landmarks, times when they were carried away by "delusion" or "contagion," and "hoodwinked from their principles." But at moments of crisis, when national independence, state sovereignty, and civil liberties were at risk, the people saw clearly, demonstrating once again "that a free government is of all others the most energetic."[7]

The Republicans' great triumph in 1800 was to set forth the libertarian principles that constituted the nation, making the United States "the strongest Government on earth." "I believe it is the only one," Jefferson explained in his Inaugural, "where every man, at the call of the law, would fly to the standard of the law, and would meet invasions of the public order as his own personal concern."[8] For Jefferson, this was not simply the apotheosis of a meaningless, high-sounding abstraction, "popular sovereignty." On the contrary, the people had rallied to his – and their own – cause in the election crisis, just as they had done in 1776: across the country, Republicans were poised to intervene if Federalists attempted to seize power. More significantly, Jefferson learned from correspondence and news reports that rank-and-file Federalists were ready to join their former partisan adversaries in resisting "invasions of the public order." By threatening to tamper with the people's will, Federalist diehards thus transformed Jefferson's narrow majority in the Electoral College into resounding unanimity – and a powerful affirmation of national identity.

Jefferson's Inaugural Address is one of the great texts in the American libertarian tradition, a blast against "political intolerance" and persecution: "error of opinion may be tolerated where reason is left free to combat it." Jefferson promised that there would be no retaliation against his Federalist foes. Instead, he sought to demonstrate the liberal and enlightened character of American Revolutionary principles in practice. For Jefferson, proud author of Virginia's Statute for Religious Freedom (enacted in 1786), religious bigotry historically had been the leading threat to liberty and obstacle to harmonious social intercourse: "we have gained little," he intoned, "if we countenance a political intolerance as despotic, as wicked, and capable of as bitter and bloody persecutions."[9]

Yet Federalists could be tolerated because they were politically impotent, not because Jefferson and his allies projected a role for them as a loyal opposition. Republicans had emerged victorious in the 1800 elections because a significant proportion of former Federalists, "real republicans, and honest men under virtuous motives," had returned to the fold. "The suspension of the public mind" during the presidential election crisis of February, "the anxiety and alarm lest there should be no election, and anarchy ensue," produced "a wonderful effect . . . on the mass of federalists who had not before come over." "The recovery bids fair to be complete, and to obliterate entirely the line of party division which had been so strongly drawn."[10]

National identity was predicated on unanimity. Americans must be conscious of themselves "as brethren of the same principle"; we must "unite with one heart and one mind." Indeed, the revolution in public opinion was so far advanced, its unanimity so assured, that Jefferson could boldly reappropriate the very term "federalist" from his former foes, now defining "federal principles" in terms of "our attachment to [a] union" of sovereign states. Toleration of "error" thus depended on a broad popular commitment to fundamental principles that left the "desperadoes of the quondam faction in and out of Congress" virtually impotent. There might be a few unreconstructed Federalists "who would wish to dissolve this Union or to change its republican form," but they represented no threat to the health of the renovated body politic: "let them stand undisturbed as monuments of the safety with which error of opinion may be tolerated . . ."[11]

"The Revolution of 1800"

Jefferson's "Revolution of 1800" was the dawning of a bright new day after "the reign of the witches," a dark night in which quiescent Americans seemed all too ready to forfeit their liberties.[12] The contrast between Republican prospects in 1798–9, when saber-rattling Federalists enjoyed a surge of popular support, and in 1801, when he read his inaugural speech before a Republican majority in the newly-elected Congress, was certainly dramatic enough to justify the new president's rhetoric. The people had suddenly and spontaneously recovered their senses. This was not the result of partisan machinations, certainly not by Jefferson himself, who had scrupulously avoided any electioneering on his own behalf. Indeed, had he and his most trusted lieutenants done *more* to bring out the vote, Jefferson could not have identified his election so completely with the American Revolution. For just as Revolutionary leadership rose on the crest of popular patriotic sentiment in 1776, the Republicans came to power a quarter-century later because the people had returned to their revolutionary first principles. Jefferson's role at both of these key moments in the new nation's history was curiously passive. When he drafted the Declaration of Independence he was not "aiming at originality," but simply sought to offer "an expression of the American mind"; in 1800, the people spoke through Jefferson yet again, for it was not the man himself but the principles he stood for that galvanized the electorate.[13]

Jefferson's supporters had made the connection between 1776 and 1800 explicit when they celebrated his authorship of the Declaration: the election was a kind of referendum, they suggested, on American Revolutionary principles. Who would be a more faithful steward of these principles than the author of the Declaration? Throughout the 1790s Federalists had basked in the reflected glory of George Washington, the "father of his country," the very embodiment of Revolutionary virtue. During his second term, Republicans attacked the Federalists for pretending to worship Washington, making him the dupe of their aristocratic-monarchical schemes; a few radicals, including Benjamin Franklin Bache, editor of the influential Philadelphia *Aurora*, attacked Washington himself for his crucial role in pushing the controversial Jay Treaty through Congress. But such attacks did little to ingratiate the Republicans with the great mass of ordinary voters. When the great general went to his final reward in 1799, Republicans joined in the national mourning, eager to raise the sainted Washington above the partisan fray.

Republicans took their cue from Washington himself, who had warned of the baneful effects of "party dissension" in his Farewell Address. Washington was the father of *all* Americans, not the creature of "a small but artful and enterprising minority of the community." With Washington thus neutralized, Republicans could then forge their own direct and exclusive link to the new nation's founding through Jefferson and the Declaration of Independence. After all, Washington's greatness was based on his selfless disregard for personal power and his scrupulous deference to civil authority. He was most worthy of praise in his devotion to the very principles set forth in the Declaration, the "glorious instrument" that had come forth "from the pen and enlightened mind of Jefferson." The "names of *Independence* and *Jefferson*" would "*forever*" be "*inseparable* . . . in the American mind," partisan operative John Beckley proclaimed in the first campaign biography in presidential history.[14] Venerating Washington, Americans gave the thanks that were due to an "indispensable man"; voting for Jefferson, they expressed their continuing fealty to the principles that had inspired Washington and his fellow revolutionaries. The election of 1800 was thus a mirror of the nation, reflecting the consciousness of a self-created American people in the legitimacy of their own authority. In raising him to power, Americans did not honor Jefferson as a *man*; they honored themselves as a *people*.

Jefferson's Inaugural Address transmuted electoral confusion and near-breakdown into a clear and decisive mandate. Where historians of the election recount confusing and conflicting outcomes in the different states – and note that John Adams would have been reelected without the additional votes that states with large slave populations gained from the three-fifths clause of the Constitution – Jefferson heard the voice of the "people." The idea that Americans in some sense constituted a single people was (and is) a fiction: surely, we nod knowingly, Jefferson must have understood this. He certainly knew that many patriotic Americans had voted against him and remained skeptical about the direction the new administration would take. There had been widespread opposition to independence in 1776, but this had only served to clarify the boundaries of the new national community and emphasize the importance of active consent and participation for its survival and prosperity. Belonging to this community was not ascriptive, based on the accident of birth; it was volitional, a matter of individual conscience and choice. But for visionaries like Jefferson nationhood was also a promise that would be fulfilled as Americans became conscious of themselves as a people. When Jefferson heard the American people speak, he anticipated that discordant elements would soon be harmonized, as they had been in the years after 1776, when the Declaration served as a touchstone of nationhood.

Jefferson's logic, like that of all nation-builders, was circular. Nationhood was both the unexamined premise and the inspiring promise. Americans became conscious of themselves as a "happy and prosperous people" as they exulted in their future prospects as possessors of a "chosen country, with room enough for our descendants to the thousandth and thousandth generation."[15] The bonds of union were familial: if they would only look far enough forward, beyond their present conflicts and prejudices, Americans would recognize this continental kinship. So too, in imagining the fulfillment of the revolutionary fathers' vision of harmonious union, successive generations would see the original design or conception more clearly.

Jefferson's celebration of the new nation's future prospects testified eloquently to his enormous sense of relief after a series of deepening crises over the previous decade had driven him to the brink of despair and the new nation to the brink of disunion. The bright vision was the counterpoint of the darker, desperate vision of counter-revolution and the loss of American independence that gripped Jeffersonians during the heyday of High Federalism in the late 1790s. Neither assessment bore much apparent relation to the actual experiences of ordinary Americans, even the small minority who were politically active. But the dialectic of disunion and union that Jeffersonians both expressed and sought to contain would have a profound effect on the course of American history. Recalling voters to their Revolutionary roots, the election of 1800 gave new life to the idea that Americans constituted a single, united people.

Who were these Americans? Jefferson's answer, as he looked forward in time and westward across space, was expansive and inclusive: separate streams of population would merge into one. But the picture was much less clear when Jefferson was elected. Each of the sixteen states then belonging to the union had a distinctive political and constitutional history: the size of the electorate varied from state to state, according to different franchise requirements; party divisions in each state reflected its particular colonial background, the impact of the Revolution and postwar dislocations, and the relation of local interests to the Atlantic economy.

Everywhere except in Connecticut and Rhode Island, where revolutionaries modified their old colonial charters, struggles over new state constitutions set the pattern for partisan conflict; in the three new states, Kentucky (1791), Vermont (1792), and Tennessee (1796), campaigns for statehood and admission to the union provided a further impetus for political mobilization. Before voters could think of themselves and act as "Americans," they had to establish their primary identities in their own states. This was true both in a procedural sense – according to the federal Constitution, the states would determine eligibility for federal elections – and in a practical political sense, as responses to *occasional* and extraordinary national political issues were shaped by the *ongoing* experience of state-level politics. Paradoxically, Jefferson's conception of a harmonious, unified, freedom-loving American people reflected his recognition of this very fragmentation: at critical moments, in 1776 and again in 1800, Americans transcended their parochial, selfish interests to embrace the common cause. In both cases, patriots rose up in defense of their liberties in *opposition* to the blandishments of the only "party," the corrupt supporters of the administration (imperial or federal), that could operate effectively across the continent.

Imagining that support for him was a spontaneous expression of true Americanism, Jefferson naturally discounted the efforts of the partisan politicians and editors who had played such a crucial role in securing Republican victories in key states. But the absence of an effective national party organization also served the purposes of local political groups, eager to tie their own electoral fortunes to a more exalted patriotic cause. For Federalist office-holders and creditors, self-interest and loyalty to the regime were often happily combined, as Hamilton had intended. Republicans only had to agree that a system that did not serve their interests was corrupt and must be overthrown. Indeed, it was much easier to think of the 1800 election as the second coming of the American Revolution, depicting Anglophile Federalist supporters of the administration as "aristocrats" and "monocrats," than to articulate and promote a national party platform that would inevitably expose fundamental differences within the Republican camp.

The Republican Appeal

The Republican heartland was in the southern states, most notably in Jefferson's Virginia and in neighboring states that had long acknowledged its leadership. If English-style "aristocracy" had taken root anywhere in the new nation, it was in this region. The domination of the "better sort" had not been seriously challenged during the Revolutionary crisis: the absence of large cities retarded the consciousness of distinctive class differences – among merchants, mechanics, landless laborers, small farmers – that gave Revolutionary politics their radical edge in the northern states. The myth of spontaneous social harmony that Thomas Paine expressed in *Common Sense* (1776) did not seem impossibly remote from the experience of enlightened planters like Jefferson, despite the old regime's obvious defects and the compelling need for constitutional reform. Because the old colonial elites were not seriously challenged during the Revolutionary crisis, republican ideologues could promote radical reforms – expanding the electorate, making more offices elective, extending religious freedom and civil liberty – without fearing for their class position. Even when conservative elements resisted the reform program, as they did with some success in Virginia, reformers would neither question the patriotism of their opponents nor seek to mobilize popular discontents to promote their program.

Jefferson's antipartisan values reflected the absence of a partisan political tradition in Virginia. During the revolutionary crisis, the ruling elite's assumption of its own right to rule was translated into the notion of a single, overarching public interest that it was uniquely prepared to serve. Talk about popular sovereignty therefore did not threaten social and political disorder: instead, the challenge for revolutionary reformers was to arouse the common folk from what Jefferson saw as their customary lethargy. The Jeffersonian obsession with "aristocracy" grew out of his anxieties about the dangerous concentration of wealth and influence in the hands of a privileged class of great landowners. To combat incipient aristocracy, Jefferson led the successful campaign against primogeniture and entail, legal devices for preserving great estates in aristocratic families; he was less successful in his ambitious efforts to guarantee a democratic distribution of Virginia's public lands, including a failed proposal in his draft of the 1776 state constitution to guarantee at least fifty acres to every white male adult. For Jefferson, "democracy" did not signify anarchy or mob rule, but was instead the only conceivable remedy for aristocracy: a vigilant citizenry, jealous of its own property rights, would never submit to the aristocratic rule of a small class of great landholders.

Jefferson's mixed record as a republican reformer in revolutionary Virginia had a profound impact on his subsequent career as a national political leader. His identification of *aristocracy* as the problem and *democracy* as its solution offered a compelling ideological framework that could be adapted to a wide variety of new circumstances. Aristocracy proved to be a protean concept, applicable for Jefferson and his followers to any regime where the state perpetuated privilege at the public's expense, whether by granting a religious monopoly to an established church or by securing exclusive rights to banks or chartered corporations like the hated East India Company.

For many revolutionary patriots, the danger of aristocracy was most immediately apparent in the burgeoning class of royal officials or "placemen" who monopolized patronage, jeopardizing the authority of home-grown gentry and galvanizing resistance to corrupt imperial rule. Independence did not eliminate the aristocratic threat. Antifederalist critics of the Constitution warned that history would repeat itself under the new national government, as the "consolidation" of power gave rise to a new office-holding aristocracy. Hamilton's administration of the Treasury seemed to fulfill these dire predictions.

The revolution did not foster deep partisan divisions among politically active Virginians, despite widespread hardship and dislocation that led to sporadic tax resistance and court closings. Debate over the future of Virginia's moribund established church presented the only serious threat of party conflict along sectarian lines, with Patrick Henry leading the charge for a multiple establishment that would have included Presbyterians and Baptists. The threat was defused in 1786 when the General Assembly, following James Madison's lead, finally enacted Jefferson's Bill for Religious Freedom (drafted in 1777). Madison clearly had sectarian strife in mind when he later argued in *Federalist* 10 that local factionalism could be mitigated and contained by "extend[ing] the sphere" of republican government under the new Constitution.[16]

When delegates convened in Richmond in 1788 to deliberate on ratification of the new Constitution, prominent Antifederalists effectively challenged Madison's analysis. Virginia's vital interests were less jeopardized by virtually nonexistent local party divisions, they argued, than by the state's prospective loss of power under the new federal regime. Madison listened closely. His reassurances to skeptical colleagues, including a promise to work for amendments that would secure states' rights and civil liberties, were sufficient to gain ratification by a narrow margin (86–76). But by committing him to a moderate, if not yet strict construction of federal powers, Madison's arguments at Richmond also prepared the way for his ultimate split with Hamilton and the administration over fiscal and commercial policy.

The political dynamic in the Virginia ratifying convention in June 1788 set the stage for emergent national party divisions. The consensus Madison attempted to forge at Richmond was grounded in the expectation that Virginia's interests would be best served under a more effective central government of strictly limited powers. If the new federal government failed to fulfill these promises, patriotic Virginians who had supported ratification would rally in defense of the state's rights and of states' rights generally. Recoiling from Hamilton's controversial financial policies, moderate Federalists like Madison thus combined with former Antifederalists to redeem the new regime from its corrupt, aristocratic tendencies. Republicanism in Virginia did not emerge as a "party" in anything like the modern sense; reaffirming the republican conception of a single, harmonious state interest, Virginia Republicans discovered threats where their revolutionary predecessors had found them, beyond the state itself, in the insidious machinations of a corrupt central government. If a respectable number of Virginians overlooked the administration's corruption, Republicans thought, it was undoubtedly because of their blind veneration for President Washington.

Jefferson's career as a revolutionary reformer began with his efforts to root out aristocracy in Virginia, most notably through a liberal land policy. When he returned from France in 1789 to take on his responsibilities as secretary of state under the new Washington administration, his concerns increasingly centered on the national government's supposedly aristocratic tendencies. The great conundrum for Jefferson, Madison, and their allies was to explain why the people's representatives in Congress could not discern and resist these tendencies. Their assumption was that the source, the free suffrage of the people, was pure, but that congressmen were too easily seduced by Hamilton when they arrived in New York or, after the relocation of the capital in 1790, in Philadelphia. A vigilant electorate that held its representatives responsible for their conduct in office offered the only security against dangerous new concentrations of power and privilege. Significantly, however, this need to monitor was not compelling in

Virginia itself, where the great majority of representatives supported the Republican position.

The rise of Republicanism in Virginia thus worked to suppress divisions within Virginia's ruling elite, even while it focused attention on mobilizing alliances with like-minded politicians and constituencies in other states and regions in order to secure the state's vital interests. Virginians had expected that their state, with its central location and advantage over the other states in population and territory, would dominate the union: the strongly nationalist "Virginia Plan," drafted by James Madison and presented to the Constitutional Convention by the state's delegation, was predicated on this expectation. But concessions to the smaller states north of Virginia on equal representation in the Senate (the Virginians wanted proportional representation in both houses) raised misgivings about enhancing federal power. Delegates George Mason and Edmund Randolph refused to sign the Constitution; Mason came back to Virginia to oppose ratification, while Randolph, after considerable agonizing, became a reluctant supporter. Many other Virginians, including Madison himself, shared their ambivalence. If agricultural Virginia did not exercise a decisive influence over the new regime, would effective power shift to the more commercially oriented north? Would the Old Dominion eventually become an outlying, tributary province of an emergent northern metropolis?

Virginian Antifederalists and their Republican successors did not raise such questions because they were small-minded localists who doubted the value of the union. Instead, they insisted, the interests of Virginia's farmers were identical with those of the great agricultural majority in every other state; therefore Virginia's preeminence was "natural," offering the best security against the concentration of wealth, power, and privilege anywhere in the union. Whatever their inclinations, Virginians would never be able to encroach on the rights and interests of their neighbors because they lacked the essential tools of metropolitan domination: large cities, great financial resources, dependent populations. Jefferson's famous celebration of agrarian virtue in his *Notes on the State of Virginia* depicted Virginia as a kind of anti-metropolis: "The mobs of great cities add just so much to the support of pure government, as sores do to the strength of the human body." "Pure [republican] government" could flourish in Virginia because of the absence of cities and the preponderance of virtuous husbandmen ("the chosen people of God"); by the same logic, republicanism would flourish in the union only so long as its "healthy parts" also held sway. Virginia's relative influence in the new federal government thus was a "good-enough barometer whereby to measure its degree of corruption": its decline would mark the rise of a new American metropolis, and therefore of a home-grown "aristocracy," intent on reversing the outcome of the American Revolution, in substance if not in form.[17]

Once the new federal regime was launched, it became apparent to Jefferson and Madison that Hamilton and his allies would manipulate republican forms to achieve their aristocratic purposes, misconstruing the Constitution into a mandate for a centralized, English-style, metropolitan government. But this recognition did not come soon enough to prevent the treasury secretary from implementing the crucial elements of his financial plan: the establishment of the First Bank of the United States, the commitment to service the national debt at its face value (a great bonanza for speculators, who bought up congressional paper obligations from veterans and other original holders at enormously depreciated prices) and, perhaps most crucially, the assumption of the states' war debts. The discrepancy between republican form and "aristocratic" substance was most conspicuous in the case of assumption: in the infamous "dinner table bargain" of 1790, Hamilton gained crucial support for assumption in exchange for locating the permanent national capital on the banks of the Potomac River. It was a bargain that the host, Jefferson, and his ally Madison would soon learn to regret.

Given Virginians' well-known fears about metropolitan domination, the removal of the capital from Philadelphia might have seemed at first blush a great triumph. After all, the new capital for many years would be little more than a village,

dependent on its agricultural hinterland in neighboring Maryland and Virginia for its very survival. But the irony of this
transaction was that Hamilton gained the substance of metropolitan rule – a consolidated national debt entailed a consolidated national revenue system – in exchange for the appearance
of a "pure" republican regime where Virginia and the other
states held sway. Just as the presence of the great Virginian
George Washington at the head of the new government reassured Americans that federal power would not be abused, so
too the promise that the capital would arise on the banks of
the Potomac (within a few miles of Washington's home at
Mount Vernon) could be taken as a pledge that the new nation's rulers would eschew metropolitan grandeur and power.
Yet, just as disenchanted Republicans came to see Washington as the pawn of Hamilton's corrupt machinations, they
also began to wonder if republican forms – the federal Constitution, as they strictly construed it; a centrally located federal
district, safely removed from any aspiring metropolis – were
sufficient guarantees of genuine republicanism. During the late
1790s, as the new capital gradually took shape, embattled
Republicans became increasingly skeptical: far from securing
republicanism, republican forms provided its real enemies with
a plausible cover for the insidious designs, seducing credulous
voters into sacrificing their hard won freedoms.

As they sought to justify their opposition to the federal administration, Virginia Republicans portrayed themselves as
authentic nationalists, true legatees of the Revolution and custodians of a Constitution that was supposed to have secured
"a more perfect union" of the states. The idea that Federalists
were secretly conspiring to reverse the outcome of the Revolution helped explain why Virginia had suffered a series of
frustratingly close, otherwise inexplicable defeats on controversial questions of national finance, trade, and foreign policy.
The counter-revolutionary threat was pervasive, yet difficult
to discern, everywhere and nowhere.

In 1794, John Taylor of Caroline offered the most systematic and influential exposition of Republican principles: an
unwary citizenry must beware of the insidious new forms of

metropolitan domination that threatened to destroy the union. Taylor claimed that a "paper junto," the secret aristocracy of "5,000" investors for whom Hamilton managed the
national debt, held the real reins of government: "Paper men
get into Congress, and govern the legislature – The bank gov-
erns the paper men – A majority of stockholders govern the
bank – And foreigners may constitute the majority – Therefore foreigners may guide the legislature of America . . ."
Through the alchemy of Hamiltonian finance, virtuous
freeholders became virtual tenants: "a funding system is a
conveyance of all the lands of the nation, subject to a rent
charge," disguised as taxation, "payable to a few persons."
Congressmen who supported Hamilton's system betrayed their
constituents. Instead of representing the "5,000,000," the
American people as a whole, majorities in Congress promoted
the interests of the corrupt "5,000." Taylor concluded that
the only means of recovering "the lost principles of a representative government" and of saving "the nation from being
owned – bought – and sold" was to flush the aristocrats from
cover. Only "a constitutional expulsion of a stock-jobbing
paper interest" could purify Congress and redeem republicanism.[18]

Taylor's stark juxtaposition of the vicious few and the virtuous (if insufficiently vigilant) citizenry jibed nicely with
Jefferson's ideas about aristocracy and democracy: both evoked
the dreaded specter of great landed estates, with the mass
of husbandmen reduced to servile dependency. The fixation
on aristocracy also enabled these Virginians to identify the
situation of their state with that of the nation as a whole: the
"paper junto" was no more than a tiny minority in any state,
even though it exercised a disproportionate influence to the
north and in Congress. From this perspective, the obvious
antidote to the aristocratic contagion was more democracy:
alerted to the immanent danger to their most vital interests,
the great mass of freeholders and taxpayers would drive the
Federalists from office. But, of course, this was "democracy"
as Virginia Republicans understood it, with a deferential populace taking its cues from enlightened leaders who recognized

and resisted aristocratic encroachments. Taylor's vastly dis-proportionate ratio – 5,000 to 5,000,000 – revealed the im-plicit elitism of Virginia Republicanism. The presumption of a single, harmonious public interest denied the very possibil-ity that popular political mobilization could fracture the body politic along partisan lines, either in Virginia or in the nation at large.

As their anxieties about an aristocratic-monarchical revival crystallized in response to Hamiltonian financial policy, Jefferson and his fellow Republicans suppressed misgivings about defects in Virginia's constitution – and in the "man-ners" of a slaveholding planter class – that had been so pro-nounced in Jefferson's *Notes*. The threat of incipient aristocracy in Virginia faded from view as Republicans' attention was riveted on the arch-demon Hamilton and the dangerous im-plications of his policies for the commonwealth's corporate interests. In any case, reformers believed they had preempted the danger of a landed aristocracy by demolishing feudal en-cumbrances and instituting a more liberal land policy in Vir-ginia and in the new national domain. "Aristocrats" would have to devise more devious, indirect strategies in their unre-mitting quest for great estates. Hamilton showed them the way: his revenue system exacting "rents" from all Virginians, high and low, redistributing wealth from its producers to a parasitic class of financiers, enriching the Federalists' invisible metropolis at the expense of its subject provinces.

The Republicans' advocacy of states' rights, culminating in the hint of nullification in Jefferson's draft of the Kentucky Resolutions, was based on the assumption of a single, har-monious interest in Virginia. The low level of popular polit-icization and partisan activity combined with the displacement of intra-elite conflict to the new national political arena to reinforce the idea of corporate identity and common interest. Taylor's diatribes showed how easily the externalized threat of incipient aristocracy could be linked with "foreign influ-ence," thus justifying Jeffersonians in identifying the particu-lar interests of Virginia with the true interest of America as a whole and in asserting their continuing fealty to the principles of the American Revolution. This identification between Virginia and the nation meant that the Federalists who controlled the national administration and held sway in so many other states were by definition illegitimate, anti-republican, and counter-revolutionary. Virginia Republicans therefore would resist the Federalist juggernaut on behalf of all Americans, offering an inspirational pattern for patriots elsewhere who sought to overthrow aristocracy and restore republican rule. In doing so, the leaders of Virginia Republicanism would not think of themselves as partisans, for they relied entirely on the initiatives of like-minded "friends" in other states to trigger the revolution in public opinion that would put an end to the Federalist "reign of witches."

The united and harmonious American people of Jefferson's Inaugural Address harked back to the patriotic national community of the Revolution. But it was an idealized image of Virginia, taking the lead against Federalism as it had against a corrupt British ministry, that seemed to authorize the new president's extravagant rhetoric. Just as Virginians had overcome divisions at earlier moments – over ratification of the Constitution, over disestablishment, over the Revolution itself – to achieve a progressive, ever more enlightened consensus, so too the American people would put the party struggles of the previous decade behind them. With the danger of counter-revolution averted, Americans would be able to take a longer view of their true interests and common destiny. But of course the new nation was not Virginia writ large; indeed, it was only possible to imagine that it might be so because of the state's peculiar historical experience and distinctive political culture. The various forms that Republicanism took in other parts of the union underscored the fragmented, heterogeneous character of American politics, and of the "people" the new nation's republican governors were supposed to represent.

Republicanism gained enough support to elect Jefferson because it appealed to so many different groups for so many different reasons. In their efforts to explain the "Revolution of 1800," historians have foregrounded one kind of appeal or another, thus suggesting that one particular group took the leading role in forging the Republican coalition. Of all interpretations, Jefferson's own – that the American "people" as a whole suddenly came to their senses – seems least plausible. Yet in discounting his own agency, or that of any national party organization, Jefferson warns us against the dangers of looking too deeply for simple explanations. His interpretation did not pretend to get at underlying causes or intentions, but instead offered a conception of the national political community that retroactively obliterated particular interests and intentions. We would properly emphasize the mythic quality of this harmonious "imagined community," and the selective forgetting it entailed. But the knowledge that this formulation barely conceals – that the republican experiment so nearly failed, that the union almost collapsed, that the American Revolution itself might have been pointless – is crucially important for us to keep in mind. Other outcomes were possible, as Jefferson certainly knew but historians too often forget.

Republicanism in the South and West

Federalists emphasized the sectional appeal of Republicanism. Jefferson and Madison acknowledged that many of their strongest supporters were drawn from the ranks of slaveholding staple producers of the southern states. Planters throughout the South shared a common interest in free access to world markets, rallying behind Republican efforts to force commercial concessions from the British through aggressive trade policy. Anxieties about renewed dependency on British markets and credit were pronounced in staple-producing states that had benefited much more from the imperial connection than had states with mixed economies to the north. The war had been particularly destructive in the South, helping to transform Anglophiliac provincial elites into revolutionary Anglophobes: in Virginia alone, 30,000 slaves escaped to British lines and countless plantations were destroyed. The planters' great fear was that old imperial trade patterns would be renewed on unequal terms that jeopardized their own independence as much as the new nation's: they were appalled by the prospect of having to resume payments to private British creditors (with accumulated interest), as promised by the Paris Peace Treaty but only finally implemented through the new federal courts under the Constitution. With their productive capacity vastly diminished, American producers found these old obligations particularly galling. Unless the new federal government acted effectively to negotiate a more equitable commercial treaty with the British – including, for instance, accommodations on slave property and other wartime losses – southern planters would end up in a more vulnerable and dependent position than they had been before the war began.

Republican Anglophobia crystallized in outraged response to the Jay Treaty (1794), a supposedly unequal alliance that preempted further efforts to renegotiate the terms of the Anglo-American relationship through trade sanctions. Over the next few years, John Taylor and other party polemicists manipulated anti-British sentiment in order to build support for their policy goals, simultaneously defining Republicanism as the political persuasion of revolutionary patriots and of southern planters who sought to reshape American political economy to better suit their particular interests. Popular Anglophobia remained a potentially potent force that resurgent Republicans would effectively exploit in 1800, but support for Republican policy prescriptions dissipated as the normalization of Anglo-American relations resulting from the Jay Treaty brought prosperity to much of the country.

Ironically, in view of their subsequent identification with arguments for states' rights and minimal central government, Republicans in the 1790s advocated the aggressive use of federal power to promote what they believed to be the new nation's vital interests. For their part, the Federalists were loath to jeopardize the increasingly lucrative trade between United States and the British Empire that produced tariff revenue (an estimated 60 percent of the total collected) essential to the federal government's very existence. With more diversified economies that had fared much better during the war – by feeding both armies, providing war materiel and exploiting other market opportunities – political leaders in the northern states were much less prone to anxieties about neocolonial subjugation to the British and therefore less concerned about developing alternative patterns of trade. Because their commercial relations with the old metropolis were so profitable, northern traders were unconscious of the sense of dependency that afflicted southern planters, reeling from the economic dislocations of the war.

Hamilton's success in setting the administration's policy on a conservative, pro-British course gave Republican political economy and foreign policy an increasingly conspicuous sectional flavor. But Virginia Republicans cherished the belief that they alone grasped the essential conditions of national independence: northerners jeopardized that independence by selfishly seeking sectional advantage. Taylor's "paper junto" thrived on unequal tax burdens, exploiting one section at the other's expense: "a few states of geographical similarity, may be exclusively taxed to any extent, although all their representatives should dissent, by the concurrence of a majority"; an "aristocracy of states" would oppress the persecuted minority, who would "occupy precisely the political station of the American provinces, whilst subject to Great Britain."[19] Southerners were not sectionalists because their northern counterparts, even when they constituted a majority, were "foreigners" or subject to "foreign influence." As Jefferson explained in 1793, the "line" between Federalists and Republicans was "clearly . . . drawn": on one side, Federalists commanded support from "fashionable circles" in Philadelphia and other cities, from "merchants trading on British capital," and "from paper men, (all the old tories are found in some one of the three descriptions)"; "on the other side are . . . merchants trading on their own capital," and therefore immune to British influence, and "tradesmen, mechanics, farmers, and every other possible description of our citizens."[20] Federalists were disproportionately clustered in the northern cities; Republicans were the natural majority *everywhere*, even where Federalists held sway.

Despite Republican advocacy of planter interests, Federalism did enjoy some support in the south. In South Carolina, great slaveholders had joined Charleston merchants to support ratification of the Constitution and many of them subsequently aligned with the Federalist administrations. The most prosperous of the British mainland colonies before the Revolution and the only one with a black majority, South Carolina was ruled by wealthy low-country planters who recognized the need for an effective central government to secure favorable terms of foreign trade and to preserve the racial order. Once the state's delegates at the Constitutional Convention were satisfied that the new government would not tamper with the institution of slavery, they eagerly joined the "nationalist" camp. Unlike reform-minded revolutionaries in Virginia, the Carolina grandees had little taste for the political mobilization of white common folk: the war years had been marked by a degree of anarchic disorder and brutal paramilitary conflict unmatched elsewhere. Well into the 1800s, elite resistance to the rising demands of back-country whites for organized and responsive government and equitable representation gave Carolina politics a strong sectional character with distinct undertones of class resentment. These struggles over representation made it difficult for the great men of Carolina to identify themselves with the "people" of the state as a whole. The myth of social harmony that justified Republican rule in Virginia was conspicuously absent in South Carolina.

The most critical difference between the two states was that Virginians could build on a long tradition of elite rule and the progressive integration of newly settled regions into the colony's political life. The stream of white settlement flowing into the Carolina Piedmont came from Pennsylvania and the Valley of Virginia, not from long-settled coastal areas; as long as they held few slaves, these largely Scots-Irish, Calvinist settlers had little in common, culturally or economically, with the established lowland elite. But the westward spread of cotton agriculture and slavery soon mitigated and ultimately dissolved these differences, thus preempting the enduring sectional and social conflicts that fostered partisan divisions in the northern states. South Carolina was nothing like Virginia in 1776, but sectional and social consolidation in subsequent decades yielded a legacy of political consensus and one-party rule that conservative Virginians might have envied.

By 1800, the Carolina aristocracy was well on the way to consolidating its authority throughout the state, but it remained to be seen how the state would align itself with the national parties. The Federalists, who saw South Carolina as their best hope south of Maryland, nominated Carolinian Charles Cotesworth Pinckney for the vice-presidency; meanwhile, the Republicans cultivated a few key political "friendships" in the state, most notably with Pinckney's cousin, Charles Pinckney, who assured Madison in October that "I have never deviated a tittle since my opposition to the British Treaty, the foundation of all our Evils & Divisions."[21] The presidential election was a question for the Pinckneys (including Federalist congressman Thomas, C.C.'s brother) and the few other families who dominated the Carolina assembly to resolve, not the occasion for rallying voters to reenact the American Revolution.

Yet the presidential decision was not made in a vacuum. For the elite to sustain and consolidate its position, it had to take into account political conditions in the state – namely the prevalence of Republican sentiment in the backcountry and among the artisans of Charleston – as well as in the union as a whole. Charles Pinckney indicated that his own support for Jefferson hinged on one key issue, foreign commercial policy; by opposing the Jay Treaty, Republicans had enlisted the support of southern staple producers who, like Pinckney, feared British commercial domination and diminishing market opportunities. Proud of their independence, Pinckney and fellow Republicans in South Carolina did not support Jefferson as committed partisans, but rather as a result of calculating their corporate and class interests. Given the recent success of black revolutionaries in Haiti and the prospect of insurrection in low-country parishes (where the ratio of blacks to whites was approximately three to one), the future of slavery was the most compelling concern, one that was increasingly shared by slaveholding planters in the west. Which candidate, Adams the New England Federalist or Jefferson the slaveholding Virginia Republican, was more likely to offer the best security for the institution? Similar questions might be asked about Indian policy and opening up new western lands. With the rapid decline of the historically lucrative Indian trade and a ravenous new appetite for fresh lands (shared by expansion-minded low-country families), the Federalists' policy of (relatively) peaceful accommodation seemed less and less appealing to Carolinians. The presumption that a Republican administration would support settler interests at the expense of Indian rights, only recently a divisive issue in Carolina, now galvanized support for Jefferson.

The emerging consensus on South Carolina's corporate interests was by no means fully articulated in 1800. What was most important for Carolina's ruling elite was to align itself with the national administration, regardless of its partisan character, in order to secure its vital interests. The incoherence of Carolina politics on the eve of the election was an accurate reflection of the indeterminacy of its outcome. But the Republicans did offer the happy prospect of a new national administration dedicated to promoting sectional interests – the security of slavery, access to fresh lands, favorable markets for staples – and once the party's ascendancy was confirmed in Jefferson's 1804 landslide, Federalism virtually disappeared in the state. Most crucially, the sectional orientation of the national party enabled Carolina Republicans to define their state's corporate interests in ways that reinforced consensus within an inclusive and dynamic elite, thus preempting partisan political challenges to their social and political authority.

The sectional appeal of Republicanism was even more pronounced in other southern and western states, where elites were much less well entrenched and political leaders had to accommodate diverse constituencies. Georgians, recognizing the need for federal support against hostile Indians and their European sponsors, quickly ratified the Constitution. Sharing the concerns of Virginia Antifederalists about the dangers of centralized authority, North Carolinians at first voted against the Constitution before finally capitulating to the threat of ostracism from the new union in a second ratifying convention, in November 1789. But both states were politically unstable and incoherent, lacking either Virginia's long tradition of gentry rule or a ruling elite like South Carolina's with sufficient self-confidence to deflect and accommodate challenges to its authority. Identification with the national Republican movement offered a valuable political resource for ambitious politicians in both states.

In North Carolina the pre-revolutionary Regulator movement climaxed in armed conflict and the virtual collapse of civil authority, weakening the prospects for effective patriot mobilization against the British. Mutually suspicious local elites from regions with distinct demographic and economic profiles competed for relative advantage, most notably in access to new western lands, reinforcing the popular equation of political office and corruption. By associating themselves with Virginian Republicans in the national political arena, North Carolina's leaders could gain some of the legitimacy and prestige so conspicuously missing at the local level. The movement of Virginia Antifederalists into Republican ranks inspired like-minded North Carolinians to follow suit; deflecting concerns about corruption and aristocracy toward a distant Federalist administration enabled local elites to coalesce, positioning themselves as virtuous defenders of vital state and regional interests.

Founded in 1732, Georgia was the newest of the revolting colonies; legally opened to slavery only in 1749, it was still lightly settled on the eve of the revolution. Protracted British occupation and the reinstitution of colonial government during the war (1779–82) retarded political development in the state, though the presence of so many Tory collaborators among the would-be ruling elite after the war gave oppositionists a potent, popular issue. Fraudulent land deals exposed the rapacious self-seeking of the new state's republican governors, further eroding respect for political authority and enabling political rivals to mobilize an outraged citizenry in support of their own aspirations. Proclaiming their loyalty to

Republicanism, the national party of virtue, James Jackson and his fellow reformers exploited popular revulsion to the notorious Yazoo grants, in which almost every state legislator accepted bribes from speculative land companies, to sweep the Yazooists from office in late 1795 elections. Jackson thus succeeded in linking his original base of support among the great planters of the eastern part of the state with western farmers and planters, fearful that speculators would block their own access to new lands.

Republicanism flourished in the south because it enabled state leaders to articulate and promote state and regional interests in the new national political sphere, and so to consolidate their own, often tenuous local authority. In states without well-established political authority, the existence of a single, overarching state interest could not be assumed, particularly when separatists overtly challenged state jurisdiction. By invoking the experience and memory of the American revolution, Republicans offered both an inspiring vision of union, within as well as among the new states, and a template for articulating and reconciling more concrete interests. Conflicting prescriptions for the national political economy made local politicians and voters more conscious of their common interests – as slaveowners or would-be slaveowners, as staple producers, as consumers and taxpayers. The definition of state interests thus emerged in tandem with controversial conceptions of the national interest. As Georgians and North Carolinians aligned themselves the Republican opposition in the 1790s, to be joined by South Carolinians at the moment of the party's rise to national power, they simultaneously consolidated their position in state politics.

This same process characterized the history of embryonic new states to the west, whether state-sponsored (Kentucky, admitted to the union in 1791), self-proclaimed (Tennessee, 1796), or formed out of the national domain, according to provisions of the Northwest Ordinance of 1787 (beginning with Ohio, 1803). Emergent elites in the new settlements depended on outside connections for prestige and power. South of the Ohio, land titles derived from old state grants,

establishing enduring familial and political connections between the former District of Kentucky and Virginia and weaker
links between Tennessee and North Carolina. Old state and
federal appointments to the judiciary, legislative councils, land
offices, military commands, and Indian agencies gave ambitious men the opportunity to accumulate wealth and valuable
political experience in the pre-statehood period. The same connections in state or national capitals that enabled these men
to gain office made them influential in their new homes, where
locals competed for office, lucrative government contracts, and
more land. If the primitive, undeveloped condition of frontier
settlements had the kind of leveling, democratizing effect that
historian Frederick Jackson Turner famously celebrated in his
"frontier thesis," it also revealed the crucial importance of
connections with eastern centers of power, influence, and credit
for successful western careers.

The Federalists' control of the national administration
should have enabled them to mobilize partisan support in the
rising new states. In the Northwest Territory (Ohio), Governor Arthur St. Clair and fellow Federalist appointees dominated the territorial government, and the army's protracted
efforts to push back the Ohio Indians guaranteed a strong
federal presence – and high levels of federal spending – throughout the 1790s. Yet even here, Federalists forfeited their competitive advantages by resisting the formation of new counties
and opposing the onset of representative government (the first
territorial legislature did not convene until 1799) and the move
to statehood itself. Rather than deploying patronage to coopt
local elites, the St. Clair administration alienated crucial constituencies, most notably the Virginians who settled in the
Virginia Military District (in the central part of what became
Ohio). Influential Virginians such as Thomas Worthington,
the new state's first governor, thus took the lead in the statehood campaign, effectively cultivating their connections with
the Republican leadership.

In the aftermath of Jefferson's election, St. Clair found himself caught between a hostile national administration and Republican mobilization of pro-statehood forces across the

Territory. No thanks to St. Clair, Federalism, with its strong appeal to Yankee settlers in the Western Reserve and in the southeastern and southwestern corners of the new state, remained an important presence after statehood. But it was the Republicans who positioned themselves as Ohio patriots, evoking memories of the revolutionary struggle against colonial rule and the more recent triumph over aristocratic Federalism. Just as importantly, Ohio Republicans could now enjoy the more substantial benefits of a cordial relationship with the national administration, the continuing source – through patronage, grants, and contracts – of local good fortune.

From the perspective of Virginia's Republican leadership, Ohio's gravitation into their party's – and their state's – sphere of influence was a natural development, confirming Virginia's centrality in an expanding federal union. That the Ohio country (which, before the land cession of 1784, had fallen within the Old Dominion's charter boundaries) would be drawn into Virginia's orbit was an article of faith for Jefferson and his friends: settlers would spread out from Virginia across the west, while the agricultural production of an expanding hinterland would flow back to Chesapeake ports, pushing Virginia itself to a higher, more complex level of economic development. As we will see, this vision of a greater Virginia as a paradigm for the nation as a whole, rather than for the south as a distinctive region, would not be fulfilled. But the assumption of a natural complementarity of interest between Virginia and the new states of the west – a complementarity that did *not* depend on the spread of slavery, which was supposedly banned from the region north of the Ohio River by Article VI of the Northwest Ordinance – was critical to the national orientation and appeal of Republicanism on the eve of Jefferson's election.

Given this almost imperial confidence in Virginia's central place under the new dispensation, Virginia Republicans could patronize new state movements without any sense of risk to their geopolitical interests. On the contrary, the proliferation of new states – like the democratic expansion of the electorate – was a sovereign antidote to "aristocracy," in this case the "aristocracy of states" that John Taylor's "paper junto" would impose on an unsuspecting union. By resisting the expansion of the union, Federalists betrayed sectionalist anxieties about losing control of the administration, thus reinforcing Republican claims to being the true representatives of the great American agricultural majority: after all, northern farmers were as hungry for new lands as their southern counterparts, and no less jealous of their rights as citizens, rights that remained imperfect as long as statehood was delayed. St. Clair's opposition to statehood, his "aristocratic" pretensions and contempt for the political capabilities of ordinary citizens (or "subjects," as he called them), was thus a great boon to territorial Republicans, justifying their professions of being true "friends of the people" – notwithstanding their own great estates, slaves, and links to the leading families of Virginia.

Republican blasts against "corruption" resonated in Ohio, where the Federalist St. Clair regime seemed determined to live up to partisan caricature. Republican advocacy of states' rights in the national debate over the Alien and Sedition Acts also played well in Ohio and throughout the west. The extreme positions staked out in the Kentucky and Virginia Resolutions – the barely concealed threat of nullification and secession – reflected the Republicans' mounting desperation about their prospects for ever gaining control of the federal government. But the Republican conception of the federal union that emerged from this great struggle over constitutional interpretation, the "federal principles" that Jefferson invoked in his Inaugural Address, was bound to be broadly appealing in the west. From the western perspective, the Republicans' support for the formation of new states and their respect for states' rights promised rapid integration into the union, not disunion; conversely, Federalist hostility to their political pretensions led ambitious westerners like the young Andrew Jackson, who signed a loyalty oath to the Spanish king, to look beyond the union for patronage and protection.

Political divisions in Kentucky mimicked those of Virginia, with a Federalist coterie of lawyers and entrepreneurs led by Humphrey Marshall (the future chief justice's cousin) playing the role of Richmond's Federalist faction. But Republicans dominated political life in the District and the new state, taking their cues from their Virginia counterparts in the new national political arena. Kentuckians had ample grounds for quarreling with each other over the future of slavery and plantation agriculture, not to mention the welter of conflicting property claims and litigation that constituted Virginia's chief legacy to the new state. But divisions on these and other issues were never synchronized neatly with national party divisions. Republican hegemony in Kentucky was assured by the state's identification with other western territories and states on a variety of national political and diplomatic issues, and was reinforced by its alignment with southern slaveholding states once the future of the peculiar institution was secured in the 1792 constitution. Political factionalism in Kentucky would therefore take place within a broad Republican consensus, with Federalists playing an increasingly marginal role after 1800.

Over the course of the 1790s, the definition of southern and western interests in the new national political sphere prepared the way for the emergence of a broad Republican coalition. National Republican leaders did not directly address southern concerns with the future of slavery, exacerbated by fears that the recently successful slave revolt in Haiti would prove contagious. But politicians who aligned themselves with the Republican opposition did take the lead in consolidating support for the institution in their respective states, and they doubtless took comfort in the fact that Jefferson, Madison, and their Virginian allies were all large slaveholders. By aggressively promoting territorial expansion, Republicans appealed to staple producers in the southern hinterland, thus strengthening the east–west connections fundamental to Jefferson's visionary geopolitics.

A turbulent diplomatic situation made the articulation of a coherent approach to foreign policy impossible, as Republicans unhappily discovered during the Quasi-War with France in the late 1790s. But Federalists were unable to turn either Republican embarrassments or their own successes to long-term political advantage in the south or in the new western states and territories. Republican identification with western interests was so complete that Federalists could make little headway in the region, even in the wake of the administration's brilliant success in opening the Mississippi to American commerce – the pivotal issue in western politics – in the Treaty of San Lorenzo with Spain (1795). Republicans generally supported lower public land prices and the rapid settlement of the national domain, though they carefully dissociated themselves from the Whiskey Rebellion that spread through the west in 1794–5, Republicans were known to share the rebels' hostility to direct federal taxes that threatened to subvert state sovereignty and aggrandize the central government. Perhaps most importantly, Republicans were contemptuous of Indian property rights and political pretensions and correspondingly responsive to settlers' statehood aspirations. As a result, when representatives from the self-created state of Tennessee (in the western region of North Carolina, ceded to the federal government in 1790) gained admission to Congress in 1796, they quickly aligned themselves with the Republican opposition. Andrew Jackson was the new state's first representative in the lower house.

Republicanism did not gain adherents in the south and west because of specific policy prescriptions in a party platform. Instead, party activists in these regions began to articulate a broad commonality of *sectional* interests – with respect to foreign trade, territorial expansion, Indian diplomacy, and (implicitly) slavery – that Republican polemicists taught them to identify with the *national* interest. Framing their appeal in general, highly abstract terms, Republicans succeeded in linking local concerns with national patriotism. As they resisted the "consolidation" of authority in the federal government, oppositionists evoked memories of the American Revolutionaries' struggle against a domineering metropolis. Their vision of a consensual union of free republican states, of an empire without a metropolis, represented the apotheosis of provincial liberties. It was a particularly compelling vision in the staple-producing south, a region that would continue to depend on distant markets and on the ability of the federal government to negotiate favorable terms of trade. The great danger was that the concentration of federal power necessary for conducting successful commercial diplomacy could be turned against the provinces themselves, enabling a core region with metropolitan aspirations to destroy the interregional balance of power and so transform self-governing state republics into subject provinces. Anxieties about provincial degradation were most pronounced in Republican Virginia, with the longest tradition of provincial autonomy and the most exalted expectations for the new republican empire. Less well-entrenched ruling elites in other states were equally vulnerable to the redistribution of power in the union, though less confident than the Virginians that they could survive its collapse. Famously "realistic" South Carolinians were not eager to face the prospect of slave insurrections without allies.

Statehood proponents in the west were most dependent on the federal government to prop up their pretensions. Unlike the proud Virginians, these political projectors had little to lose and much to gain by closer connections with the union. Yet the Federalists, fearful of both the dilution and the regional redistribution of power, failed to exploit these integrative, nationalist impulses in the new settlements. In contrast, the Republicans eagerly catered to western ambitions, promising that the rights of new states as well as old would be secured against metropolitan encroachments once the Federalists were driven from power. From the perspective of aspiring elites, this was the best of both worlds: the political legitimacy and material benefits that came with incorporation in the union were not offset by having to accept a subordinate position in the national political arena. On the contrary, the practical implication of the state equality principle – most conspicuously in the federal Senate – was that these lightly populated new western states would wield disproportionate power. But, as Republicans flatteringly suggested, westerners would exercise this power as true representatives of the great natural republican majority in the nation as a whole, not as political opportunists whose claims to preeminence in their own communities were tenuous at best.

Throughout the south and west, Republicanism's appeal was far from radical. Everywhere, the most pressing concern of politically active classes was to consolidate their authority and legitimacy and to integrate them into the union on the most favorable terms. Though there were significant social dimensions to political factionalism in most places, divisions tended to coalesce along sectional lines with discontent focusing on inequitable representation and corrupt or otherwise inadequate administration: agitation for new states constituted the most extreme expression of local sectionalism. Every southern and western state either dealt with these divisions, more or less successfully, or was itself the product of them. The result of sectional politics was to retard the development of political parties that expressed conflicting interests within local communities. The Revolutionaries' inspiring conception of a single, harmonious, and harmonizing corporate interest continued to be salient precisely because political activity continued to focus on defining and delimiting those communities. As a result, the radical potential of the Republicans' rhetorical campaign against "aristocracy" was muted in the south and west, where even great slaveholding planters from the very best families could take the lead in defending local rights. Where aristocracy was thus displaced, and so identified with distant, despotic metropolitan rule, everyone – and no one – was a "democrat."

Republicanism in the North and East

In the mid-Atlantic and New England states, Republicanism emerged in opposition to local political establishments. The Republican vision had enormous appeal for some voters, while others saw political advantage in forging ties with the national opposition movement. Whatever their motives, northeastern Republicans could succeed only if they could mobilize expanding electorates to break with entrenched elites. Republicanism in the northeast, far more than in the south, was thus the creation of local politicians and operatives, particularly the editors and polemicists of a burgeoning partisan press. As an opposition movement that exploited local discontents with the traditional order, Republicanism could serve as a plausible vehicle for democratic aspirations. At the same time, however, it was difficult for Republican office-seekers to overcome their insurgent status and present themselves as "natural" leaders of their communities. To their frustration, Federalists continued to enjoy strong popular support throughout the period, particularly in New England.

The colonial histories of the northeastern states shaped the character of Republicanism in the region. Before independence, some states already had long experience with factional or partisan conflict; many had confronted, or been threatened by, major political and constitutional changes. Pennsylvania, Delaware, and Maryland had been proprietary colonies, governed by individuals or families who had received grants directly from the Crown; in order to attract settlement, these proprietors framed colonial governments with active and responsible legislatures. Connecticut and Rhode Island retained their original colonial charters and were, to an extraordinary extent, internally self-governing. The remaining northern states had been royal colonies, administered directly by the Crown. But New Hampshire, New Jersey, and Massachusetts had all started life under charters and came under Crown control only in the aftermath of the Glorious Revolution; in its first decades New York had been a Dutch colony. Distinctive traditions of provincial autonomy, the experience of sudden, sometimes "revolutionary," regime change, and histories of broad popular political participation set the stage for the coming of the American Revolution in the northern states. Political factionalism was a more or less familiar phenomenon everywhere when revolutionaries broke with the empire and began the process of constitution-writing and state-building.

Pennsylvania, which eventually became the linchpin of Jeffersonian success in the north, affords the classic example of how early national politics built on colonial and revolutionary foundations. Since William Penn framed the colony's

government in 1682, politics largely centered on battles between supporters and opponents of the Penn family propri-
etorship. As the imperial crisis spread across the continent with
the enactment of the Stamp Act in 1765, the anti-proprietary
Quaker party (including future patriot Benjamin Franklin)
remained so obsessed by the their grievances against the Penns
(most notably on land and tax policy) that they pressed the
Crown to make Pennsylvania a royal colony. This suspicion
of concentrated, hereditary political power soon took a more
conventional, antiroyalist form as Pennsylvanians created a
government for themselves under their radical, ultrademocratic
1776 constitution. Partisan struggles between "Constitutionalist" defenders of the new regime and their "Republican"
opponents laid the foundation for the fights of the 1790s.

By concentrating extraordinary power in a unicameral
legislature chosen by annual elections, the 1776 constitution
seemed designed to promote political factionalism. Executive
power was exercised by a popularly elected twelve-man council, led by a president. A Council of Censors, to be elected
every seven years, was charged with determining whether
amendments to the constitution were required. Partisan battles over the election of the first Council, in 1783–4, were intense. Anti-constitutionalist Republicans (not to be confused
with the Jeffersonian Republicans of the 1790s) wanted to undo
most of the 1776 constitution, calling for a bicameral legislature, a single governor with greater powers, and higher population thresholds for assembly districts (a measure which would
curtail the power of less populous western counties). Although
anti-constitutionalists lost this battle, they ultimately won the
war. As their numbers increased in the existing assembly, they
were able to recharter the controversial Bank of North America
and to secure both Pennsylvania's ratification of the federal
Constitution of 1787 and a new state constitution in 1790.

Despite their highly partisan nature, the debates over the
federal Constitution and Pennsylvania's constitution did not
lead directly into divisions between Federalists and Republicans in the 1790s. Many who eventually counted themselves
among the ranks of the Republicans, notably future governor

Thomas McKean, were advocates of constitutional revision. Still, as partisan ranks coalesced in the run-up to the congressional elections of 1792, a rough correspondence emerged between those who had favored constitutional reform on the federal and state level and those who, like Robert Morris and Thomas Fitzsimons, now embraced the federal government's nationalizing measures under treasury secretary Alexander Hamilton. Many of the most prominent "Anti-Federalists" in Pennsylvania had opposed constitutional reform, including westerners James Findley and Albert Gallatin and Philadelphians Alexander James Dallas, James Hutchinson, and Jonathan Dickinson Sergeant. The Federalists were able to overcome formidable opposition in 1792, largely because the state's representatives were still elected at large, and Philadelphia and the eastern counties – Federalist strongholds, as well as the epicenter of electioneering activity – exercised disproportionate influence. Intrastate battles about the distribution of local power remained the primary motivating force in Pennsylvania politics.

It took national and international developments to align the electorate along the Federalist–Republican axis. The galvanizing events were the federal excise tax leading to the Whiskey Rebellion and the debates surrounding the Jay Treaty. Discontent among Pennsylvanians both west and east pushed the Pennsylvanian Anti-Federalists into the political orbit of the national Republican movement. The new partisan consciousness came into focus in the 1796 presidential election. As Pennsylvania chose its slate of presidential electors, voter turnout in the western counties was high, tipping thirteen of the state's fifteen electors into Jefferson's column. The vote was nonetheless extraordinarily close, with fewer than 300 votes separating the highest-polling Republican elector from the lowest Federalist. At the start of the Adams administration, Pennsylvania was thus almost equally divided between Federalists, still dominant in the east, and Republicans who dominated in the west. In 1799 Governor Thomas Mifflin, generally seen as a nonpartisan figure, retired, making way for the election of avowed Republican Thomas McKean.

The rise of Republicanism in Pennsylvania was again precipitated by controversial federal measures. In 1798, as John Adams prepared the United States for war with France in the wake of patriotic furor over the XYZ Affair (when three agents of French foreign minister Talleyrand – known in dispatches as "X," "Y," and "Z" – demanded a bribe of 240,000 dollars before opening talks with American envoys), the Federalist Congress passed a direct tax in order to raise funds for an army. The tax was to be based on the number of each household's windowpanes, and federal enumerators were met with vigorous resistance in many eastern counties – an uprising known as Fries' Rebellion, after John Fries, a militia captain who led one of the protests and was subsequently imprisoned. In short, invasive congressional legislation, authored by Federalists, had turned many eastern districts to the Republican cause. McKean was elected governor that year, and a year later, after a contentious debate in the state legislature, Pennsylvania gave a bare majority (8–7) of its electors to Jefferson and Burr over Adams and Pinckney. Thus, in 1800, Republicanism was ascendant in Pennsylvania. Federalism was by no means defeated, however, and the state continued to foster a political climate in which partisan battle was the norm.

The history of Republicanism followed a similar trajectory in New York State. Colonial politics in New York were even more contentious than in Pennsylvania, with factiousness pivoting on rivalries between the Livingstons and the Delanceys and their various connections. In the aftermath of the Glorious Revolution, New York's royal governors distributed vast manorial estates in the Hudson Valley to the Livingstons, Van Cortlandts, Van Rensselaers, and other prominent families. Though the question of how much influence these "manor lords" wielded over their tenants is a subject of vigorous scholarly debate, they played a conspicuous role in New York political life well into the nineteenth century. Seeking to gain advantage and augment their limited powers, New York's royal governors dispensed land and patronage, and as they did so, political factions coalesced and fell apart. Competition between the "court" faction – supporters of the governor – and "coun-

try" – his opponents – was such a predictable phenomenon in
New York as to seem normal, well before the imperial crisis.

If New York's response to the revolution was shaped by its
prior history of factiousness, the revolution transformed the
character of political alignments. In the decade before 1776,
the Delanceys held the upper hand over their great rivals, the
Livingstons, but their successful manipulation of royal patronage suddenly became a major liability. As in other states, the
revolution saw an opening of the political process in New York,
as more of the "middling sort" found their way into office.
George Clinton, an Ulster County lawyer who was first elected
to the Provincial Assembly in 1768, epitomized this development. After brief service in the Continental Congress and as a
militia general, Clinton was elected governor in 1777. With
the support of the Livingston family, the New York electorate
returned him to the governorship again and again until 1795.
Clinton was a committed Whig and republican, but no radical: he consistently supported property rights and strongly
condemned Shays's Rebellion. In supporting Clinton and the
rising middle class he patronized, the Livingstons sustained
their leading role in New York politics. In the 1780s, the
Clintonians were opposed by many of the remaining landed
families, who lent their support to the emerging nationalist
group of politicians, led by former Continental officers, such
as Philip Schuyler and Alexander Hamilton, and men who
had been staunch nationalists in Congress, such as John Jay.
The most serious defeat suffered by the Clintonians was the
ratification of the federal Constitution by the New York convention, which Clinton had actively opposed. But the
Clintonians would remain a potent force in New York in the
1790s and beyond.

As in Pennsylvania, the activities of the new federal government altered the terms and tenor of politics in New York,
aligning opposing factions along national lines. Alexander
Hamilton's prominent role in the first Washington administration guaranteed some opposition from Hamilton's enemies
in New York. Initially, there was little animus against the treasury secretary's financial program in New York political cir-

cles. By the end of 1790, however, Chancellor Robert R. Livingston joined Governor Clinton in publicly criticizing aspects of Hamilton's "funding system," notably the assumption of state debts by the federal government and the creation of a national bank, which many Clintonians feared would combine with Hamilton's existing Bank of New York, which he helped found in 1784. In 1791, Hamilton's enemies scored significant victories: the state assembly sent Aaron Burr to the Senate, and, in assembly elections later that year, the Clintonians added several new members to their ranks, including Melancton Smith, Hamilton's chief opponent at the state ratifying convention in 1788. At the same time, the emerging Antifederalist coalition forged alliances with forces outside the state, most importantly with the Republicans of Virginia. Clinton and Livingston could both build on prior political friendships with prominent Virginians: Clinton was a longtime correspondent of James Monroe's and Livingston knew James Madison from their service in the Continental Congress. In the summer of 1791, Madison and Jefferson made their famous journey through upstate New York and New England, paying visits to Livingston as well as to Aaron Burr. The collaboration between the Virginians and New Yorkers would grow stronger in the 1790s and ultimately prove crucial for the success of the Republican revolution. It is no coincidence that both Burr and Clinton would serve as vice-president under Jefferson and that Clinton retained the office during Madison's first term.

Links with emerging national parties invigorated political factiousness in New York. While Clintonians exploited Republican connections, their opponents took advantage of ties with the Washington administration, particularly with Hamilton, who continued to exercise extraordinary influence even after he left the Treasury in 1795. The French Revolution provided a further stimulus to the polarization and mobilization of the electorate. Inspired by enthusiasm for the transatlantic revolution, Democratic-Republican Societies sprang up across the state, helping the Republicans win six of the state's ten congressional districts in the 1794 elections. Yet New York

Republicans found it difficult to maintain a united front. In 1795 Governor Clinton announced his retirement, and many Republicans vied to succeed him. Abraham Yates got the party's nod ahead of Burr, but was left to run against the respected Federalist John Jay, who was in London engaged in diplomatic negotiations. The election was a setback for the Republicans, as Jay defeated Yates by over 1500 votes, or six percentage points. There were several reasons for the Federalists' success: property requirements for suffrage were tighter for in-state elections, and the new communities on the frontier turned out heavily for Jay. Yet, as New Yorkers greeted their new governor with jubilation when he returned home, discontent was emerging with the commercial treaty he had just negotiated with Great Britain.

As in Pennsylvania, the controversy over the Jay Treaty cemented ties between local Republicans and the emerging national movement. When the terms of the treaty first became known, New Yorkers of all backgrounds rose in protest, venting their outrage in public meetings and newspaper polemics. Within a few months, however, the anti-treaty tide had begun to turn: most residents of New York City and of nearby areas in its commercial orbit now favored acceptance of the treaty. Republicans who hoped that popular discontent with the treaty would consolidate their power in the state proved sadly mistaken. The Federalists succeeded on two fronts: in 1796, all twelve of New York's presidential electors voted for John Adams and six of ten congressional districts were now in their hands. Federalists and Republicans remained at relatively equal strength during the Adams presidency. It was divisions within Federalist ranks that opened the door for the Republican triumph in 1800. As Hamilton was opposed to President Adams's policy of negotiation with France, Federalists in New York divided between supporters of the administration and their Hamiltonian critics. During the state assembly elections of 1800, Federalist divisions opened the way for the victory of Republican Burrites in several key New York City districts. Controlling the assembly, Burr ensured that New York's twelve electors voted for Jefferson and himself. A swing of only a few hundred popular votes had enormous electoral implications: a state which had strongly supported Adams in 1796 now voted for Jefferson in 1800, thus guaranteeing Federalist defeat in the national election.

Republicans did not fare so well in New England. Not a single elector in this six-state region would vote for a Republican until Jefferson's landslide victory of 1804; the few successful Republican candidates for Congress largely hailed from the rural and agricultural periphery, including Vermont and the western and central districts of Massachusetts. The Federalists were more deeply entrenched in longer settled, more populous and prosperous districts. Although some of these districts elected Republican congressmen, particularly as Jefferson's popularity crested during his reelection campaign in 1804, they were among the first to jump ship as the administration stumbled through the successive crises of the Embargo and the War of 1812. Federalists not only offered a political program that was more appealing to most New England voters, but they also developed effective party organizations to ensure that their sympathizers got to the polls.

The history of Republicanism in Massachusetts illustrates the challenges faced by the political opposition in New England. Massachusetts Republicans had to cobble together a coalition of diverse, disconnected interests from across the state. They appealed most successfully to the ambitious and upwardly mobile, aspirants to higher status and position who had been shut out of established networks of advancement and patronage. Merchants in secondary ports, urban mechanics, and western farmers all hoped the insurgent movement would enable them to overcome their traditionally marginal position in colonial and state politics. The first recruits to Massachusetts Republicanism were former Antifederalists, including Elbridge Gerry, James Winthrop, and John Hancock's circle in Boston, whose suspicions about their opponents' motives seemed confirmed when they were excluded from the new administration's patronage networks. Worcester's Levi Lincoln and other representatives of the agricultural interior were also drawn into the Republican orbit. The party was even more successful further west. In Berkshire County, a region only tenuously integrated into the state's commercial economy, John Bacon was elected to Congress in 1800, marking one of the party's first great electoral successes. Urban mechanics, under the leadership of Boston's Benjamin Austin, also rallied to the Republican cause.

Jefferson recruited some of his most important allies in second-tier maritime communities. Marblehead, Salem, and Lynn, as well as more modest entrepots in the District of Maine, including Saco and Wiscasset; and peripheral communities such as Barnstable on Cape Cod and the island of Nantucket, all became Republican hotbeds. Marblehead was the home of Gerry, and Salem of the Crowninshield family. George Crowninshield and his five sons epitomized the aspiring New England merchants Jefferson came to see as central to his vision of an inclusive and expansive political economy. Shut out of the lucrative British trade by the wealthy Boston houses, the Crowninshields dispatched their ships anywhere they could, to the Far East, India, and, most frequently, to the European continent. Trading with the Mediterranean, France, and ports on the North Sea, the Crowninshields exemplified the sectors of the mercantile community most hurt by the ratification of the Jay Treaty and then by the Quasi-War with France. Other merchants in similar positions, including Orchard Cook and James Swan, threw in their lot with the Republicans. Jefferson also gained significant popular support in the fishing and whaling communities of Cape Cod, Nantucket, and Martha's Vineyard: because the New England fisheries sent only a small proportion of their catch to Britain, their interests were often overlooked by the Federalists. While Federalist policies benefited elite, urban, mercantile interests, and middle-class yeomen with market access, there were many in Massachusetts who did not directly benefit from Federalist rule. During the 1790s they increasingly supported Republican candidates for office.

Republicanism was on the rise in Massachusetts in the 1790s, but it was not until after Jefferson's election that his party enjoyed major success. Elbridge Gerry's narrow loss in the gubernatorial campaign of 1800 promised better things to come. By 1807, after several more years of partisan struggle against a surprisingly resilient Federalist establishment, Republicans finally achieved a rough parity with their opponents. Federalists throughout the region responded by developing an increasingly sophisticated party infrastructure, with caucuses and committees of correspondence. They were ready to recapture voters and offices when the national administration's ill-starred commercial policies, culminating in "Mr. Madison's War" of 1812, wreaked havoc on the region's economy. Republicanism's progress in Massachusetts and the other New England states thus proved fitful. During times of peace and general prosperity, Jefferson's party could successfully mobilize a widening coalition of the ambitious and the aggrieved; the apparent irreversibility of Republican success at the national level even led establishment figures such as John Quincy Adams to turn their coats. But these centripetal tendencies, drawing New Englanders ever more closely into the union as Jefferson and his Republican colleagues defined it, would be offset by powerful counter tendencies during successive crises in the Atlantic trading system. As New Englanders became increasingly conscious of their region's distinctive and disadvantageous position in the union, alienated Federalist elites reinvigorated their hold on popular loyalties.

Conclusion

What defined Republicanism as a national movement was not the distinctive character of its appeal in one part of the country or the other – this survey only hints at the various forms it assumed – but rather its ability to bridge deepening sectional cleavages. The rise of Republicanism illuminated and exacerbated the very sectional tendencies it sought to contain and transcend. During the "reign of witches," when Jefferson and his colleagues despaired of ever redeeming the federal government from its Federalist masters and retreated to their base of support in Virginia, Republicanism threatened to become an overtly sectional movement. Yet even in these dark days, em-battled Virginians sustained crucial intersectional alliances with powerful factions in Pennsylvania and New York. And when their fortunes suddenly and dramatically improved, the Re-publicans' determination to build coalitions that would sus-tain the union became paramount. The rise of Republicanism in New England, however halting, encouraged Republican leaders to believe in the possibility of a progressively more perfect and harmonious union.

Virginia Republicans did not consciously exploit the local partisanship of other states and sections. State-level politics were rooted in concerns about local interests and shaped by distinctive histories of partisan competition. These vigor-ous traditions of partisanship and popular mobilization, so conspicuously absent in the Republican heartland in the south and west, were critical to the party's success to the north and east. The Republican revolution depended on, and was transformed, by traditions of political mobilization that were largely unfamiliar in Virginia itself. Jefferson never embraced party competition as an end in itself, but he always admired the vigorous political institutions and civic culture that, for instance, enabled New Englanders to mobilize against his Embargo. His proposals for republican reform in Virginia, culminating in his conception of the "ward republic," consti-tuted his ultimate tribute to the vitality of local political life to the north.

The ideological appeal of Republicanism was also trans-formed by its progressive spread beyond the plantation south. In states where Republicans were in the minority, to the north, anti-aristocratic, anti-metropolitan rhetoric took on a much more radical, social dimension. Here, much more plausibly than in Virginia, Republicanism could be seen as the vehicle for democratic aspiration. Of course, the genius of Repub-licanism was that it could be so many different things to its growing legion of followers. As opposition factions across the nation embraced Republicanism, they redefined the movement in their own image. Yet even the most cynical and opportun-istic partisans believed that they shared common principles and were moved by common impulses with fellow Republicans elsewhere. No real national party organization was therefore necessary, or so Republicans who defined themselves as the "people" – and Federalists as the people's counterrevolutionary enemies – liked to think. This is why Jefferson barely recognized the crucial role of party operatives and printers such as William Duane in making possible his election in 1800. For Jefferson, it was not the politicians but the people themselves who had saved the day by reenacting and reaffirming the Revolution.

NOTES

1   TJ, First Inaugural Address, 4 Mar. 1801, Merrill Peterson, ed., *Thomas Jefferson Writings* (New York, 1984), 493.
2   TJ to Joseph Priestley, 21 Mar. 1801, Andrew A. Lipscomb and Albert Ellery Bergh, eds., *The Writings of Thomas Jefferson*, 20 vols. (Washington, DC, 1903–4), 10:229.
3   TJ to James Lewis, Jr., 9 May 1798, ibid., 10:37.
4   "ELECTION OF A PRESIDENT," *National Intelligencer* (Washington, DC), 16 Feb. 1801.
5   TJ to Priestley, 21 Mar. 1801, Lipscomb and Bergh, eds., *Writings of Jefferson*, 10:229–30.
6   "For the National Intelligencer," "LETTER from a respectable citizen to a Member of Congress, on the ELECTION of a PRESIDENT," *National Intelligencer* (Washington, DC), 21 Jan. 1801; "ARISTIDES," "ON THE ELECTION OF A PRESIDENT, No. 11," ibid., 5 Jan. 1801; "ELECTION OF A PRESIDENT," ibid., 16 Feb. 1801.
7   TJ to John Dickinson, 6 Mar. 1801, Lipscomb and Bergh, eds., *Writings of Jefferson*, 10:217.
8   TJ, First Inaugural Address, 4 Mar. 1801, Peterson, ed., *Jefferson Writings*, 492.
9   Ibid.
10 TJ to Joel Barlow, 14 Mar. 1801, Lipscomb and Bergh, eds., *Writings of Jefferson*, 10:222.
11 TJ to William B. Giles, 23 Mar. 1801, Lipscomb and Bergh, eds., *Writings of Jefferson*, 10:240; TJ, First Inaugural Address, 4 Mar. 1801, Peterson, ed., *Jefferson Writings*, 493.
12 TJ to Spencer Roane, 6 Sept. 1819 ("Revolution of 1800"), Lipscomb and Bergh, eds., *Writings of Jefferson*; TJ to John Taylor, 12 June 1798 ("reign of witches"), ibid., 10:46.

13 TJ to Henry Lee, 8 May 1825, ibid., 16:118.

14 John Beckley, *Address to the People of the United States with an Epitome and Vindication of the Public Life and Character of Thomas Jefferson* (Philadelphia, 1800), reprinted in Gerald W. Gawalt, ed., *Justifying Jefferson: The Political Writings of James Beckley* (Washington, DC, 1995), 183.

15 TJ, First Inaugural Address, 4 Mar. 1801, Peterson, ed., *Jefferson Writings*, 493.

16 Jacob E. Cooke, ed., *The Federalist* (Middletown, Conn., 1961), no. 10 (Madison), 64.

17 TJ, *Notes on the State of Virginia*, ed. William Peden (Chapel Hill, NC, 1954), Query XIX (Manufactures), 165.

18 [John Taylor], *Definition of Parties: or, the Political Effects of the Paper System Considered* (Philadelphia, 1794), 27, 7, 5, 15.

19 John Taylor, *An Argument Respecting the Constitutionality of the Carriage Tax; Which Subject was Discussed at Richmond, in Virginia, in May, 1795* (Richmond, 1795), 16–17.

20 TJ to Madison, 13 May 1793, J. C. A. Stagg et al., eds., *The Papers of James Madison: Congressional Series*, 17 vols. (Chicago and Charlottesville, 1959–91), 9:88–9.

21 Charles Pinckney to JM, 26 Oct. 1800, ibid., 17:427.

2

Little Republics

> "It is by dividing and subdividing these republics from the great national one down through all its subordinations, until it ends in the administration of every man's farm by himself; by placing under every one what his own eye may superintend, that all will be done for the best."
>
> *Jefferson to Joseph C. Cabell, 2 February 1816.*[1]

Except for occasional retreats to his Poplar Forest plantation in Bedford County, Virginia, Thomas Jefferson rarely traveled far from Monticello during his retirement years. Maintaining a low profile on the most controversial political issues of the day, he devoted renewed energy to the cause of public education. By 1816, when he wrote his famous letter on ward republics to Joseph C. Cabell, his Albemarle County neighbor and coadjutor, Jefferson's campaign to establish a state university and locate it in the nearby village of Charlottesville was poised for success. The new University of Virginia reflected its founder's conception of the role of learning and public service in sustaining the commonwealth. But as this letter reveals, it was only a small part of his vision for a thoroughly republican Virginia. The fate of the republic depended not only on the education of its ruling elite, but also on the virtue and vigilance of a well-informed citizenry.

In his 1779 Bill for the Diffusion of Knowledge, Jefferson first proposed his pyramidal system of public education, based on universal primary education (for girls as well as boys) and narrowing through selective grammar or secondary schools (for boys) to culminate in university education for the meritorious few. Part of a comprehensive revision of Virginia's laws designed to establish a firm foundation for the commonwealth's experiment in republican self-government, Jefferson's education system would assure that the white male property-owning adults who constituted the "people" in their civic capacity were sufficiently well-informed to curb the self-aggrandizing designs of their would-be rulers. Yet though the legislature eventually adopted many of Jefferson's proposals, the Bill for the Diffusion of Knowledge failed. At a time when war-weary Virginians were pushed to the limits of their resources (if not their patriotism), Jefferson's proposal and schemes like it in other states were anathema to taxpayers. There were also good ideological reasons to question the need for such a massive expenditure of public funds on institutions that primarily would benefit a small elite class. And revolutionary patriots had already proven vigilant in defense of their liberties without the benefit of tax-supported schools. After all, as Jefferson himself had proclaimed, the most fundamental truths were "self-evident" to the common understanding. To suggest that the people were too ignorant to govern themselves was to betray the bias of an aristocratic ruling class.

Looking ahead to the advent of public schools in the nineteenth century, historians of education generally lament the short sightedness of revolutionary legislators with their self-serving libertarian scruples about public spending. They underscore the contrast between the visionary Jefferson – or his friend and counterpart Benjamin Rush in Pennsylvania – and the stingy taxpayers who resisted their schemes. There undoubtedly is something to be said for such characterizations. But Jefferson himself came to see that there were other, perhaps more appropriate ways to guarantee popular enlightenment. In 1816, he was much more concerned with expanding the scope of citizen activity at every level, "placing under every one what his own eye may superintend." A farmer knew what was best for his farm, a father knew what was best for his family. Popular sovereignty was thus not a fiction, fashioned to justify a republican elite's right to rule, but proceeded upward as every honest citizen participated in his own government. The challenge then was not simply to make sure that the highest public servants were well educated, the design of

Jefferson's university, but to guarantee that government at
every level was truly republican, resting on the active consent
of citizens. Against the implicitly hierarchical, aristocratic bias
of his 1779 bill – in which "knowledge" and authority were
"diffused" from a republican intelligentsia – Jefferson offered
in 1816 a much more democratic, decentralized, bottom-up
conception of politics and education. Enlightenment was ex-
istential, proceeding from the full exercise of every citizen's
natural capacities within the appropriate sphere of activity.

The development of Jefferson's thinking on education over
the course of his career reflected the rapidly changing character of American republican society. His scheme for ward republics translated the abstraction of popular sovereignty into
an elaborate federal scheme: household and nation would be
linked in an ascending series of "republics," each "sovereign"
in its own sphere. He thus collapsed traditional distinctions
between government and society, making every family farmer
his own governor. In the Jeffersonian scheme, family government was the foundation of civil order.

Republican Fathers

In Jefferson's ideal republic public schools would enable revolutionary fathers to teach their sons how to govern themselves.
But the first order of business in the early American republic
was to secure its independence. Jefferson's conception of the
ward republic was shaped by his turbulent career in public
service. While his political opponents recoiled at the supposed
"excesses" of democratic politics and sought to widen the distance between governors and governed, Jefferson and his Republican allies emphasized the continuing need for popular
political mobilization. The Republican Party was supposed to
perpetuate and institutionalize the patriotic fervor of the revolution; it was a kind of school for good citizens, keeping the
fathers vigilant and mobilizing them against internal and external threats. Partisan politics – educating the fathers – thus
took precedence over an elaborate and expensive system of

public schools to educate the sons. This reversal of priorities represented Jefferson's accommodation to political reality. So, in his ward republic scheme, the political organization of the neighborhood necessarily preceded any provision freeholders would make for the support of schools.

Jeffersonian Republicanism constituted a bridge between the world of high politics and the society of scattered villages and rural neighborhoods in which most Americans lived. In celebrating the virtue of yeoman farmers, Jefferson was simply recognizing this social reality. The paradox was that as his politics became more democratic, reflecting more accurately the new nation's predominantly rural and agricultural character, American society itself began to change in unexpected and unpredictable ways. Jeffersonianism thus looked forward to a more inclusive democratic politics, even while fixating on an increasingly anachronistic vision of a citizenry composed of virtuous and independent freeholding farmers. As long as these opposing tendencies were held in balance, Republicans could sustain the illusion that, as Jefferson told newspaper editor William Duane, they "are the *nation*."[2] After all, the vast majority of white male Americans were either farmers, or aspired to be farmers, or identified with the values farmers supposedly exemplified.

Jeffersonianism appealed to a generation of republican fathers, authorized by nature's laws to govern families for their own good. The equality of Jefferson's Declaration of Independence was the equality of "men," and through them, of their families; it promised that American fathers would never have to submit to the kinds of degradation characteristic of aristocratic regimes – in which all men, and their families, were unequal. The population of the early republic, like that of colonial America, was predominantly organized in nuclear families: like their agricultural counterparts, artisans and mechanics in towns and cities thought of themselves as heads of self-contained households. In all parts of the country, the population was extraordinarily young: in 1790, 49.6 percent of the white male population was under the age of 16; the average household size was 5.79. The age structure reflected the plentiful subsistence made possible by a favorable ratio of land to total population, early family formation, and the high percentage of live births; on the eve of the Revolution, the annual birthrate in colonial America was approximately 50 to 55 for every 1,000 colonists. Historically, family size was largest in southern New England and other long-settled regions where family farming predominated. In some of the more long-settled and heavily populated areas, large families and the progressive subdivision of estates over several generations decreased average farm size to the limits of economic viability well before the revolution. But if the surplus population of young men were willing to move, opportunity beckoned elsewhere: in the cities, where a chronic scarcity of labor kept wages relatively high (by European standards) and in newly opened frontier regions, where fresh, highly productive land was cheap. Dynamic growth thus propelled both the rapid expansion of settlement and new concentrations of population in rising villages and towns.

In 1800 the United States was overwhelmingly rural and agricultural; only 6 percent of the population lived in "cities" (with a population of 2,500 or more). Yet if cities were still small, they were growing dramatically: Philadelphia and New York, the two largest colonial cities, with populations of 40,000 and 25,000 respectively in 1775, each counted more than 100,000 inhabitants by the turn of the century. While the population of the United States as a whole grew a remarkable 35 percent from 1790 to 1800 (from 3,929,214 to 5,308,483), and another 36 percent in the following decade (to 7,239,881) the area of settlement also grew rapidly, thus sustaining favorable ratios of population to land.

The most striking characteristic of this population was its mobility. The association between horizontal mobility – across space – and vertical mobility – rising in wealth and status– was already well established in colonial Anglo-America. The revolution gave a powerful new impetus to these dynamic tendencies. The war removed political obstacles to new settlement, "pacified" the frontier, and exposed soldiers to opportunities in distant parts of the country. Opportunities to purchase lands at competitive prices expanded dramatically with the opening of state and federal land offices, the distribution of military bounty lands, and proliferating private land speculations. Historians disagree about the effects of these opportunities on the "average" American farmer: if it was possible for young men to replicate the careers of their fathers, thus reinforcing traditional agrarian values, a dynamic market also encouraged new forms of enterprise. The spread of settlement was driven by *commercial* agriculture, with the greatest rewards going to those who embraced "modern" values and successfully exploited distant markets; buying and selling land could be an end in itself, and not just the means toward subsistence. The apparent contradiction between backward-looking "republican" values and forward-looking "liberal" values, between the market as means and as end, troubled contemporaries much less than it does modern scholars. Indeed, it was the genius of Jeffersonianism to obscure the distinction, celebrating both the farmer's independence of the market and his enterprise in pursuing market opportunities. Jefferson's yeoman farmer was thus a republican everyman, an idealized image with as much cultural resonance for the urban artisan as for his country cousin. The common ground for both, containing and transcending ambivalence about the market, was the apotheosis of the republican father and head of household.

The American Revolution has often been depicted as a struggle of sons against fathers, culminating in a reconfiguration of marriage and family life along consensual, affective, and sentimental lines. There is no question that patriots fashioned themselves as "sons" (of liberty) and "brothers" in their resistance to the supposed abuses of patriarchal authority by the English king and their mother country. But this was less a revolt against patriarchy than an effort to perfect and justify paternal rule, freed from the "dead hand" of aristocracy. Jefferson, the great republican theorist, saw no contradiction in casting himself as "the most blessed of the patriarchs" in his life at Monticello.[3] His animus was instead directed at the tyranny of the fictitiously immortal family, the aristocratic lineage that made men and families unequal, regardless of their merits. Even the beneficiaries of an aristocratic regime – the favored few who were born to rule – lacked the natural autonomy and independence of a republican father who provided for his own family and prepared his sons to establish their own independent households when they came of age. The legal fiction of aristocracy, enforced in reality by the power of the state, was that family pedigree – the accident of birth – determined the fortunate (or unfortunate) heir's station in life. For Jefferson, this was the secular analogue of the Calvinist doctrine of predestination: Adam's hapless progeny were powerless to determine their own fate; needless to say, Adam himself could take no satisfaction in providing for his sons, since his only legacy to them was the taint of sin and eternal damnation. Adam was thus the model for founders of family lineages, entailing the sin of aristocracy – a slavish dependency on the caprice of fortune – on successive generations. Jefferson's republican patriarch was Adam's antitype, the good father whose benevolent authority was perfect and unfettered and therefore in accord with nature's laws.

American revolutionaries juxtaposed the "natural" nuclear families that were the building blocks of republican society with the "artificial," extended, and transgenerational families of corrupt aristocratic regimes. The civic well-being of the republic was a function of the soundness of its component parts. For consent to be a durable foundation for government, it was essential that citizens confront each other on equal terms: republican fathers governed their families, free from outside interference and according to the dictates of nature. "Nature" was the crucial premise here. In the republican scheme, the only legitimate dependencies were those determined by nature, to secure the independence of families and perpetuate the race.

Wives and Mothers

Households in the early republic were never completely autonomous, nor was paternal authority absolute. Republican families were created by free acts of consent between independent agents of equal moral standing. Though their civic identities were thereafter "covered" by their husbands, wives supposedly exercised a crucially important – if necessarily subordinate – role in family governance. Men who failed to respect and honor their wives earned the opprobrium of their neighbors. Fathers who failed to acknowledge the independence of their adult children or who sought to extend their authority beyond their own households also defied nature: the republic – the fathers of the state in their collective capacity – would not sanction such arbitrary exercises of authority. Nor were fathers free to exploit or abuse their authority over family dependents; to borrow the formulation of the contemporary German philosopher Immanuel Kant, it was imperative to recognize the moral integrity of every individual as an "end" in him- or herself, not as the "means" toward other ends, regardless of his or her contingently and temporarily dependent condition. Religious congregations sometimes disciplined errant members; outraged neighbors might intervene where violations of community norms were most egregious; and all citizens were in theory amenable to legal sanctions.

As a practical matter, however, society in general and the "state" in particular were ill-equipped to interfere in the domestic sphere. This liberal, laissez-faire stance was strongly reinforced by republican ideology and was most conspicuous in gender relations. The promise of republicanism extended to all free, white males, for sons could aspire to the household independence and civic dignity that their fathers possessed. But females could aspire to nothing on their own behalf; as dependent, passive "citizens," they were represented in civic life by fathers and husbands. In the Anglo-American legal tradition, the dependent status of married women was rationalized by the doctrine of *coverture*: the *feme covert* was "covered" by the male who exercised legitimate authority over her and any property she possessed. Women were not completely erased in legal practice: in default of male protectors, single adult women with sufficient property could support themselves in independent, if defective, households; widows could claim dower rights, generally to the income from a third of their husbands' real property, during their own lifetimes. But these qualifications of coverture did not constitute any significant recognition of women's rights. To the contrary, the complexities of family law reflected the imperfect fit between the social ideal, in which everyone belonged to some household or other, and the occasional failure of families resulting from fathers' premature death, absence, or incompetence. Women's highly circumscribed property rights helped sustain the household regime, minimizing the liability of society as a whole for female survivors of family failure.

Demographic conditions in Anglo-America were extraordinarily conducive to family formation and survival: longer life expectancies combined with early marriages to assure that most fathers could expect to live until their sons and daughters in turn formed new households. When Jefferson imagined himself a "patriarch" or George Washington urged migrants to the West to fulfill "the first and great commandment, *Increase and Multiply*," they were commenting on these propitious material conditions.[4] Fecund women and a fertile continent, "with room enough for our descendants to the thousandth and thousandth generation," made the United States "nature's nation."[5] The natural role for women was reproduction, a high policy imperative in a lightly populated new nation seeking to extend its control over a vast continent. By any conventional standard, the United States was militarily weak, vulnerable as much to centrifugal forces within a tenuous union of states as to the machinations of neighboring imperial powers and their Indian proxies. But the Americans had one great advantage in the contest for continental empire: the highest birthrate in the western world. Benjamin Franklin offered a remarkably precocious analysis of American demography in 1751, predicting that the American population would double every twenty-five years: "in another Century . . . the greatest Number of *Englishmen* will be on this Side the Water."[6] After the revolution, Yale President Ezra Stiles accurately projected a population of 50,000,000 by 1876. Even "if the present ratio of increase should be rather diminished in some of the elder settlements, yet an accelerated multiplication will attend our general population, and overspread the whole territory westward for ages."[7] Both writers were patriotic visionaries, linking population, wealth, and power to America's rising glory, whether as part of the British Empire or as a new nation. Although they conceded that immigration contributed to population growth, they emphasized that a high birthrate was its primary source. By fulfilling their "natural" role as mothers, American women were the ultimate source of awesome power, guaranteeing the inexorable spread of republican civilization across the continent. Jefferson and other early advocates of "manifest destiny" had this glorious role for women in mind as they envisioned the transformation of "virgin land" into a productive landscape of family farms.

Foreign observers also noted the political significance of growing population and expanding settlement. Over more than a century of conflict for hegemony in North America, French imperial officials had been obsessed with Anglo-American fertility; Spanish officials inherited these concerns when the trans-Mississippi region was ceded to Spain in the Peace of Paris in 1763. Frontier settlers were not necessarily fearsome fighters; European professionals and Indian auxiliaries were usually better armed and much more amenable to command. But rapid population growth promised superior manpower and surplus wealth that would one day support a formidable military force. For anxious American commentators, that day was assuredly forthcoming – but had not yet arrived. During Jefferson's presidency, Tennessee congressman John Rhea predicted that the American position would *become* impregnable within a generation, as frontier sons reached maturity and the surplus population of the eastern states swelled the western settlements: if peace could be preserved for another twenty years, "the prosperity, happiness and power of the United States of America will remain fixed on a basis not to be moved by the united efforts of nations."[8]

The westward movement of American population was punctuated by war and would not have been possible without the exercise of state power. But its primary dynamic was demographic (and epidemiological) and economic, not military. A favorite rationale for the expropriation of Indian lands was that white settlers put them to "higher," more productive use: nature's bounty, properly "improved," could sustain a much larger population. But, of course, the higher uses settlers had in mind – namely producing agricultural surpluses for distant European, Caribbean, and American markets – precluded the traditional forms of land use that had sustained Indian populations for centuries. Jefferson interpreted the cultural encounter between white settlers and native inhabitants in terms of reproductive regimes. Countering the suggestions of Comte de Buffon that animal species, including humans, tended to degenerate in the New World, Jefferson insisted that Indians were fully capable of achieving the highest level of civilized development. The explanation for their savage state was *cultural*: Indian men chose to resist civilization – and jeopardize the survival of their race – because they exercised despotic sway over their women, interfering with the "natural" process of reproduction by forcing them to do men's work. This was why Indians, with the leisure to cultivate their skills as warriors, could be – for a brief moment – such dangerous enemies. But the next generation, disappearing from the face of the land while white Americans became "as numerous as the leaves of the trees," would be unable to sustain their enmity.[9] Ultimately republican civilization would triumph because of the enlightened way Americans treated their women.

A high birthrate was the best possible proof that American families were organized in accord with nature's laws. The "natural equality" of women, their freedom to fill their roles as wives and mothers, was best secured under the republican dispensation because male household heads did not exploit their superior physical power to oppress them. With the Indians, Jefferson wrote in his *Notes on Virginia*, "force is law.

The stronger sex therefore imposes on the weaker. It is civilization alone which replaces women in the enjoyment of their natural equality. That first teaches us to subdue the selfish passions, and to respect those rights in others which we value in ourselves."[10] The enlightened treatment of women thus was not simply a question of political prudence, as the American people guaranteed their future hegemony over the continent, but also revealed that self-restrained republican fathers had crossed a threshold of *moral* development. By recognizing women's moral autonomy and integrity – their "natural equality" *within* the family – republican men transcended their own savage natures. An unfriendly reader might conclude that Jefferson conceived of women merely as breeders, whose "nature" reduced them *below* the level of civilized men. But the "equality" of women – like the freedom and equality of men – constituted an achievement *of* republican civilization, exalting women above the men who impregnated them and provided for them and their children. "Nature," the fertility both of the continent and of the women who populated it, signified the great potential that enlightened republican men who recognized its laws would develop for the greater glory of mankind.

Republican families were little republics, the building blocks of an enlightened social order that accorded with nature's design. The republican father's moral identification with dependent family members provided the most perfect, "natural" justification for his authority. Yet if this conflation of part and whole, father and family, recalled the traditional justification of monarchy, with subject-children – dependent members of the body politic – submitting to the benevolent authority of royal fathers, republicanism also expressed powerful anti-patriarchal impulses. When revolutionaries sought to secure their property rights and thus guarantee their role as providers and protectors of their families they provided a republican rationale for traditional paternal authority: the patriarchal principle of sovereignty was not so much abolished as relocated, from kingdom to household, so that it now conformed to nature's laws. At the same time, however, Jefferson and fellow patriots envisioned a progressive social order that would enable all citizens, including women, to fulfill their human potential.

Republican men might conceive of this fulfillment in familial terms, linking a fantasy of perfect paternal power with their selfless devotion to the well-being of dependents. Even while the republican ideal of self-governing families reaffirmed and reinforced the father's independent role in representing his family to the outside world, it also provided a new domain for female agency and influence within the domestic sphere. Republican paternalism could be turned against the abuses of patriarchal power. Abigail Adams famously asked husband John to "Remember the Ladies": "I cannot say that I think you very generous" to them, she explained, "for whilst you are proclaiming peace and good will to Men, Emancipating all Nations, you insist upon retaining an absolute power over Wives."[11] In her *Gleaner* essays (1792–4), Judith Sargeant Murray proclaimed the right and responsibility of women to support themselves and their families when husbands and fathers failed to perform their expected roles. Though these critics operated within the conceptual framework of gender difference, reminding men that the ultimate justification for male authority was the welfare of families, they also made it clear that "the Ladies" were perfectly capable of making moral judgments on male behavior. With the selfless devotion so characteristic of their sex, republican women were also prepared to take on male roles when necessary, however unnatural these roles might ordinarily be. Revolutionary republicanism thus simultaneously justified conventional gender distinctions while authorizing women to claim a position of moral equality, if not superiority.

The independence of the male citizen in the civic realm, beyond the household, was predicated on fulfilling his responsibilities to dependent family members. Only then would he vindicate his right to be free from the control of other men and govern his own family. Moral men would not only sustain family government, thus providing a secure foundation for a republican social order, but would also look beyond their own immediate self-interest to recognize the common good of *all* the families who collectively constituted the "people." This was the logic of female influence: both at home and in society, republican women domesticated and moralized the "boisterous passions" of republican men, enabling them to develop their moral potential. As American republicans learned from Lord Kames (Henry Home) and other great moral philosophers of the Scottish Enlightenment, an innate "moral sense" defined human nature itself. "The Creator would indeed have been a bungling artist," Jefferson concluded, "had he intended man for a social animal, without planting in him social dispositions."[12] Jefferson and the moral philosophers did not define "nature" *against* civilization, but instead insisted that civilization progressively fulfilled nature's design. The new republican regime would be *more* civilized than its corrupt European counterparts because it better enabled Americans to realize their true natures as moral beings. Women would play a critical role in fulfilling this revolutionary promise.

Women were recognized as citizens in the new American republics, but they could not participate fully in civic life. With the exception of a relatively small number of unmarried property-owning women who voted in New Jersey until 1807, women did not vote, hold public office (with the exception of a few postmistresses), or serve on juries or in the military. Yet women were often present in public places – in salon society, in election-day crowds, and even in the audiences that crowded law courts and legislative halls – and public men sought their approval and support. The paradoxical justification for gender hierarchy was the sentimental conceit that men fulfilled their better natures by identifying with dependent, but morally superior females. In other words, truly enlightened men cultivated their capacity for feminine feeling; to the extent they were successful, they could *represent* their women, thus justifying their erasure from civic life. In retrospect, this fictive or "virtual" representation strains credibility. Yet it did serve to give republican women civic identities that were, to some ambiguous extent, independent of their husbands and fathers.

Republican fathers also claimed the rights to "represent"

women in economic transactions. They may or may not have recognized the contributions these women made to the household economy, whether in producing, processing, and exchanging goods for family consumption or market exchange, but husbands certainly understood that their wives' dowries could provide crucial resources for establishing farms or other businesses. And though it was difficult to secure women's distinct property rights in marriage – except in states where equity jurisprudence mitigated the rigors of coverture – fathers' continuing solicitude for married daughters could limit husbands' authority in practice, particularly given the possibility of gaining further resources through inheritance. In republican theory, enlightened men provided both for their families and for the common good because they were autonomous and responsible moral agents; in reality, republican men often found themselves constrained by – and dependent on – complex family networks.

The marriage union had extraordinary ideological significance for revolutionary republicans. Everywhere in the western world, family life was increasingly construed in sentimental, affective terms. Americans were unusual, however, in identifying the choice of marriage partners with the formation of family households that were the building blocks of the republican edifice. Young women who freely chose their mates thus found themselves in the vanguard of the republican assault on patriarchal tyranny. Their free choices provided a new gloss of legitimacy to traditional doctrines of coverture and female subordination. At the same time, however, the idealization of marriage as an affective, consensual union led to a gradual liberalization of divorce laws that at least implicitly recognized women's "rights." The sentimental celebration of female virtue would have profound implications for the constitution of bourgeois family life in subsequent decades. In courtship, young women were empowered to make moral judgments about the character of courting males; after marriage, husbands' performance as household heads constituted a continuing test of their character in the world of men. The character of the republican husband and father was tested by his ability to "govern" his family effectively and benevolently, and this was, paradoxically, most conspicuous in his *wife's* day-to-day management of the household economy.

Virtuous women were vulnerable to bad choices in the marriage market because they were so ignorant of the ways of the world. The exaltation of romantic love constituted both a denial that there even was a marriage market, governed by the material concerns of prospective mates and their families, and an implicit recognition that women in particular needed reliable criteria for assessing the character of future husbands. If there was a carnivalesque dimension to courtship, with young women reigning supreme over their future lords and masters, it also provided the opportunity for courting males to display romanticized versions of character traits – enterprise, perseverance, and fidelity – that would stand them and their dependents in good stead later in life. The burgeoning sentimental literature of the day, much of it imported from England but including as well the work of some of the first successful (and often female) American novelists, was addressed specifically to the cultural problem of choice in courtship, of communicating the kind of knowledge that would enable virtuous women to imaginatively transcend, but not to compromise, the innocence that made them desirable and valuable as mates. William Wells Brown's *The Power of Sympathy* (1789), the "first" novel written by an American, was a derivative reworking of the themes of seduction and betrayal churned out by English writers. Subsequent writers such as Susanna Rowson, author of the best-selling *Charlotte Temple* (1797), adapted the genre more compellingly to American locales and social settings. These novels invariably offered a gallery of fam ily portraits resulting from the choices young women made, some happy and others pathetic. Their message was ambivalent: on one hand, virtuous innocents who could not discern the true character of their suitors were doomed to victimhood; on the other, more thoughtful heroines exhibited the superior discernment that would guarantee their future happiness.

The common concern was with *knowledge*, the need to interpret the self-representations of suitors. The concern was exacerbated by the conscious duplicity of fortune hunters and seducers who were so adept at manipulating romantic conventions and at presenting themselves as authentic lovers, motivated by the most laudable and "natural" impulses. In seeking to distinguish nature and artifice, reality and appearance, sentimental women engaged with a fundamental problem in republican culture. Women would suffer more catastrophically and conclusively from *their* bad choices; mobile, enterprising men could always make a fresh start. But the welfare of the commonwealth also ultimately depended on the reciprocal trust and fellow feeling of male citizens. The domestic sphere was a microcosm of the larger society: a society of deceivers and seducers, of maximizing, amoral men, was fundamentally corrupt and could not survive. This was why Montesquieu had written that "virtue" was the soul, or animating principle, of a republic. Americans embraced a "softer," more modest version of this precept. "I go on this great republican principle," James Madison told the Virginia Ratifying Convention in June 1788, "that the people will have virtue and intelligence to select men of virtue and wisdom."[13] This was the bourgeois virtue of the workaday world, a virtue that derived from – and was exhibited in – the domestic sphere.

Sentimental novels mediated between two economies, material and sexual, providing female readers with crucial knowledge about their social and cultural roles. Modern readers tend to be suspicious and contemptuous of the cult of sentimental feeling, emphasizing the dangers of mystifying and denying these supposed economic realities. But such an approach is reductive and anachronistic, for the challenge to women and men in the early republic was to reconcile exalted cultural norms with the mundane realities of family life. Readers could learn a good deal about sex, and particularly about the dangers of unwanted pregnancies, from these novels; they could also contemplate the disastrous material implications of bad romantic choices. Not coincidentally, the rage for sentimental novels *coincided* with the emergence of a new reproductive regime in which women exercised more control over their sexuality. Sentimental writers correctly emphasized the increased risks to women in a mobile society, where the extended family networks of village society no longer operated effectively to regulate household formation and provide for the welfare of neighbors. Romantic courtship kept courting men at a safe distance from vulnerable women, providing a buffer zone of sublimated sentiment and highly stylized behavior. Denial and postponement of sexual favors both enhanced female bargaining power in courtship and anticipated a domain of growing female influence within marriage.

Fathers and Sons

Thomas Jefferson impregnated his wife, Martha Wayles Skelton Jefferson, six times. No sons lived past infancy; one daughter, Lucy, died of whooping cough at age 2, survived by her two older sisters, Martha and Maria. Martha Jefferson died in 1782, after giving birth to Lucy. Daughter Maria Jefferson (Eppes) lived long enough to become a mother herself, dying in 1804 at age 25. Only Martha Jefferson (Randolph) survived her father, producing twelve children; Maria had two children before her premature death. The frequent presence of so many of these children at Monticello gladdened the retirement years of their grandfather. The mortality figures in the Jefferson family were high, but not unusual. Childbirth was a time of great danger for both mother and child: the ever present possibility of early death provided ample material for sentimentalists who extolled feminine virtues, further underscoring the importance of postponing and regulating sexual activity.

The sentimental Jefferson lavished extraordinary love and attention on his daughters. Martha, known in the family as "Patsy," played a particularly important role in Jefferson's life after her mother's death. "I have placed my happiness on seeing you good and accomplished," Jefferson admonished her in 1783 (when she was 11 years old), "and no distress which this world can now bring on me could equal that of your disappointing my hopes. If you love me then," he concluded on a characteristically manipulative note, "strive to be good under every situation. . . ."[14] Daughters had to be carefully educated in order to properly fulfill their "natural" role in the family circle. Jefferson recognized as well that his daughters should be prepared for unfortunate contingencies – "the chance that in marriage [Martha] . . . will draw a blockhead I calculate at about fourteen to one," he told a French correspondent – that might require them to assume male responsibilities.[15] But a young female's highest aspirations should be to ornament and improve the domestic sphere, not to follow the unnatural example of promiscuous Parisian aristocrats who encroached on male prerogatives. The contrast with America was striking. You should be content to stay in Philadelphia, Jefferson advised the young matron Anne Willing Bingham, where "the society of your husband, the fond cares for the children, the arrangements of the house, the improvements of the grounds, fill every moment with a healthy and an useful activity."[16]

Male self-interest in promoting this idyllic image of domestic bliss is obvious. But for Jefferson there was a crucial moral and altruistic dimension to his conception of gender roles. Male energies were mobilized to create a domestic sphere in which men submitted to female influence. Most crucially, republican daughters were educated to take on the exalted roles of wife and mother in new, independent households, not to serve the selfish dynastic ambitions of great aristocratic families. The defining characteristic of republican domesticity was the social reproduction of the autonomous household form. This is what made republican fathers moral: their absolute authority in family government prepared the way for the eventual succession of the rising generation. Fatherhood was thus a form of stewardship. Eschewing the aristocratic delusion of immortality, in which the "dead hand of the past" shaped family destinies across generations, republican fathers recognized that, "by the law of nature, one generation is to another as one independant nation to another." The authority of the republican father, like the sovereignty of an "independant nation," was contingent on the reciprocal recognition of fathers and sons. Fathers were sovereign, but they held power – and property – in trust, or "usufruct," for their children.[17]

In Jefferson's republican vision, the dynastic impulses of aristocratic families gave way to an inclusive conception of the "people" as a great family of families. Enlightened citizens understood that their own best interests were inextricably tied to those of fellow citizens; recognizing the independence of the households formed by their own children, fathers collectively would be solicitous for the welfare of *all* households. This redirection of loyalty and identity, from particular families to the "country" as a whole, came easily to Jefferson. Without any sons of his own, he saw himself as a disinterested patron and mentor of talented younger men, promoting their moral and intellectual development and preparing them for careers in public service. Jefferson's interest in public education grew naturally out of this sublimated, diffuse conception of paternal responsibility. Republican ideology and revolutionary experience encouraged patriot fathers to think of themselves as a single generation: regardless of their ages, they were all "sons of liberty" and brothers-in-arms. Their children necessarily constituted another, distinct generation. Thinking in these schematic terms led Jefferson and his contemporaries to conceive of their republican experiment as "a new order *of* the ages," a fundamental reordering of generational relations. The great challenge was to perpetuate the republic, guaranteeing that future generations would enjoy the great boon of self-government. Education represented a public investment in the rising generation, an intergenerational transfer of property that fostered socially useful skills rather than perpetuating unequal estates. Young men who benefited from this public largesse would recognize the need to make similar provisions for their own children, thus sustaining the patriotic spirit of their revolutionary fathers.

Ambitious proposals for comprehensive public education may have produced meager results, but they did address a fundamental social and cultural concern. Aspirations to household self-sufficiency gained a powerful new ideological sanction in the revolution, and a fluid and dynamic economy encouraged enterprising young men to form new families. But opportunities for aspiring household heads reflected the erosion of traditional forms of patriarchal authority based on control of a limited supply of land or other forms of property, including the right to exercise a particular craft. Republican conceptions of paternal benevolence implicitly acknowledged both the inability of particular fathers to provide for – and control – their sons in the traditional fashion and their collective capacity, as custodians of the commonwealth, to maximize the opportunities of the rising generation as a whole.

The attenuation of traditional patriarchal authority was accelerated both by the extraordinary mobility of the American population and by the emergence of free labor markets in urban areas. As distances between households grew, the power of extended family connections diminished accordingly; the exploitation of family labor and of apprentices, fictive children subject to patriarchal rule, increasingly gave way to contractual relations with free workers. These developments did not originate with the revolution, but revolutionaries *were* required to come to terms with them, to discover principles of social order and cohesion in the absence of traditional forms of patriarchal power. They had to answer critics of the new republican regime, who believed that the revolution could not survive the centrifugal forces it unleashed, and overcome their own profound misgivings. In rejecting the paternal authority of George III, had Americans jeopardized the foundations of family government, turning sons against their fathers?

Social contract theory offered a theoretical solution to the problem of anarchy. Once their freedom to act as independent agents was secured, autonomous individuals would *come together*, freely consenting to republican self-government. In parallel fashion, liberal political economists explained how the enlightened pursuit of self-interest would lead to reciprocally advantageous exchanges in free markets, thus promoting the public good. Yet both of these accounts required a leap of faith. Were citizens – or participants in market transactions – capable of calculating their own long-term best interests? The problem had two dimensions, practical and normative. First, republicans would have to overcome formidable epistemological obstacles: in a world of deceptive appearances and conscious misrepresentations, would the principles of social action be as "self-evident" as the language of the Declaration of Independence so confidently suggested? And even if enlightened citizens *could* see clearly, would they be inspired by the same vision of individual and collective happiness? Jefferson and other revolutionary republicans resolved (or deflected) this normative dilemma by invoking a unitary, ordered conception of nature, governed by laws that would become progressively more apparent to enlightened mankind. But this did not mean that the republican form of government could survive only where citizens were either philosophers (or angels). On the contrary, the genius of republicanism was to build on the solid foundation of the people's common sense by coordinating the kinds of knowledge citizens gained in their ordinary pursuits with appropriate spheres of authority.

"State a moral case to a ploughman and a professor," Jefferson told his nephew Peter Carr, and "the former will decide it as well, and often better than the latter, because he has not been led astray by artificial rules."[18] The devolution of authority in Jefferson's scheme of ward republics made sense not only because the farmer knew what was best for his farm (and presumably would be receptive to new knowledge that would increase productivity) but because the father knew what was best for his family. Practical moral precepts derived from a proper understanding of family relationships and responsibilities: the mysteries and "artificial rules" and of "higher," elite education were more likely to obscure than illuminate those precepts. Family life was the best school of morality. In Jefferson's new republic all families – and all generations – were equal, as nature designed them to be, thus guaranteeing the perpetuation and progress of the race. In the reciprocal recognition of each generation's "sovereignty," fathers and sons would meet on a high moral plane: the benevolent impulses that governed families would suffuse republican society as a whole. The more perfect union of republican fathers and their independent households would be grounded not merely in prudential calculations of self-interest but in the ties of love and affection that spontaneously emerged from – and were cultivated in – properly constituted families.

Bonds of Brotherhood: The Associational Impulse

Self-interest alone could not sustain the republic. Individuals seeking their own, immediate advantage were vulnerable to corrupt influence; failing to provide for the welfare of future generations, they would not identify with one another as members of the people, a great family of families. Jefferson recognized the need for more powerful and enduring bonds of union when he drafted the Declaration of Independence. Disdaining the language of prudence and calculation, Jefferson and his congressional colleagues "mutually pledge to each other our Lives, our Fortunes and our sacred Honor."[19] The imperial crisis, as it was recapitulated in the Declaration, was a family quarrel. When the king betrayed his paternal responsibilities, his aggrieved children turned to one another to vindicate the claims of the "living generation." In doing so, filial obligations gave way to fraternal bonds. The patriots' willingness to give up their lives for their imaginary family was both reproof to the despotic father – who was now making war on his own children – and justification for the new republican regime.

But Jefferson and his colleagues knew that this new American family or "people" was their own invention, a desperate improvisation at a time of revolutionary crisis. Suspicious congressmen encountered each other as strangers with conflicting interests and alien attitudes. Their tenuous union was based more on the grand abstractions of republican ideology – translations of English constitutional principles into various and distinctive provincial idioms – than on the shared historical experience and collective consciousness of a single "people." Conceptions of American nationhood reflected this paradoxical imperative. In order to overcome their misgivings about challenging monarchical authority and to assure themselves that their bold enterprise might just possibly succeed, patriots had to imagine themselves brothers, members of the same great family. This invocation of family ties constituted a revolutionary leap of faith that could only be fulfilled in the future, as patriot brothers became the fathers of a great people.

In the meantime, however, patriots would have to act together, *as if* they were brothers. Much of the political conflict of the revolutionary and early national periods reflected ambivalent responses to this political imperative. Thrown together in intensely intimate and highly stressful political contexts – in revolutionary committees and congresses and then in new state and national governments – patriots forged both fraternal friendships and fratricidal enmities. As historian Joanne Freeman has persuasively argued, political partisanship was fueled by an "honor culture" in which policy issues were inevitably translated into personal terms. Honor, the sensitive self-regard traditionally associated with proud aristocratic lineages, was now linked with conflicting conceptions of the public interest – thus pointing to a "modern" conception of party competition in a pluralistic democracy – but retained a powerfully personal, apparently "pre-modern" dimension. It would be a mistake, however, to exaggerate the distinction between "modern" and "pre-modern" elements in the party divisions of the early republic. The great challenge for revolutionary statesmen was to reconcile abstract political principles with lived personal experience, making revolutionary aspirations to independent nationhood seem real, both to themselves and to the "people" generally. Alexander Hamilton felt compelled to duel with Aaron Burr in order to preserve his "ability to be in future useful, whether in resisting mischief or effecting good, in those crises of our public affairs, which seem likely to happen": his devotion to the republic demanded the ultimate sacrifice.[20] The need to mediate the universal and the particular, the public and the personal, defines modern politics. Party leaders no longer fight duels because they have found other, more "sophisticated" ways to mobilize their followers.

Revolutionary patriots were inspired by the loftiest ideals, devoted themselves not only to the welfare of their country but to the future happiness of the whole human race. Yet this did not mean that they could easily transcend the personalistic politics of the old regime. On the contrary, republicanism simply extended the scope of the aristocratic honor culture, encouraging enterprising men of modest pedigree to assert their patriotism and virtue, traditional prerogatives of the ruling class. Historians of republican ideology have shown that print culture was the crucial medium for this process of democratization. The "bourgeois public sphere" of print – the myriad pamphlets, newspaper essays, and broadsides that publicized patriot principles – afforded new opportunities to able penmen, however obscure their background. In this cool, supposedly impersonal world of print, pseudonymous patriots could strike neo-classical poses as disinterested advocates of the common good.

Yet the revolutionary "republic of letters" did not have stable, well-defined boundaries, nor would it always be governed by canons of good taste and erudition. Print was a dynamic, protean medium that could be deployed in unexpected ways. Staunch patriot John Adams, author of the *Novanglus* letters (1775) and other important contributions to the literature of revolution, recoiled at the vigor and vulgarity of Thomas Paine's best-selling *Common Sense*. Unlike Paine, Adams continued to be enamored of the mixed and balanced government that Whigs believed characterized the uncorrupted British constitution. But Adams was less disturbed by Paine's message (both men called for an immediate break with Britain) than by the vernacular immediacy of his language. Paine's direct form of popular address, unmediated by traditional cultural authority, was the literary analogue of simple democracy. This subversive, democratic tendency would become increasingly powerful over the next few decades, as political leaders sought to mobilize public support for controversial policy positions. The result was a progressive *transformation* of the public sphere, and therefore of how an increasingly politicized people defined itself. Dispensing with the implicitly genteel conventions of dispassionate, reasoned argument, newspaper editors fomented a politics of personality and partisanship. A "cool" medium became increasingly heated, thus confusing and conflating "private" and "public" and enabling individual citizens to identify with people or the nation as a whole.

Recent scholarship on the origins and construction of national identities has illuminated the limitations of a static notion of the public sphere, focused on the ability of an emerging "bourgeois" class to discover (and disguise) itself in print. Revolutionary print culture enabled Americans to identify with one another over great distances, simultaneously obliterating differences and promoting a sense of intimacy. The significance of this collective consciousness, however "false" it may now seem to us, was to promote and synchronize political action toward concrete goals in specific local settings. Under the aegis of publicity, an atomized and homogenized "people" did not retreat to private spaces to coolly contemplate the wider world; instead, citizens joined one another in an expanding array of associations to express and enact their civic identities. The revolution, with its committees, militia musters, and mobs, was the practical model for this democratized public sphere. Far from being impersonal and abstract, the civic life of the early republic was intensely personal and local, encouraging individual citizens to take conspicuous public stands on the controversial issues of the day. Politics was not simply the business of privileged insiders (though, of course, it would always be that), but a compelling concern for all good citizens conscious of the universal significance of the new nation's republican experiment. This consciousness of meaningful connection to a transcendent whole – the genius of modern nationalism – justified the ongoing mobilization of partisans in ritual reenactments of the revolution that transformed American public life. Partisan identities gave citizens a more concrete sense of their "sovereignty," encouraging them to act locally while linking those localities with each other and with the wider world.

Deep divisions within an expanding political nation constituted the crucial dynamic of this democratization of civic life. The presence of powerful internal enemies, false patriots who would betray the revolution – whether by leaguing with Britain to erect a new aristocratic, monarchical regime (as Republicans charged Federalists), or by cynically unleashing the forces of anarchy and disorder that made a mockery of republicanism in revolutionary France (as Federalists charged Republicans) – sustained a sense of revolutionary crisis that justified continuing popular political mobilization. Voters were thus the moral equivalent of soldiers, willing to sacrifice all for the good of their country – and eager to gain whatever advantage they could, material or otherwise, over factious foes. If professions of patriotism concealed a mixed multitude of motives, they also authorized partisans to question their opponents' intentions. This characteristic juxtaposition of exalted principle and withering skepticism accelerated the democratization of discourse. As polemicists flushed out their quarry, stripping away the masks of anonymous opponents and probing their "characters," traditional distinctions between the better sort and common folk, private and public, progressively eroded.

Political democratization was spearheaded by partisan political editors who played increasingly critical roles in local politics. William Duane, editor of the Philadelphia *Aurora*, the leading national organ of the Republican party (the only major opposition paper that survived, barely, during the worst days of Federalist oppression in the late 1790s), was the prototype of a new class of editor-politicians who proliferated in subsequent decades. The "Revolution of 1800" would have been impossible without Duane and his fellow partisan editors. Not only did Duane help sustain the Republican cause – at a time when Jefferson, Madison, and other supposed "leaders" were virtually immobilized by the Federalists' repressive measures and popular enthusiasm for war against France – but he also served as an important political operative in Philadelphia and Pennsylvania Republican politics, bringing national political issues down to street-level by organizing local election tickets, getting out the vote, and distributing patronage. But Duane got few thanks for his efforts from the Republican elite he so ably served. Jefferson preferred to think that he owed his election to a broad, spontaneous, popular reaffirmation of revolutionary principles, not to the specific agency of partisan activists like Duane, often with dubious social backgrounds. In other words, elite leaders were more comfortable with abstract conceptions of popular sovereignty than with the mechanics (in both senses of the word) of political mobilization. The ambivalence about the democratization of political life that characterized Jefferson and its other ideological sponsors resulted from this cognitive dissonance. Jefferson made the most exaggerated claims for the epochal significance of his election precisely because of his unwillingness to acknowledge his debt to party activists such as Duane.

Though his personal ambitions were thwarted by the gentry leadership of his party, Duane heralded a new era in the history of party politics. His street-level success in translating ideological principle into partisan practice was made possible by the democratization of civic life. Partisan political mobilization was only the most conspicuous manifestation of a general tendency for American men to form associations. Fraternal union was not only an ideological imperative but a practical necessity for individual citizens who needed to pool limited economic and cultural resources as well as votes in order to achieve personal and collective goals. The associational impulse itself was not new, particularly in cities where groups like the St. Andrew's Society and the Sons of St. Patrick (formed in Philadelphia in 1749 and 1771) offered welfare benefits and cultural comfort to Scottish and Irish immigrants respectively. By the time of the Revolution philanthropic leaders had also begun to establish an infrastructure of hospitals, poor houses, schools, and libraries in Philadelphia and other large cities. After independence, however, the cultural authority of traditional social elites was increasingly diluted as ordinary citizens took the initiative in forming new groups and establishing new institutions. Groups such as the Masons, once the sole preserve of the urban gentry, formed new lodges in country towns, appealing particularly to ambitious, upwardly mobile young men from modest backgrounds.

Membership in fraternal or religious organizations gave citizens portable identities in a mobile society where the traditional sources of social knowledge characteristic of stable rural neighborhoods and village communities were no longer effective. Success in business depended on a man's "character"; in the absence of neighborly knowledge, group affiliations helped establish his trustworthiness and respectability. Every group presumably vetted new members, certifying their reliability to counterparts in other localities. In this way, associational life replicated the decentralized federal character of the new constitutional regime, reinforcing both local community identities and the consciousness of belonging to the "imagined community" of the nation as a whole.

Civic entrepreneurs in new settlements would replicate the institutional structures of the towns and neighborhoods they had left behind: town founders from over-populated Connecticut were particularly successful in exporting Yankee civic culture to Ohio's Western Reserve and further to the west. In these contexts "replication" meant adaptation and innovation: though extended family and neighborhood groups moved to the frontier, every new community included a large proportion of strangers. Local institutions and associations did not grow out of long-established kinship, friendship, and patronage networks that had facilitated civic development in the east. Nor could these groups rely on the prestige and authority of the state, as could established churches in every New England town and village (except in the new state of Vermont). Instead, the voluntary principle triumphed. Americans were joiners because it was in their interest – whether material or spiritual, or both – to belong to a variety of different groups; they were not simply following in the well-trod footsteps of their forefathers, even where associations sustained a sense of religious or cultural distinctiveness.

The rapid disestablishment of state churches throughout the country – the last establishments were dismantled in Connecticut, in 1818, and in Massachusetts, in 1833 – gave a powerful boost to voluntarism in religious life, as evangelical preachers who competed for members and financial support promoted a culture of revivalism and vital piety. Every religious and civic group had to justify itself to would-be members who were free to choose the groups they would join. In this highly mobile environment there was a premium on vigorous, voluntary assertions of group identity – for instance, in the new birth of converted Christians, or in Masonic initiation rituals – and a corresponding disparagement of inherited, ascriptive status, the hallmark of traditional, aristocratic regimes. The republican emphasis on consent thus permeated all aspects of American culture, from courtship and family formation to proliferating voluntary associations designed to serve every conceivable social and economic purpose.

Civic entrepreneurs recognized that order could no longer be enforced, nor could energies be mobilized and coordinated, by the exercise of traditional authority in a hierarchical social structure. When Jefferson invoked the individual's "pursuit of happiness" as the fundamental premise of the new regime, he thus suggested that social motivation and responsibility had to be *internalized*. The challenge was to assure that citizens shared a common worldview, projecting and pursuing happiness in harmonious ways that promoted the common good. For Jefferson, the solution was to clear away the intellectual rubbish of the old regime of privilege and prejudice and so enable the enlightened republican citizen to *look within* himself – to his own moral sense – to decipher nature's laws. But the opposite was more nearly the case, for the practical education of the republican citizen was *external and other directed*, learning how to interpret and anticipate the actions of other citizens in a fluid social environment. The modern conception of the "self," constantly negotiating or "fashioning" an identity in rapidly changing social conditions, was the necessary fiction of the age. The fiction was that individuals were truly autonomous and independent, and therefore capable of giving their consent. The social reality, which Alexis de Tocqueville so brilliantly analyzed in *Democracy in America*, was that unprecedented social freedom produced extraordinary conformity, that "individualism" gave rise to homogenized mass culture.[21]

Observers have explained the apparent paradox of order in anarchy by invoking God, or Nature, or the Market, or some combination of the three. But the paradox is a function of the way the problem is framed. Convinced of their own indispensability, privileged classes of the old regime naturally would see the republican revolution as a prelude to a reign of chaos; for their part, republicans would reverse the compliment, portraying aristocracy and monarchy as the unnatural sources of conflict and misery. The simpler, less ideologically charged explanation is that Americans had always been forced to fabricate social identities by voluntarily joining in group enterprises, and that the exaltation of popular sovereignty was a result of this social experience. Jefferson invoked these twin themes of mobility and choice when he identified "expatriation" as the central narrative thread of American colonial history: in their decision to come to the New World, freedom-loving emigrants simultaneously asserted individual and collective identities: "for themselves they fought, for themselves they conquered, and for themselves alone they have right to hold."[22] The revolution simply accelerated and illuminated a well-established social and cultural dynamic. Conscious both of their individual rights and of the need to cooperate with others to achieve *any* political, social, or economic goal, citizens simultaneously affirmed their identities both as individuals and as members of ever more inclusive social solidarities, culminating in patriotic identification with the American people.

Independence made Americans conscious of themselves as a distinct people, but it did not transform American culture. Still looking to the British metropolis for cultural standards, Americans remained cultural provincials. This was true even where revolutionaries claimed to be most original, in their "discovery" and application of republican principles that were only "self-evident" to them because they were so steeped in the British Whig tradition. American patriots came to congratulate themselves on their provincial defects, insisting that their *distance* from the corrupt metropolis made them all the more virtuous. Drawing on the familiar association of the "country" party with righteous opposition to "court" corruption, American republicanism represented the apotheosis of provincialism. Americans may have "turned the world upside down," but the revolution simply reinforced their traditional frames of reference, underscoring the juxtaposition of center and periphery, metropolis and province, "new world" and "old." Revolutionary patriots imaginatively transcended their provincial identities, advocating the "rights" of all mankind and asserting that their new republican constitutions expressed the natural genius of a free people. But these grand abstractions could not fill the cultural void. If Americans were not provincial Britons, who were they? A generation of historians, antiquarians, and mythographers, including David Ramsay, Jeremy Belknap, Mercy Otis Warren, John Marshall, and Washington's popular biographer, Parson Mason Locke Weems, sought to provide answers: the revolution itself, properly memorialized, constituted a glorious (if somewhat compressed) instant history worthy of a free people; the converging colonial histories of each state took on new interest in light of the movement toward independence.[23] But these histories would gain value and significance only if the republican experiment succeeded, if *future* generations of patriots saw themselves as part of the unfolding narrative. In other words, American "history," like the character of the American people itself, was protean and prospective, contingent on an unknown future. In their pursuit of happiness, provincial Americans were also pursuing their identity.

Individually and collectively, Americans had to make their way without the familiar landmarks of a mature society. Forced by circumstance to improvise a new civic culture, Americans at the same time remained slavishly dependent on metropolitan norms and standards. The efforts of cultural patriots to define a distinctive language and literature, like those of the historians to give the Americans a history of their own, reflected their acute consciousness of the problem. Lexicographer Noah Webster, whose great *American Dictionary of the English Language* was published in 1828, sought to distinguish American from British English, imputing enormous cultural significance to existing (and trivial) differences in usage while urging his countrymen to adopt his own (more "natural" and therefore republican) scheme of phonetic spelling. There was a growing market for products such as Webster's, though less because of their patriotic agenda than because they appealed to ambitious readers eager to "improve" themselves. For socially mobile Americans, improvement continued to be measured by metropolitan standards. Educational reformers such as Benjamin Rush of Philadelphia thought republican schools should jettison classical languages and learning, but the people would not be satisfied with merely vocational education. Latin survived and prospered in the academies and colleges of the new republic because of popular aspirations to genteel learning that could no longer be suppressed and contained by a hierarchical social order.

Cultural nationalists chafed at the new nation's continuing subservience to the metropolis. Like their political counterparts, revolutionary intellectuals aspired to be founders, generators of new values appropriate to the new republican regime. But their own social and cultural aspirations drew them inexorably into the great "republic of letters" that linked American provincials with the centers of European enlightenment. The revolution led Jefferson and a few fellow travelers to turn from Britain to France for cultural inspiration and authority, substituting a self-consciously progressive definition of "civilization" for the slavish, almost instinctive imitation of all things English that traditionally characterized provincial American elites. But this hypersensitivity to the latest, most enlightened trends in European thought and fashion simply reinforced the traditional role of the "better sort" in America, to serve as cultural mediators and exemplars of metropolitan gentility for their benighted countrymen.

The University of Virginia was the institutional embodiment of this cultural imperative. Jefferson's goal was to bring enlightened learning to his beloved commonwealth, producing a new republican ruling class in his own (provincial) image; not coincidentally, he also intended to create an edifying and inspirational model of architectural good taste that would spur the rebuilding of Virginia. Not surprisingly, when Jefferson sought to recruit professors for his university, he sent his agent Francis Walker Gilmer to Europe; the only Americans on the original faculty were George Tucker, professor of moral philosophy, and John T. Lomax, professor of law. After his own rigorous education in classical and modern learning and a life-time of correspondence and conversation with enlightened Europeans, Jefferson's faculty recruitment strategy came natu-rally. In effect, Jefferson had gone to Europe to become an American, a personal quest that would be replicated in his university's curriculum.

The new nation was, in fact, better able to produce scholars and teachers to staff its educational institutions than Jefferson acknowledged. To Jefferson's way of thinking, however, this intellectual class was indelibly tainted by twin heresies of "priestcraft," a traditional association with established and evangelical religion, and "aristocracy," the supposed tendency of a reactionary, Anglophiliac elite to resurrect the old, pre-revolutionary regime. European intellectuals with the right republican credentials, such as English radical Thomas Cooper, were more eligible for positions of cultural authority in the new nation than were their provincial American counterparts (the freethinking Cooper's appointment to a professorship in 1819 scandalized proper Virginians; Cooper accepted another position in South Carolina well before the new University opened its doors in 1825). In making such judgments, Jefferson challenged the cultural independence of home-grown intel-lectuals even while betraying a characteristically provincial in-feriority complex. Americans were hardly good enough for their own country; until institutions like the University of Vir-ginia could produce a truly republican elite, the new nation would continue to depend on enlightened Europeans for cul-tural leadership.

Jefferson was not the only cultural patriot who simultan-eously bemoaned and exemplified American provincialism. Exponents of high literary culture and the fine arts who hoped to find a prestigious – and remunerative – place for them-selves in the new republic as producers of a distinctively "American" culture met with massive popular indifference. American consumers had little interest in patronizing provin-cial writers and artists when the market was flooded with the products of metropolitan culture; because Congress did not accede to the international copyright agreement until 1830, enterprising printers could cut prices further by churning out cheap, pirated editions of British publications. Ambitious American artists sought training and patronage in Europe: Pennsylvanian Benjamin West, who emigrated in 1760 became a highly successful court painter in London; young John Trumbull, son of Connecticut's revolutionary governor, studied with West in London after the revolution – and visited Jefferson in Paris – before returning to America. Aspiring writers also sought the imprimatur of publication and critical acceptance in the former mother country. Well into the nineteenth century, American writers such as Washington Irving and James Fenimore Cooper established their reputations in England before being taken seriously at home. Cooper was the first American to make a living as a novelist; Philadelphian Charles Brockden Brown, a lawyer and partisan polemicist, gained a modest reputation from his gothic novels such as *Wieland* (1798) and *Arthur Mervyn* (1799–1800); the "Connecticut Wits," a small coterie of Federalist poets including Timothy Dwight, John Trumbull (no relation to the painter), David Humphreys, and Joel Barlow (who became an enthusiastic Jeffersonian), produced patriotic epics and political satire in the course of busy careers as lawyers, preachers, and educators.

The provincial artist's dilemma was double-edged. The first challenge was to find subject matter that was distinctive enough to justify his own – and the new nation's – lofty aspirations, but at the same time could meet the familiar, utterly conventional standards that were rigorously enforced by metropolitan arbiters of good taste. According to these standards, the American scene – so devoid of rich historical associations, so banal and transparent – offered little of interest to the refined sensibility. Celebration of the continent's natural grandeur implicitly conceded the point, for there was little grandeur in the human environment. Natural and pastoral motifs also fit neatly into well-established metropolitan literary and artistic traditions. But they did not appeal much to Americans who were too busy "improving" nature and developing its economic potential to dilate on the sublime or awesome.

Jefferson's much-anthologized passages on the beauties of nature underscored the prevailing popular indifference, setting off by contrast his own more rarefied perceptions. Cultivated European visitors would be amply rewarded for taking the trouble to cross the Atlantic to see the Natural Bridge (which Jefferson owned) or the Potomac River gap in the Appalachian Ridge, "one of the most stupendous scenes in nature." Yet there "are people who have passed their lives within half a dozen miles, and have never been to survey these monuments of a war between rivers and mountains, which must have shaken the earth itself to its center."[24] Jefferson emphasized his social and esthetic distance from his more practical-minded countrymen in such brief passages, but the bulk of his book, with its exhaustive catalogues of natural resources, showed that he shared his neighbors' instrumental attitude toward nature. In either case, the message to European readers was the same: come to the new world, whether to behold its natural wonders or to participate in its economic development. Jefferson thus once again struck a characteristically provincial note: even as he lauded Virginia's and America's *potential* for development – and for achieving the economic independence that its political pretensions required – he acknowledged that fulfillment of this potential depended on the continuing importation of European capital and expertise.

Cultural aspirations and economic development were linked. The kind of artistic and literary attainments that gave a nation an exalted character in the community of nations depended on the emergence of a cultural elite with sufficient leisure, resources, and collective self-confidence to generate its own values and standards. The crucial question was how a democratic society without great concentrations of wealth and privilege could support cultural production of any sort. It gradually became clear, to the consternation of cultural nationalists, that "public" support would not take the place of traditional forms of court and aristocratic patronage. The "people" might be willing to make patriotic sacrifices on the battlefield in order to secure America's political independence, but taxpayers showed little enthusiasm for publicly supported education, much less for patronizing arts and letters: if anything, the disestablishment of state churches marked a retrenchment of public investment in cultural institutions. In effect, the republican fiction of a monolithic "public" was pulverized, pluralized, and privatized. Cultural leaders would have to be entrepreneurs. Just as the clergy would have to win converts and financial support in a highly competitive religious marketplace, educators, writers, and artists would have to cultivate and respond to genuine popular demand for their services and products.

Drawn disproportionately from the ranks of the well-educated, wealthy, and privileged, aspirants to cultural leadership were as ambivalent about the claims of consumers in the emerging cultural marketplace as republican statesmen were about the escalating demands of voters in hotly contested elections. Yet there were extraordinary new opportunities for cultural as well as political entrepreneurs who could cater to popular tastes. The "people" were justifiably suspicious of the pretensions of would-be aristocrats, recognizing the discrepancy between metropolitan gentility and poor provincial imitations: Jefferson and his fellow Republicans exploited such popular prejudices in promoting their own pretensions to leadership. But just as Jefferson advocated a more refined, virtuous, and meritorious conception of leadership – promising the electorate better value for their votes – the cultural marketplace constituted an expanding arena for socially (and spiritually) ambitious consumers to improve themselves and rise up in this world (or the next). From the elite perspective, a more democratic culture was by definition vulgar and degraded, conflating high and low, aristocratic and plebeian. But for new consumers, the cultural marketplace provided new openings to the wider world, fostering rising social expectations by offering popular scripts for their pursuit of happiness.

Historian Richard Bushman has described this market-driven, increasingly pervasive democratic ethos as a culture of "respectability," a republicanized version of "gentility" that eschewed the excesses of aristocratic luxury and corruption. We now recognize respectability as the ideology *of* the marketplace, the so-called "bourgeois" values that flourished with the rise of capitalism. But students of consumption and behavior have shown that the market served as the medium for defining and pursuing more traditional social and cultural agendas, enabling participants to fashion themselves according to all manner of improving scripts. And the popular understanding of improvement, entrepreneurs recognized, was deeply conservative, transcending – and thus justifying – steady habits, hard work, and the accumulation of property. Property itself, in the form of the rapidly expanding world of consumer goods, was invested with extraordinary cultural significance, embodying the values and aspirations of ambitious Americans. Property accumulation might be an end in itself for the hypothetical "capitalist," but as the eminent German sociologist Max Weber and other critics of capitalist culture have shown, this capitalist was an ascetic, other-worldly sort, driven by his faith in some transcendent good.

The real world of the early American republic was not populated by ideal types. By the standards of the old world, where accumulating wealth and exercising power was supposed to be the exclusive province of an aristocratic elite, there were extraordinarily large numbers of self-seeking profit-maximizers in America who showed alarmingly little respect for traditional social distinctions; frauds, counterfeits, and confidence men proliferated in a mobile, opportunistic society where King Mammon now reigned. Moralizing clergymen and culture critics held forth on these themes to popular acclaim and were duly rewarded in the marketplace. As they enjoined their countrymen to aim for higher and better things, republican and evangelical moralists articulated appropriate behavioral standards and cultural values for anxious strivers.

The most remarkable development in the cultural history of the early republic was the success of the clergy, now deprived of the state support they had enjoyed in most colonies, in creating a valued and honored place for itself in local communities across the continent. Preachers of the Gospel marketed their wares in the cultural marketplace with flair and sophistication. Throughout the early republican era, sales of religious publications of all sort – from learned theological commentaries to the most humble tracts and manuals – far outpaced all other forms of publication. Unlike their secular counterparts, religious leaders had a clear agenda – winning souls – and could recognize and exploit genuine popular demand. Not coincidentally, American evangelicals from the time of Jonathan Edwards (1703–58) and his many students had secured for themselves a leading position in the vanguard of Protestant Christendom as theologians and revivalists.

In the wake of the Revolution, evangelical clergymen were well prepared to meet new marketplace challenges. Their efforts, culminating in a series of revivals beginning in the late 1790s (the "Second Great Awakening") helped make the new United States the most dynamically "Christian" nation in the world. Most importantly, the rapid progress of Christianity (measured in dramatically increasing numbers of churches, clergy, and converts) showed that the marketplace could generate social order and cultural homogeneity even as it offered consumers unprecedented freedom of choice. Under the new dispensation of voluntary contributions, Christians demonstrated an extraordinary willingness both to support the clergy and invest in their own and their communities' social and cultural improvement.

Christianity and republican ideology both had profound, complementary influence in shaping the new American culture of middle-class respectability. Deists like Jefferson, who considered evangelical Christianity a dangerously reactionary force, inimical to freedom of thought and therefore to the progress of civilization, were somewhat perplexed by this development. But evangelicals recognized Jefferson as an ally. Presbyterians, Baptists, and other dissenters were grateful to Jefferson for leading the fight against the Anglican establishment in Virginia: whatever his intentions may have been, his Bill for Religious Freedom (enacted in 1786) enabled evangelical sects to Christianize the commonwealth. When, as president, Jefferson's arduous critical study of the Bible led him to conclude that he was in fact a "Christian" – at least according to his own, highly idiosyncratic understanding of the term – he tacitly accommodated to the changing cultural landscape

and acknowledged his enormous debt to his evangelical supporters. He may finally have recognized that there was a fundamental congruence, not a contradiction, between his own
republican faith in the progress of civilization and the evangelical Christian's quest for an authentic, unmediated relation
with God.

Jeffersonianism and evangelical Christianity both flourished
in a world where political and cultural authority was radically decentered and diffused and where ordinary people were
free to vote, worship, and otherwise pursue their happiness as
they saw fit. If Americans were more likely to define their
highest aspirations in religious rather than political terms, they
recognized no Jeffersonian "wall of separation" between the
two domains. (Unlike most of his countrymen, Jefferson was
notoriously secretive about his own religious beliefs.) Private
piety was both deeply personal, hidden from the view of others, and transparently public, for God's grace enabled believers to lead better (if still sinfully imperfect) lives. Evangelical
Christianity appealed to Americans as much for its promises
of self-improvement as for its spiritual consolations. With the
help of fellow believers, Christians would be better able to
resist temptations which the market made more promiscuously
available and therefore to become sober, disciplined, and productive citizens. In the "alcoholic republic" where all social
pathologies seemed traceable to drinking, temperance was the
evangelical reformer's great panacea, the mother of proliferating efforts to control and eradicate disease, crime, and pov-
erty. Crucial to all these campaigns was a new conception of
the respectable, well-ordered "self" that was the product both
of Enlightenment psychology and the evangelicals' practical
divinity.

Christianity provided the missing dimension to Jefferson's
republican faith. Preachers offered practical advice about how
to link the business of everyday life with transcendent values
and therefore to make manifest the natural sociability, the
capacity for moral improvement, that Jefferson and other
Enlightenment moralists imputed to all men (and which made
them "equal"). The problem with Jefferson's more secular

vision of republican politics was that its skeptical account of the inevitable abuses of public power (all rulers were potential "aristocrats") reduced the public sphere to its lowest common denominator: public service, as Jefferson himself frequently observed, was a miserable, thankless vocation: "a dreary scene where envy, hatred, malice, revenge and all the worse passions of men are marshalled, to make one another as miserable as possible."[25] It was a necessary evil that could only be justified by imputing a higher value to "society," the world *beyond* politics where man realized his full potential, and particularly to the domestic domain, where republican fathers exercised sovereign authority for the good of their natural dependents. But Christian democrats, with their faith in the possibility of individual and collective redemption and improvement, did not recognize Jefferson's dichotomous distinctions between society and politics, home and the world. The tendency of their thought and practice was dynamic, integrative, and associative, to bring Americans ever closer together in pursuit of personal and collective goals. By contrast, the bonds of union among Jefferson's mutually jealous "little republics" were always tenuous, more a stipulation of faith in the inevitable progress of civilization toward some imagined future harmony than a practical program for collective action.

Conclusion

Americans undertook their grand experiment in nation-making without a distinctive national history and culture. They had to look *elsewhere* for their social and cultural cues. As republicans, who acknowledged no superior authority, they looked to each other; as provincials, who aspired to higher levels of refinement and civilization, they continued to look to the European metropolis. Self-fashioning, the pursuit of social mobility and improvement, thus reinforced the cult of respectability and conformity. In continuing to fashion themselves after metropolitan models, provincial Americans yet again strove to conform, reinforcing conventional standards that both gave direction to their personal strivings and made individuals more intelligible to each other.

Common cultural standards, like membership in proliferating associations that facilitated social action, provided Americans with much needed social knowledge about each other. Americans were famously curious – they needed to know who they were dealing with – but they were also credulous: they had to accept each other *on faith*. After all, the born-again Christian was confessedly a bad character who, by the grace of God, could be entrusted by his fellow believers with the most sacred responsibilities. Americans had to be believers: thus they flocked to churches, where belief was sanctioned and reinforced, as well as to other groups where they discovered themselves in each other.

Jefferson's political theory offers a window into the new republican social order. His celebration of the household form and of republican paternalism resonated both with the experience and aspirations of many Americans; his hostility to concentrations of political and cultural power appealed to – and helped sustain – a provincial hostility to the metropolitan authority that is the most enduring legacy of the American revolution. Yet Jefferson's scheme was at the same time far too static and narrowly political. Americans would not simply come together in his "little republics" to defend their liberties and transact public business, only to withdraw to their private domains. Constantly on the move, they would join in a dizzying array of associations to achieve their various goals. They would take their cues from each other – and from the proliferating institutions and associations that competed for their attention, their money, and their faith.

The end of the old regime thus did not mean the elimination of cultural authority, but rather its diffusion and redefinition. Ultimately, the *source* of that authority was less important than a general willingness to play by the rules of the game, to embrace the logic of a market society and culture with a fervent faith in the higher purposes it served. Alexis de Tocqueville captured the apparent paradox of cultural unity in social diversity in his discussion of "individualism," the cultural expression of the sovereign self that held sway in Jeffersonian and Jacksonian America. Republicans, who were obsessed with "virtue" and "character," recognized that authoritative behavioral cues and sanctions no longer flowed from the monarch to his subjects, or from the metropolis to its provinces. Republican culture sponsored the proliferation of new groups and new social identities: its genius, the genius of American nationalism, was to connect these identities, enabling citizens to be "good Americans" through their loyalty and sentimental identification with their families, with their local communities, and with the many groups they joined – churches, fraternal associations, business enterprises – as they pursued their happiness.

NOTES

1 TJ to Joseph C. Cabell, 2 Feb. 1816, Andrew A. Lipscomb and Albert Ellery Bergh, eds., *The Writings of Thomas Jefferson*, 20 vols. (Washington, DC, 1903–4), 14:421.

2 TJ to Col. William Duane, 28 Mar. 1811, ibid., 13:29.

3 TJ to Angelica Schuyler Church, 27 Nov. 1793, Julian Boyd et al., eds. *The Papers of Thomas Jefferson*, 27 vols. to date (Princeton, NJ, 1950–), 27:449.

4 Washington to the Marquis de Lafayette, 5 Dec. 1784, John C. Fitzpatrick, ed., *The Writings of George Washington*, 39 vols. (Washington, DC, 1931–44), 28:4.

5 TJ, First Inaugural Address, 4 Mar. 1801, Merrill D. Peterson, ed., *Thomas Jefferson Writings* (New York, 1984), 494.

6 Franklin, "Observations Concerning the Increase of Mankind, Peopling of Countries, &c.," 1751, J. A. Leo Lemay, ed., *Benjamin Franklin Writings* (New York, 1987), 373.

7 Stiles, *The United States Elevated to Glory and Honour*, 1783 Connecticut Election Sermon (2nd edn., Worcester, 1785), 60.

8 Rhea to his constituents, 8 Apr. 1806, Noble E. Cunningham, Jr., *Circular Letters of Congressmen to Their Constituents, 1789–1829*, 3 vols. (Chapel Hill, NC, 1978), 1:429.

9 TJ to Kitchao Genoway, 27 Feb. 1808, Lipscomb and Bergh, eds., *Writings of Jefferson*, 16:426.

10 TJ, *Notes on the State of Virginia*, ed. William Peden (Chapel Hill, NC, 1954), 60.

11 Abigail Adams to John Adams, 31 Mar. and 7 May 1776, Lyman

Butterfield, ed., *Adams Family Correspondence*, 2 vols. (Cambridge, Mass., 1963), 1:370, 372.

12 TJ to Thomas Law, 13 June 1814, Lipscomb and Bergh, eds., *Writings of Jefferson*, 14:142.

13 Madison Speech, Virginia Ratifying Convention, 20 June 1788, John P. Karminski et al., eds., *The Documentary History of the Ratification of the Constitution*, 16 vols. to date (Madison, Wisc., 1976–), 10:1417.

14 TJ to Martha Jefferson, 28 Nov. 1783, Boyd et al., eds., *Jefferson Papers*, 6:360.

15 TJ to Marbois, 5 Dec. 1783, ibid., 6.374.

16 TJ to Anne Willing Bingham, 7 Feb. 1787, ibid., 11:123.

17 TJ to James Madison, 6 Sept. 1789, ibid., 15:395, 392.

18 TJ to Peter Carr, 10 Aug. 1787, ibid., 12:15.

19 The Declaration of Independence as Adopted by Congress, 4 July 1776, ibid., 1:432.

20 Hamilton, "Statement on Impending duel with Aaron Burr," [28 June– 10 July 1804], Harold C. Syrett and Jacob Cooke, eds., *The Papers of Alexander Hamilton*, 27 vols. (New York, 1961–87), 26:278–81.

21 Alexis de Tocqueville, *Democracy in America*, trans. Phillips Bradley, 2 vols. (New York, 1945), 2:8–12, 98–101.

22 TJ, "Draft of Instructions to the Virginia Delegates in the Continental Congress" [July 1774], Boyd et al., eds., *Jefferson Papers*, 1:122.

23 David Ramsay, *The History of the American Revolution*, ed. Lester H. Cohen, 2 vols. (1789: Indianapolis, 1990); Jeremy Belknap, *The History of New Hampshire*, 3 vols. (Boston, 1792); Mercy Otis Warren, *History of the Rise, Progress and Termination of the American Revolution, Interspersed with Biographical, Political and Moral Observations*, ed Lester H. Cohen, 2 vols. (1805; Indianapolis, 1988); John Marshall, *The Life of George Washington, Commander in Chief of the American Forces, During the War which Established the Independence of His Country, and First President of the United States*, 5 vols. (Philadelphia, 1804–7); Mason Locke Weems, *The Life of Washington*, ed. Peter S. Onuf (1809 eds.; Armonk, NY, 1996).

24 TJ, *Notes on Virginia*, ed. Peden, 19–20.

25 TJ to Martha Jefferson Randolph, 8 Feb. 1798, Edwin Morris Betts and James Adam Bear, eds., *The Family Letters of Thomas Jefferson* (Charlottesville, 1966), 155.

3

Pursuits of Happiness

"Those who labour in the earth are the chosen people of God, if ever he had a chosen people, whose breasts he has made his peculiar deposit for substantial and genuine virtue."
Jefferson, Notes on the State of Virginia.[1]

In his *Notes on the State of Virginia* Thomas Jefferson celebrated his state's and the new nation's agricultural economy. If the republican experiment were to succeed in America, it was because of a happy "mediocrity" of condition that enabled citizens to treat one another as true equals and therefore to govern themselves on the basis of consent. Without a privileged class of great landed aristocrats, who lorded it over humble and dependent neighbors, any talented and enterprising young man could seize the great opportunities offered by a rapidly expanding economy. Status and condition were not fixed, as they were in the old world. Americans were free to pursue happiness in their own ways, and their success would come in accumulating property and forming families and, most importantly, in enjoying the personal autonomy and independence that enabled individuals to be truly free. Happiness lay in the pursuit itself, in the self-determination of free men who cast off the shackles of a hierarchical social order that denied the humanity and natural rights of the vast majority of its subjects.

In Jefferson's celebration of agrarian virtue, the independent, self-governing yeoman farmer moved to the fore while the state faded into the background. The history of civilization through its successive stages was transposed across space – from the savage wilderness beyond the frontier of American settlement to its ultimate degeneration and corruption in Europe – with Euro-Americans precariously poised somewhere in between. But Jefferson knew that there was no escape from history or from Europe. Instead, his pastoral fantasy evoked an image of patriotic Virginians and Americans securing their equal standing and just deserts *within* the Atlantic trading system. The American farmer would not be immune to the "casualties and caprice" of the marketplace because he had withdrawn into virtuous isolation, but rather because he and his fellows used government to successfully assert their just claims. When Jefferson recommended that "our work-shops remain in Europe," he was recommending a division of labor in an interdependent Atlantic economy. His ultimate goal – free trade on equal terms – relied on the very exercise of state power that his pastoral vision apparently banished: "Our interest will be to throw open the doors of commerce, and to knock off all its shackles, giving perfect freedom to all persons for the vent of whatever they may chuse to bring into our ports, and asking the same in theirs."[2] Jefferson did not wish for the state to fade away, but rather wanted its energies utilized to create opportunities for free men to improve themselves. He and his Republican colleagues thus articulated a coherent vision of how the machinery of government should interact with the economy's producing and commercial sectors. We now know this field of study as "economics"; in Jefferson's time it was known, perhaps more accurately, as "political economy."

Far from wanting to remove themselves from European commerce and civilization, Americans sought a more perfect, reciprocally beneficial relationship with the Old World that would guarantee their economic prosperity as well as their political independence. (Jefferson's *Notes on Virginia* was itself a promotional tract, offering a prospectus for the state's expansion and development.) Jefferson and his fellow republican statesmen recognized that the prosperity Americans enjoyed *as a result* of commercial exchange with Europe enabled them to accumulate the property that was in turn the basis of the independence they claimed *from* Europe. In practical terms, then, independence depended on historically contingent conditions, most notably on access to European markets, where there was vigorous competition for American staple products. Thomas Paine expressed this fundamental contingency most eloquently in *Common Sense* (1776): Americans would be able to set the terms of trade because their exports "are the necessaries of life, and will always have a market while eating is the custom of Europe."[3] Of course, the colonists would not command the full benefit of their natural advantages – namely a seemingly boundless supply of fertile land – until they recognized their own strength and renounced their unnatural subordination to Britain. Once they engaged in the European trading system on fully equal terms, Americans would enjoy the prosperity that nature's bounty promised them.

Paine's argument seemed compelling to patriotic Americans on the eve of independence, helping them to imagine a new order of things – or perhaps to recognize an already existing, "natural" order – in which provincial Britons would be transformed into independent Americans. But the political conflicts and economic vicissitudes of the next quarter-century showed that Paine's common-sense principles would not be easily put into practice. In a perfect world, American supply would meet European demand free from the distorting commercial regulations and arbitrary and excessive revenue burdens of British mercantilism. But American independence did *not* lead to the end of mercantilism and the initiation of a free trade regime in the Atlantic trading system. On the contrary, the revolution accelerated the deterioration of the old European balance of power and intensified international rivalries, thus guaranteeing that commercial regulation would become an even more crucial tool of statecraft.

The periodic interruption of trade also provided opportunities for rising manufacturers to compete in home markets. Jeffersonians were famously ambivalent about this inadvertent byproduct of global political dislocation: by lessening its reliance on European imports, a vigorous manufacturing sector would secure the new nation's economic independence and thus enable it to negotiate more advantageous commercial treaties; but when the import trade returned to normal, peacetime levels and manufacturers clamored for protective tariffs, export-oriented staple producers rediscovered the virtues of free trade and the international division of labor. Protection, they then charged, was little better than highway robbery, enriching the favored few at the expense of the vast majority of farmers and planters, the real producers of wealth. Successive periods of war and peace thus underscored the critical importance of state power for enabling Americans to pursue their happiness by exploiting their "natural" advantages in the Atlantic economy. But Americans learned to be equally sensitive, to the point of paranoia, about how state power could be used to their disadvantage.

Recognition that the free trade millennium was not yet at hand and that Americans themselves would have to pursue neo-mercantilist policies in order to negotiate favorable commercial treaties with recalcitrant European powers provided a major impetus toward federal constitutional reform. In the great party divisions of the 1790s, Republicans identified themselves with the interests of agricultural staple producers who wanted to improve the terms of trade with foreign consumers. Jefferson and his ally James Madison criticized the Federalist administration for its unwillingness to adopt an aggressive national commercial policy: the United States should force Britain to relent on its restrictions on American participation in the lucrative West Indian trade by threatening high duties on British imports. Later in the nineteenth century, Jefferson's ideological heirs reversed the position, recognizing that their prosperity depended on supplying rapidly developing British markets for American staples – particularly cotton – and not on forging new trade relations elsewhere. Southerners then preached the new free trade gospel, quoting chapter and verse from Adam Smith's *Wealth of Nations*, as they advocated an end to a protective tariff regime that emerged after the War of 1812 and which, they claimed, favored northern manufacturers and diverted profits from staple producers. During the era of the early republic, however, Republicans had not yet embraced Smith's teachings – or shed the revolutionary

Anglophobia that animated their campaign against Federalism and ultimately led them to fight another war for American independence in 1812. During these years Republicans were just as likely as their Federalist opponents to endorse constructive state interventions in the economy, particularly in the realm of foreign commercial policy. This aggressive state action had its costs: some regions and economic interests felt forgotten amidst the Republican ascendancy, while agricultural staple production encouraged the perpetuation of the institution of race-based chattel slavery and the new lands that were turned to cultivation and settlement had to be wrested from their Native occupants. But the republican vision of political economy naturalized these developments and the role of the state faded from view. State power would thus become the rhetorical bogeyman of succeeding generations of doctrinaire republicans, even though it was, in reality, its *modus vivendi.*

American Commonwealths

As long as they remained in the empire, Americans were constrained both externally, by mercantilist regulations designed to benefit the metropolis, and internally, by the traditional assumption that the state should reinforce – and if necessary create – the hierarchical distinctions and unequal privileges that would transform colonial societies into plausible replicas of the metropolitan model. Freed from imperial rule, the colonies could become true republics, or "commonwealths," as Massachusetts, Pennsylvania, and Virginia – the most important new states – all fashioned themselves. Economic historians have underscored the importance of the commonwealth ideal in the political economy of the new states. State power was not to be abolished, but instead dedicated to the general benefit of the entire citizenry. American farmers and planters knew that they could not take markets for granted. The market did not exist in the contract theorists' "state of nature," before the organization of political society, but was itself the product of state action. Without an activist federal state that could aggressively negotiate more favorable terms of trade in the Atlantic trading system, and without activist state governments that could promote infrastructural development, they would have no access to markets at all.

The commonwealth ideal had both a social dimension, in its anti-aristocratic, leveling bias, and a geographical dimension: no locality or region would claim the kind of primacy that the British metropolis had exercised over its American provinces. Fears of metropolitan domination were most clearly expressed in the movement to relocate state capitals away from the old colony capitals and port cities where British influence had been – and continued to be – most conspicuous. As, for instance, Philadelphia and Charleston gave way to Harrisburg and Columbia, state governments were reoriented inland, away from the old viceregal capitals where colonial "court" parties held sway and toward the interests of the "country." Agrarian republicans may have sought to insulate state governments from foreign influence and the influence of the great transatlantic traders. But they were equally likely, as commercial farmers, to be interested in improving their access to distant markets through state governments that were now more responsive to their interests. The goal was not to extricate polity and economy, but rather to guarantee the equalization of benefits that came from both.

American revolutionaries believed that their new state constitutions restored the proper relationship between government and society that had once characterized the British Empire. If, in embracing the teachings of John Locke and the social contract theorists, Americans could trace their own beginnings to a prehistorical "state of nature," their understanding of what nature entitled them to was historically determined, the result of their experience in the British Empire and the Atlantic trading system. Governments had played a crucial role in the economy throughout colonial history, most notably in distributing lands and other public goods, setting standards for exports such as tobacco and wheat, offering bounties for indigo and other exports, and incorporating groups or licensing individuals to perform crucial functions on behalf of the larger community. After independence Americans continued to rely on pervasive state activity in the economy.

Where citizens of the new republics differed from subjects of the English king was in their profound hostility to government-sanctioned franchises or monopolies – like that granted by Parliament to the East India Company in 1773 for the sale of tea in the American colonies – that did not serve any generally recognized public purpose or that secured privileges or advantages to particular classes at the public's expense. In a hierarchical social order where all men were created unequal, the unequal distribution of public benefits followed naturally. But American republicans embraced a new conception of the public good premised on the equality of citizens that was fundamentally incompatible with aristocratic privilege. Their new republican governments would collapse the distinction between government (or administration) and society that had proven to be the fundamental flaw of the British imperial constitution. The republican symmetry between politics and society would be reflected in the lower houses of new state legislatures which were perfectly representative, being in John Adams's words "in miniature an exact portrait of the people at large."[4]

In overthrowing British rule, revolutionaries might imagine that they were freeing themselves *from* the incubus of tyrannical government. At the same time, however, the revolution raised Americans' expectations about how they could use governmental power to promote their various – and often conflicting – interests. Responsive, activist governments deriving their authority from the consent of the people would facilitate Americans' myriad private pursuits of happiness. Before producers could calculate rationally and trade freely they needed a stable currency, enforceable contracts, and secure markets. Free trade within the American union also required the imposition of a new federal layer of government that could enforce uniformity, comity, and the rule of law to preserve peace and facilitate private transactions. And as long as other nations sought to protect or project their interests through commercial regulation, the federal government also would have to be prepared to act vigorously in the diplomatic arena.

Agriculture and Improvement

The economy of the early republic was dominated by agriculture. In an underdeveloped, overwhelmingly rural country, located on the periphery of an increasingly global economy, there were only limited opportunities for enterprising Americans to pursue in other economic sectors, and these were all more or less subsidiary to agriculture. Local land shortages, exacerbated on the eve of revolution by imperial policies that discouraged taking up new lands, spurred the growth of provincial cities which supported a limited range of home manufactures. But agriculture was by far the most dynamic sector of the economy. American farmers and planters enjoyed comparative advantages in the Atlantic trading system, most notably a vast reserve of fertile and inexpensive land and easy access to distant markets made possible by the Anglo-American merchant fleet; cheap British credit facilitated the expansion of commercial agriculture and periodic frenzies of land speculation. Adam Smith and his fellow political economists agreed with ambitious American farm-builders that the future prosperity of the American colonies, within or outside of the empire, depended on the expansion of agricultural production.

Historians offer starkly conflicting interpretations of what farm-building settlers hoped to accomplish as they brought new lands under cultivation. Disagreement hinges on the meaning of the "independence" sought by aspiring freeholders. Were American farmers most concerned with gaining freedom from external control, whether by aristocratic landlords in a traditional social order with a limited supply of land or by merchants and creditors in a modernizing, market economy? Or were enterprising farmers more interested in participating in, not escaping from, market relations? Perhaps, as scholars have begun to argue, the opposition is false and misleading.

Farmers who sought "competency," the accumulation of sufficient land and other resources to secure a family's present
comfort and future prospects, necessarily responded to market opportunities; anxieties about threats to their economic
independence made them into maximizing "improvers." This
is not to say that they were therefore "capitalists" for whom
the accumulation of property was an end in itself; ambitious
farmers of a speculative bent were more likely to imagine themselves as landlords with vast estates. But farm-builders did
have some sense, whatever their motives and mentality, about
how their own enterprises fit into the global economy. They
understood the distinction between production for markets,
the defining characteristic of commercial civilization, and savage subsistence. Without markets, land speculators and settlers would waste their capital and labor and the settlement
frontier would retreat. Consciousness of these risks and opportunities guaranteed that westerners (broadly defined) would
be a major force in the discussions of political economy during the revolutionary and early national periods.

The political economy that American republicans crafted
after the revolution, which emerged in the various actions
of constitution-making and legislation at both the state and
federal level, consciously sought to preserve avenues for commerce and competition that were the lifeblood of the independent citizen. Hence, the young American governments faced
the related challenges of adapting existing commercial agriculture to an Atlantic economy in which they no longer had
the privileges that came from membership in the British Empire, and of bringing new regions and new producers into the
ambit of trade. As the interstate market was very limited in
the 1780s and 1790s, the expansion of American commerce
necessarily meant the expansion of the export trade. Republicans sought to expand American commerce overseas in a manner that would equalize benefits to each region and each state.
A carrying trade centered in one region would provide the
means by which agricultural staples from other regions could
find buyers, while a federal government would ensure that no
one region or interest placed any other in a dependent posi-

tion. The result would be an American economy: a dynamic, export-oriented economy, responsive to all political and economic interests, but especially those far from the metropole. It would be a state-sponsored economic regime that would facilitate competition and provide opportunities for industrious improvers, rather than use government monopolies and patronage to reward an undeserving, aristocratic few.

While the political economy that emerged after the revolution depended on state power, it was not predicated on any great structural transformation in the arenas of production. Republicans such as Jefferson, Madison, and Monroe imagined an American economy based on the same activities of agriculture and commerce that existed before 1775. During the colonial period, different regions had developed different export crops within the imperial trading system. Rice was the leading crop in the lower south (South Carolina and Georgia), accounting for more than half (55 percent) of average annual exports before the revolutionary crisis intervened; indigo, providing dye for the British textile industry, represented another fifth of the region's exports. Tobacco dominated in the Chesapeake colonies of Virginia and Maryland, constituting almost three-quarters (72 percent) of exports, with grain playing an increasingly important secondary role (19 percent). The transition to wheat, primarily for export to the West Indies, accentuated the continuity of the northern Chesapeake region with neighboring Pennsylvania and the other middle colonies (New Jersey and New York), where grain dominated (with 72 percent of exports). No other export crop or product – including flaxseed, wood, iron, and livestock – accounted for more than 7 percent of this diversified region's exports. With no great staple export, New England also depended on a diversified array of products, with fish (35 percent), livestock (20 percent), wood (15 percent), and whale products (14 percent) leading the way. The timber resources of New England's forests were also put to use by coastal shipbuilders, whose vessels were utilized both by the fishermen who braved the George's and Grand Banks, and the enterprising merchants who expanded New England's role in both the coastal and Atlantic carrying trades.

The revolution disrupted all of these lucrative trade patterns. The commercial privileges that the American states had enjoyed as colonies were gone, and the war itself wreaked havoc on the economies of many localities. The lower south was particularly hard hit by the war. Hundreds of plantations were destroyed and thousands of slaves lost during extended periods of British occupation and patriot counter-offensives; as many as 20,000 slaves evacuated with the British forces at war's end. Rice exports plummeted (from approximately 155,000 barrels per year before the war to less than 25,000 barrels in 1782), while the indigo industry virtually disappeared with the elimination of bounties colonial producers had enjoyed under the navigation acts. Despite these losses, however, the region remained well endowed with the highest concentration of enslaved labor in the new nation and with a fertile hinterland that was still largely undeveloped at independence. With the introduction of new varieties of cotton suitable to the drier upcountry, innovative planters found a lucrative solution to their problems. Cotton production was still very limited in 1790 (when an estimated 3,000 bales were produced), but took off in the next decade, reaching 100,000 bales in 1801. Cotton accounted for almost half of the 30,000,000 dollars increase in the value of American exports between 1791 and 1807. By the 1830s, when annual production exceeded 1,000,000 bales, cotton was undeniably "king" of the American export economy.

Not all sectors of the pre-revolutionary agricultural economy were equally prosperous. Before 1776 tobacco growers had long suffered from stagnant and falling prices and had amassed enormous debts (estimated at 2,000,000 pounds) to British creditors. Jefferson and his fellow planters believed that the dismantling of the British Navigation System (which required that tobacco and other "enumerated" crops be sent only to Britain) would give them direct, more remunerative access to their ultimate consumers (as much as 85 percent of the colonial tobacco crop was reshipped to the European continent). Jeffersonian hopes for the transformation of the Atlantic political economy were disappointed, however, as British merchants, with their superior credit and marketing facilities, continued to dominate the American export trade. Tobacco production eventually returned to and exceeded prewar levels, but the annual value of exports stagnated at approximately 6,000,000 dollars, beginning in 1802; by 1803 it had already fallen behind cotton as the leading American export.

Stung by the fickle tobacco markets and the postwar recession, planters were eager to exploit market opportunities resulting from foreign crop failures and the disruptions of the French revolutionary wars, and they moved into the production of grain and other foodstuffs, another great Jeffersonian panacea. But though it was clear to political economists that the United States, and particularly the middle states, enjoyed a "natural" comparative advantage in the Atlantic economy as exporters of foodstuffs, markets were unusually sensitive to changing political and environmental conditions. Grain producers found the erratically enforced regulation of trade with the British West Indies, the leading market for American agricultural exports during the colonial period, particularly galling. Yet again, Republican opponents of British mercantilism hoped that aggressive commercial diplomacy would give American producers better access to their customers – in this case, to regain the advantages of trade *within* the British Empire that were jeopardized by independence.

The revolution was less devastating to the north, but recovery was also less dramatic. New Englanders benefited most from the general revival of trade after the inauguration of the new federal government. While staple producers to the south sought new markets for their exports or, in the case of cotton planters, to exploit the insatiable appetite of the British textile industry for raw cotton, New England shipbuilders and merchants moved aggressively into the carrying or reexport trade, taking the place of European carriers whose merchant fleets were decimated or redeployed during the great maritime conflicts of the French revolutionary wars. Earnings from the carrying trade (including both domestic exports and reexports) skyrocketed from 5.9 million dollars in 1790 to 42.1 million dollars in 1807; the total value of reexports rose from a minuscule 300,000 dollars to a staggering 59,643,558 dollars over the same period. American domination of the Atlantic trade, and the increasingly important position of merchants in both New England and the emerging middle state metropolises of New York and Philadelphia in the new national economy, is reflected in the growing proportion of American-owned ships entering US ports: in 1790 American ships represented 59 percent (355 of 606) of all entries; by 1807 the proportion had risen to 93 percent (1,116 of 1,203). The carrying trade, and the mercantile infrastructure it nurtured, came to be, arguably, the most vibrant sector of the American economy.

The carrying trade played a crucial role in Republican political economy. As advocates of commercial agriculture, Jeffersonians looked with favor on a vibrant mercantile sector. They thus engaged in an aggressive commercial diplomacy that was supposed to open the British West Indies to American ships and force belligerents to respect neutral rights. Promotion of the carrying trade constituted only one part of a larger program to link farmers and planters to distant markets. Improving internal avenues of transportation and communication was a complementary policy imperative. Republicans who opposed the "consolidation" of authority in a strong central government believed that a dynamic economy would foster a harmony of interests that would bind the union together.

The lack of adequate transportation facilities, both within and between states, was an enormous impediment to the realization of the Jeffersonian vision. The biggest obstacle to market participation by agricultural producers was the high cost of transporting goods across land.[5] Some parts of the country, including the Chesapeake watershed, were well served by a natural system of rivers that gave staple producers easy access to overseas commerce. Jefferson's *Notes on Virginia* exulted in this region's future prospects of development based on potential connections with the great Ohio–Mississippi river system. But even in Virginia's case, "nature" needed a helping hand from man – in other words, state-sponsored internal improvements – in order to fulfill its potential. Beginning with the organization of the Potomac Company, jointly sponsored by Virginia and Maryland in 1784, visionary statesmen and investors sought to link the Chesapeake with the Ohio country by canal navigation. Meanwhile, competitors in Pennsylvania and New York sought to promote their states' development through rival projects. Though the Potomac project ultimately proved a costly failure, the canal-building mania spurred economic development in the two northern states; New York, the aptly named "Empire State," finally won the race westward with completion of the Erie Canal in 1824. Canals linking the Great Lakes and the Ohio River watershed quickly followed.

Canals were the most conspicuous improvements, but in the shorter run turnpikes made more of a difference to agricultural producers in settled regions who sought better access to markets. While turnpikes had little effect on long-distance travel – roads remained rough and tolls were easily circumvented, thus rendering most turnpike companies unprofitable – they did promote market penetration of the hinterland. Every decrease in transport costs made commercial agriculture viable over a more extended territory, thus providing new opportunities for enterprising farmers – and their sons.

The emerging transportation infrastructure also had the unintended consequence of accelerating the growth of the American manufacturing sector. Jefferson's treasury secretary Albert Gallatin noted the multitude of benefits a national system of internal improvements would bring in his 1808 report to Congress. These initial projections were supported four years later in the analysis of the 1810 Census, prepared for Gallatin by Tench Coxe. As he analyzed the census returns, Coxe could not help but notice how pervasive manufacturing enterprises had become in the young republic. Small-scale manufactures arose just about anywhere settlement occurred, as "manufactures commence with our first settlements, and aid their progress in its earliest stages," since frontier settlers had easy access to raw materials, as well as immediate needs imposed by the necessity of building their communities.[6]

Coxe reformulated the prescription of Jefferson's *Notes*: America's workshops need not be in Europe, but could lie "adjacent to agriculture."[7] It was, in fact, beneficial that they do so. American manufactures provided a ready market for all manner of agricultural raw materials. "The commerce among the several states, in the American Union, in the raw materials, manufactures and provisions of our country, is a branch of trade more certain than any other."[8] On the eve of a war caused by the need to defend American producers' access to overseas markets, Coxe saw clearly the potential benefits of a diversified American economy that could grow, process, and manufacture entirely within its borders.

The interests and experiences of the vast majority of Americans guaranteed stiff resistance to any program promoting manufactures, even with war looming on the immediate horizon. Farmers and planters had no interest in policies that might jeopardize their profits. Because of disruptions of European production during the French revolutionary and Napoleonic wars, American foodstuffs, particularly wheat, commanded unprecedentedly high prices. The resulting prosperity seemed to confirm Paine's belief, elaborated in the learned discourses of physiocratic economists, that agriculture was the ultimate source of wealth and that farmers would be rewarded accordingly for expanding production; while the Old World was caught in the vice of expanding population and diminishing resources described by English demographer the Reverend Thomas R. Malthus in his famous *Essay on the Principles of Population* (1798), New World farmers were able to make up the growing deficit. Thus while Coxe and other Republican economists looked forward to a progressive union of agriculture, commerce, and manufactures, most Americans continued to believe that the national interest was best served by the export of staple products. And because "nature" seemed to decree their favored position, Americans were prone to forget that every exchange in the interdependent Atlantic economy depended on state action.

The Politics of Development

Americans' pursuit of happiness led them to embrace many uses of state power, to negotiate favorable terms of trade with foreign powers, to get their goods to market through state-sponsored internal improvements, to gain secure titles to productive lands, to protect infant manufactures from ruinous competition with cheap imports. They also relied on governments to promote business enterprises of all sorts by creating corporations, granting franchises, and limited delegations of state power. The state was thus to be found everywhere in the early republic. But it did not present a single, monolithic face. Instead, the republican conception of popular sovereignty disguised state power by conflating state and society. In a complex federal polity that sustained the legitimate authority of distinct, overlapping jurisdictions, state power was still further diffused and disguised. Americans may have rejected the strong, centralized government that British imperial administration threatened to impose on the colonies, but they did so in order to preserve the constitutional rights of responsive local governments that had upheld their rights as Englishmen and facilitated their various private pursuits.

The revolution confirmed and strengthened the American commitment to constitutionally limited, decentralized government, spurring rising expectations about what responsive governments could do to promote both private and public interests. In the immediate aftermath of the revolution, the inability of governments at every level to meet these expectations led to a general crisis of legitimate authority that led to the successful movement for federal constitutional reform. The ratification of the new Constitution did not result in the emergence of a powerful British-style central government, notwithstanding the best efforts of Alexander Hamilton and his fellow Federalists. Instead, by apparently guaranteeing the survival of the federal system as a whole and by establishing American credibility and credit with European governments and bankers, the new regime enabled governments at every level to operate more

energetically. The vicious cycle of the postwar "critical period" was thus made virtuous: the capacity of governments to
respond effectively to popular demands reinforced their legitimacy, which in turn inspired the ambitious, sometimes visionary new schemes of state action that characterized the
commonwealth era.

The key issue in American political economy throughout
Jefferson's age was to determine how the new nation would
fit into the Atlantic economy. Well into the antebellum era,
the staple producers who dominated the economy depended
on export markets. This meant that all Americans, directly or
indirectly, were subject to the vagaries of a collapsing European diplomatic system. It followed logically that the first great
national political parties – the Federalists and the Republicans of the "first party system" – emerged out of conflicts
over foreign policy issues. The federal government's diplomatic
stance toward Britain, the former metropolis, and France, its
revolutionary ally, potentially affected every region and interest in the union. Americans anxiously calculated the relative
impact of these conflicting policy orientations. In doing so,
they learned to suspect the motives of at least some of their
countrymen. This growing consciousness of difference stood
in uneasy counterpoint to the revolutionary republican assumption of a transcendent harmony of interests. Convinced that
the enlightened pursuit of private interest should draw Americans together, not drive them apart, Federalists and Republicans alike were quick to interpret disagreements over policy
as fundamental threats to the nation's survival. Projecting the
most malign motives on to their opponents, paranoid partisans came close to destroying the union they professed to cher-
ish.

The ideological ferment of the French revolutionary era made
conflicts over political economy seem extraordinarily porten-
tous, with the future of western civilization hanging in the
balance. But it would be mistaken to conclude that the escalating, increasingly hysterical rhetoric of the 1790s was much
ado about very little. The status of the United States as an
independent nation was fundamentally problematic, and not

simply because this "new order for the ages" was such a radical departure from European constitutional forms. The most significant fact about these former British colonies was that their respective economies were so imperfectly integrated with each other and, by contrast, so closely tied to Europe and particularly to Britain. By the late 1790s, under the aegis of both the Jay Treaty and the Quasi-War with France, Great Britain garnered the lion's share of American exports and was the dominant source of American imports. For example, in 1799, the British Empire received over a third of the total dollar value of American exports, while it was the source for 47 percent – almost half – of the value of everything that Americans imported that year.[9] Britain remained the United States' leading conduit to continental markets; as they had been before 1776, British capital and credit continued to be critical to the operation of the Atlantic commercial system as a whole, and American engagement with this system in particular. Revolutionary Americans were precocious nationalists, anticipating modern conceptions of the nation or "people" as the foundation of legitimate authority. But the economic foundations of American nationhood were not yet in place, and could only be glimpsed in the conflicting designs of the opposing parties for the continent's future development. Simply put, American economy and polity were not yet fully integrated. In the short run any systematic effort to bridge the gap would necessarily draw the United States into closer political alliance with one or the other of the metropolitan powers; either alignment would underscore Americans' continuing dependence on Europe and thus the incompleteness and insufficiency of their revolution.

By their own lights, Federalists and Republicans were all patriotic Americans. The source of their conflicts was in the absence of a consensus about what – beyond repelling an invasion by a foreign power – patriotism actually entailed. In a federal republic where popular sovereignty was embodied in ascending levels of government, the image of the whole would always be inflected by local, provincial loyalties. Americans did not shed their provincial identities after 1776, but their

provincialism became more diffuse and less obsessively fix-
ated on the British metropolis. If, on one hand, the revolutionary conception of American nationhood provided a new
cosmopolitan framework within which these provincial identities could be sustained, Americans were profoundly ambivalent about the need for a national metropolis – a central place,
to which and from which prosperity and power would flow –
in their republicanized empire. Their solution, to locate the
capital in a new, centrally located federal district, distant from
existing urban centers, institutionalized their ambivalence.
Americans could not do without a national capital – and *some*
kind of central government – but they could prevent the dangerous concentration of wealth and power by keeping the capital at a safe distance from port cities that were too closely tied
into foreign trade and were therefore too vulnerable to foreign influence. But if Americans could thus preempt the emergence of an American metropolis, they could not so easily
disengage from an Atlantic trading system in which they remained dependent on a distant metropolis.

Partisan political controversy in the early republic revolved
around conflicting prescriptions for dealing with the problem
of metropolitan power. Federalists sought to secure American
independence by establishing an energetic central government,
an American metropolis, that could deal more effectively with
its European counterparts. Eventually, as Hamilton promised
in *The Federalist*, the United States could aspire to exercise
the kind of imperial hegemony in the New World that Britain
once exercised over its American colonies and "be able to in-
cline the ballance of European competitions in this part of the
world as our interest may dictate."[10] In the meantime, however, Americans would have to recognize that their best interests as a secondary power in the European system lay in
accommodating themselves to Britain, the dominant maritime
power and their chief trading partner. In response, Republicans embraced an approach to the metropolitan problem that
was at once more conservative, in its systematic opposition to
Federalist state-building, and more diplomatically ambitious.
Inspired by a vision of free trade, in which no single power

could assume a metropolitan role, Jefferson and his colleagues advocated an aggressively anti-British commercial diplomacy.

Jefferson's commercial diplomacy crystallized during his years as American envoy to France, from 1784 to 1789. Drawing inspiration from Congress's Model Treaty of 1776, a blueprint for commercial reciprocity between the United States and its trading partners that eschewed political alliances, Jefferson envisioned dismantling the mercantilist regimes that inhibited free trade and entangled the New World in the never-ending cycle of European wars. Given Britain's maritime dominance and its determination, as set forth in Orders in Council limiting American participation in the lucrative West Indies carrying trade, Jefferson's conception of commercial freedom reflected a markedly anti-British bias that sustained the bitter animosity of the revolutionary war years. More direct trade with the European continent, where a large proportion of American exports were ultimately consumed, would guarantee Americans a fairer return for their contributions to world trade. In practice, this meant that France, the great continental power, would emerge as a counterweight to Britain, bidding up staple prices in free competition for American goods. Jefferson thus tilted toward France well before the French Revolution established the ideological affinity of the "sister republics" in their global struggle against the reactionary forces of the old regime. His diplomatic orientation was over-determined, combining revolutionary animosity to the former metropolis and radical republican aspirations for world transformation with a more concrete sense of the new nation's interests – and particularly those of staple-exporting planters like Jefferson himself – in the Atlantic economy.

Jefferson's free-trade vision, and its corollary, the rights of neutral, noncombatant powers like the United States to continue to trade freely during wartime, epitomized the anti-mercantilist, anti-metropolitan thrust of his revolutionary republicanism. Had it been possible to implement such a regime, it was undoubtedly true that a wide array of interest groups from every part of the union would have been its beneficiaries. Jefferson thus always assumed that the enlightened pursuit of self-interest would reinforce the commitment of patriotic Americans to secure their economic as well as political independence; conversely, opposition to his political economy could only signify insufficient patriotism and continuing subservience to the old metropolis. Free trade would mean higher prices for agricultural products, but the expanding volume of commerce would also benefit the shipbuilders and merchants of the "eastern" states. In effect, Jefferson and his Republican colleagues thought that independent Americans could have it both ways, enjoying continuing access to the markets, capital, and credit the British Empire had formerly afforded them while gaining free, direct access to the rest of the world. Ironically, the free-trade vision was appealing to Americans precisely because of their experience with it in the empire. Because it was so obviously in Britain's own interest to sustain a free trade with the United States after independence – approximately a third of British exports, primarily manufactured goods, were sent to the colonies before the war – Jefferson was convinced that the Americans had a strong bargaining position in extracting commercial concessions. He interpreted the Federalist administration's unwillingness to assume a more aggressive diplomatic posture against Britain as a revealing indication of their counter-revolutionary bad faith. Advocates of the new federal Constitution had promised that American diplomats would be able to negotiate commercial treaties on more favorable terms. But instead of a commercial accord with Britain that would help initiate the free-trade millennium, John Jay's mission to England in 1794 led to an agreement that seemed to confirm American subservience to the mother country's political and economic interests.

The Jay Treaty determined the subsequent course of Jeffersonian commercial diplomacy, drawing a clear line between those who continued to embrace the free- trade vision and the more short-sighted, selfish interests of those who relied on closer ties with Britain. When Jefferson rose to power in 1801 and an interval in the European wars gave Americans some respite from the diplomatic cross-pressures of the 1790s, he was confident that he could now construct a true union of interests that would redeem the revolution's promise. The Republican party provided the vehicle for this reorientation of American political economy. In New England, for instance, merchants in secondary port cities such as Salem and Newburyport in Massachusetts, and those who sought alternatives to the traditional Anglo-American trade, provided ready recruits to Jefferson's cause. Republicans gained ground everywhere that economic interest groups had chafed under the Federalists' commercial policy, including urban artisans and manufacturers who struggled to survive against the flood of cheap British imports. The paradox of Jeffersonian political economy was that the promise of free trade, predicated on escaping from British commercial domination, necessarily entailed a degree of protectionism that was broadly appealing to disadvantaged sectors of the economy. Free trade under existing conditions would simply perpetuate British hegemony over dependent and underdeveloped provincial economies, preempting the emergence of a true free trade regime, in which all participants competed on equal terms.

Jeffersonian Republicans thus embraced a "neo-mercantilist" political economy as the most efficacious means toward the ultimate end of free trade. Once again, the exercise of state power was crucial both to the immediate prospects of specific economic interest groups and to the long-term prosperity of the entire nation. Historians have persuasively argued that Jefferson, the "half-way pacifist," misguidedly turned to commercial diplomacy as an apparently cheap and painless alternative to war, one that would preempt development of the kind of centralized, war-making state apparatus favored by High Federalists. But the reverse is also true: for Jefferson, an aggressively anti-British commercial policy represented the continuation – and hoped-for completion – of the revolutionary war by other means. The goal of economic independence, like other national security concerns, was ultimately reducible to the question of self-preservation, where the first law of nature justified any and all necessary exercises of state power. The implementation of commercial regulations curtailed the economic freedom of individual traders and might even abrogate their civil liberties, as in the case of the Embargo of 1807–9, when the Jefferson administration attempted to suppress foreign trade completely. War necessarily suspended the exercise of natural rights which could only be fully enjoyed within a republic that was at peace with the world. And Jefferson was always prepared to wage war against the new nation's enemies, whether rebellious slaves, hostile Indians, counter-revolutionary foreign powers, or even fellow Americans who would not submit to the will of the people. But state power was always the means, never the end.

The basis of Republican political power was the great agricultural interest, and particularly the staple export producers of the plantation south. But the future of the party depended on building a nationwide coalition of interests. Jeffersonian thus emphasized a broad division of labor in which merchants connected farmers and planters with distant consumers and small-scale "home" manufacturers met the growing needs of local markets. If, as the French economist Turgot and other "Physiocrats" argued, agriculture was the ultimate source of value and therefore had pride of place in the Jeffersonian scheme, vigorous commercial competition in a truly free market was crucial to its smooth operation. Farmers may have distrusted merchants, whose first loyalty was always to their own fortunes and not to any particular "country," but they recognized that merchants were indispensable middle men in the international economy. In a free-trade regime, competition among merchants would take the place of patriotic attachments, forcing them to find the best markets for agricultural products and thus enhancing the wealth of the nation.

The major internal obstacle to free trade, famously excoriated by Adam Smith, was the tendency of merchants and manufacturers to form state-sanctioned combinations in order to monopolize particular trades. The absence of strong state authority in America mitigated such "corrupt" uses of power, particularly at the federal level, and state governments generally used the corporate form to promote private enterprise rather than privilege (though the distinction was often controversial). But if the multiplicity of jurisdictions and interests pointed toward commercial freedom within the American union, the new nation's foreign trade was much more vulnerable to mercantilist constraints. In their never-ending competition for relative advantage, nation-states imposed commercial regulations and distributed corporate privileges in order to generate crucial revenue and secure vital strategic interests. The United States was no exception to this rule: Jefferson's determination to minimize direct taxation and other forms of politically controversial interference in the domestic economy made the uninterrupted flow of import duties all the more critical for the federal government's survival. And if the new nation wanted Britain and its other trading partners to liberalize the terms of trade, it would have to be prepared to impose commercial regulations of its own. Political competition within the Atlantic states system thus required the radical expansion of state authority at the same time that proponents of republicanism and economic liberalism sought to limit government interference within the domestic economy. This fundamental ambivalence about the role of the state determined the conflicted future course of Jeffersonian political economy.

Americans did not turn to a single, monolithic metropolitan government to advance their interests, as they had been forced to do before independence. Now they could shop among jurisdictions in an expanding political marketplace, seeking advantage at different levels of the federal system or moving from state to state. The extraordinary mobility that so conspicuously distinguished the American system was by no means confined to opportunistic elites. Ordinary farmers moved from place to place to take up fertile new lands, and even modest success could be translated into political office and social status in new frontier settlements. The rapid expansion of the union and creation of new governments assured a chronic shortage of qualified lawyers, office-holders, and politicians. In the dynamic political marketplace there was ample opportunity for the ambitious, both to use the system and to become part of it. The paradox was that political activity was so pervasive and so unremarkable that it became virtually invisible; like the market economy it mimicked and promoted, the political market seemed to emerge spontaneously, as if by nature's decree, to recognize and reward the most meritorious. Republicanism was thus to politics what liberalism was to economics: systems that were not the product of "accident or force" – that is, of historical contingency – but that instead derived their legitimacy from their conformity to human nature and nature's laws.

Slavery, Commerce, and the State

Unspoken in nearly all the debates between contending interests about the shape of the Republican political economy were the fates of those whose happiness was not to be pursued or even considered. The commercial development of the American republics was predicated, in large part, upon the labor of enslaved African Americans. Slave labor produced the new nation's most lucrative export crops, and was thus instrumental to any vision of prosperity entertained by Jefferson and his collaborators. Nothing within the republican credo prevented a perfect republic from also being a slave society, and thus many of the state-republics of the American union were – their continued commercial development was intertwined with the maintenance of the institution of race-based chattel slavery, and its attendant legal and social apparatuses. In the age of transatlantic democratic revolution, an institution like slavery, which was rooted in a fundamental conception of human inequality, looked increasingly anachronistic to many. Although many Republican intellectuals, steeped in readings of natural law and the rights of man, had qualms about slavery, they also found in the same literature of Enlightenment an emerging science of racial difference. Republican thought answered the intellectual dilemma of slavery with the cold, hard science of race, and as a result, some of the sharpest social boundaries in the new nation were drawn along racial lines.

According to the republican theory so eloquently articulated in Jefferson's Declaration of Independence, "all men are created equal." But natural rights doctrine presented a conundrum, for the original equality could only be translated into practice when a particular people, acting on the premise of common interests and a shared identity, successfully asserted and defended those rights against all other peoples. In theory, a republic's legitimacy derived from its fidelity to universal, natural rights principles; in practice, a republic – like any other regime – came into existence through the forceful exercise of will by a political community on behalf of its exclusive claims to rule over a specific territory. As the revolution itself made clear, might necessarily preceded right; having vindicated their pretensions on the battlefield (with considerable help from their French allies), Americans could then exercise their natural rights to a fuller extent than any other people in world history. This made them a unique, *exceptional* people, determined to preserve their national independence, as the first law of nature enjoined, against any and all hostile powers. In short, men could only exercise their rights as men *within* a republic. Other sovereignties could claim, in the name of their own peoples, the benefits of the law of nations, but only the American republics could truly represent the natural rights of individuals.

The confusion of power and consent, of the forceful assertion of exclusive claims with universalistic pretensions, was at the core of revolutionary American national identity. Within the American republics, where a dynamic and expansive political marketplace enabled citizens to follow myriad paths toward happiness, the crucial role of state power in nation-making disappeared from view. By the same logic, however, the exercise of power was starkly conspicuous at the new nation's territorial and racial boundaries; here is where we now see the most egregious violations of the natural rights principles the revolutionaries espoused. The contradiction is apparent to us because we no longer understand, as did Jefferson and his colleagues, that the republican self-constitution of a people must precede any effective rights claims of individuals.

Modern-day cosmopolitans tend to discount and disparage

the idea of the nation as a natural social and political form, asserting instead that all humans constitute a single great community and that national governments are legitimate only to the extent that they uphold the fundamental rights of their citizens. But revolutionary Americans thought differently. That they constituted a particular people was a self-evident fact of political life amply confirmed by the revolution – a struggle for their national existence against a hostile English people who sought to reduce them to a condition of submission and slavery. The war for independence was also fought on other fronts, against other peoples: against enslaved Africans, a captive nation whose liberation could only come at the expense of the freedom of white Americans, and against Indian nations whose interest in preserving their ancestral lands led them into counter-revolutionary, anti-republican alliances with hostile European powers. The revolution itself was only the first phase of a series of military and diplomatic conflicts that kept American republicans in a continuing state of war, despite their pacific professions, throughout the era of the early republic.

White Americans knew that the institution of slavery was based on the continuous exercise of force. Their great anxieties about the possibility of slave insurrection and actual warfare between the races were justified during the revolution by Lord Dunmore's invitation to Virginian slaves to fight with the British. In the 1790s, the ultimately successful struggle of black revolutionaries in nearby Santo Domingo (modern Haiti) to establish the first black republic – and the second republic in the western hemisphere – kept these anxieties at a high pitch. That the contagion could easily spread to the mainland was chillingly confirmed by Gabriel's Rebellion in Virginia, failed uprisings in 1800 and 1802 that led to brutal reprisals (twenty-seven slaves were executed) by a badly shaken state government. Chronic resistance against the institution by individuals and small groups of slaves seemed particularly ominous when put into a larger geopolitical context. During the Quasi-War with France, rumors circulated that a Franco-African army was about to descend on the slave states. Whenever war threatened – again with France during the Louisiana crisis of 1802–3, and with Britain in the successive crises culminating in the War of 1812 – the fear that America's enemies would enlist rebellious slaves as an auxiliary force seemed increasingly credible. In subsequent decades of the antebellum era, anxious southerners may have exaggerated the danger of slave revolts; outside intervention no longer seemed likely and the coercive machinery of the slave states (and of a union dedicated to preserving the institution) was increasingly effective. But Americans in the early republican era were not paranoid to fear insurrectionary movements among their slaves. In response to these fears, Jefferson and other reformers broached the possibility of gradual emancipation and colonization of former slaves. Few anti-slavery activists at this early day, with the exception of Quakers and a handful of other Christian sectarians, were primarily motivated by humanitarian concerns. They were more likely to be concerned with preserving the republic by eliminating the leading threat to national security.

The dimensions of that potential threat were daunting. In 1776, enslaved Africans and African-American creoles constituted approximately a fifth of the total population of the United States. The number of free blacks, usually mixed-race descendants of white mothers (whose status determined that of their children) was at this point very small – two related developments in the era of the early republic that would have fateful consequences for the future of the union. At independence, slavery was legally established in every one of the original states; only the new state of Vermont, organized in 1777 but not recognized by the other states and admitted to the union until 1791, banned the institution. Every state north of the Mason–Dixon line (separating Maryland and Pennsylvania) took at least the first cautious steps toward emancipation over the next twenty-five years, however, beginning with Pennsylvania in 1780. The emerging distinction between slave and free states in turn reinforced the concentration of the black population in the staple-producing southern states. Despite increasing numbers of blacks in the largest northern cities, the northern states tended to whiten, with blacks representing a declining proportion of populations including growing numbers of European immigrants.

Emancipation schemes, usually very gradual – in 1800, New Jersey became the last northeastern state to adopt an emancipation law, but the number of slaves in these "free" states did not drop below 1,000 until 1840 – were inspired by a mixture of motives. A temporary drop in slave prices after the revolution led some observers to question the institution's continuing economic viability. After Virginia legalized private manumissions in 1782, and many planters chose to liquidate their investments in slave property, the state's free black population surged, matching parallel developments throughout the upper south. Religious and ideological scruples about slaveholding played an important part in many of these manumissions, most famously in the case of Virginian Robert Carter of Nomini Hall, a zealous religious seeker who freed more than 500 slaves. But such scruples were often difficult to disentangle from material and prudential concerns. St. George Tucker, a prominent Virginian jurist and planter, was clearly conscious of the dissonance between republican freedom and chattel slavery in the Commonwealth when he proposed a gradual emancipation scheme in his *Dissertation on Slavery with a Proposal for the Gradual Abolition of It in the State of Virginia* (1796). Yet neither Tucker nor his friend Jefferson could envision a biracial republic. Jefferson condemned slavery for its demoralizing effects on both blacks and whites in his *Notes on Virginia*, calling "the whole commerce between master and slave" the "perpetual exercise of the most boisterous passions, the most unremitting despotism on the one part, and degrading submissions on the other"; clearly, there was no republican foundation here.[11] Tucker instead advocated the creation of a racial caste system, with black freedmen constituting a permanent laboring class claiming only limited civil rights. Jefferson, a more rigorous republican who could not tolerate the ambiguity and quasi-aristocratic hierarchy of a regime in which all men were so conspicuously not equal, argued instead for expatriation and colonization. Equality required homogeneity and reciprocal respect among citizens: the continuing presence of African Americans, whether as slaves or as nominally "free" people without rights, jeopardized the civic health of the commonwealth. As Jefferson wrote in the wake of Gabriel's Rebellion, this "blot or mixture" on the body politic must be eliminated.[12]

Had slave prices continued their postwar decline, economic self-interest might have conspired with religious principles and republican prudence to set slavery on the road to extinction, at least in the upper south where blacks were outnumbered by whites. But the rapid recovery of the economy of the lower south, where enterprising whites had always depended on slavery to produce rice, indigo, and other staple exports, soon provided a lucrative market for surplus slaves in the Chesapeake region and reversed the brief downward trend in slave prices. Well before the invention of the cotton gin helped open the southwestern frontier to the explosive development of the union's most valuable export crop, South Carolinians and Georgians were committed to the perpetuation of slavery. Despite the existence of black majorities, lower south planters wanted more slaves and successfully resisted agitation, which their Chesapeake counterparts supported, for an immediate ban on the international slave trade.

At the Constitutional Convention in Philadelphia and in subsequent congressional deliberations, South Carolinians assumed a precocious proslavery posture that anticipated their leading role in later intersectional controversies. But this first generation of pro-slavery politicians differed from its successors in its realistic assessment of the role of state power in sustaining the institution. In a period of chronic political and diplomatic instability, states with large slave populations could have no illusions about being able to repress slave insurrections without outside assistance. Awareness of this overriding security threat explains why lower south politicians were so eager to establish an energetic central government and why so many of them later aligned with the Federalists, notwithstanding the aversion of many northern Federalists to the institution of slavery. A strategic alliance with these potential opponents, predicated on a common commitment to a strong federal state, was slavery's best guarantee. As long as the federal government was committed to upholding the institution, as it was under the new Constitution, slave state interests were far better served within rather than outside of the union. The key issues were national security and access to foreign markets on favorable terms, both of which depended on a strong federal government. In a region that had enjoyed such extraordinary prosperity within the British empire, and where leading planters recognized the positive role the metropolitan government played in making their fortunes, there were fewer pretensions to self-sufficiency than in the north. This geopolitical realism muted the appeal of the kind of doctrinaire republicanism preached by Jefferson and his allies. If Jefferson could envision a new American (or Virginian) empire, oriented westward and exploiting the great system of rivers that opened up the continent, Carolinians and Georgians continued to look eastward toward European markets.

The federal government was pledged not only to defending the slaves states from internal as well as external enemies, but was also committed to upholding slaveowners' property rights by guaranteeing the return of fugitive slaves. Congress thus passed an Act in 1793 establishing federal jurisdiction over fugitive slave cases and making good on the Constitution's promise that persons "held to Service or Labour" who escaped from "service" should be "delivered up" to their rightful owners (Article IV, Section 2). In a union consisting entirely of slave states, federal provisions for securing slave property would have flowed naturally from each state's obvious self-interest. But in a union of slave and free states, the republican premise of equality and homogeneity could not be sustained: Constitutional provisions favoring slavery, including the notorious three-fifths clause which gave them additional voting power in the House of Representatives, institutionalized this inequality and expanded the scope of federal authority accordingly. As long as the new nation's geopolitical situation remained insecure, as it would until the conclusion of the War of 1812, and as long as the southern states controlled Congress, realistic slaveowners did not worry excessively about encroachments on their states' "sovereignty" by a domineering central government. They understood, better than most other Americans, that the exercise of public power was the fundamental precondition and concomitant of their private pursuits of happiness. Slavery originated and was sustained by acts of violence; slaves could only become "property," to be passed on from generation to generation, where the power of the state was continuously exercised in support of the institution.

State governments played the most crucial role in perpetuating slavery, just as they took the lead in promoting the interests of key sectors of the economy through internal improvements and other exercises of state power. Most importantly, legislatures defined the legal status of slaves in slave codes that sought to minimize as much as possible the inherent tensions of a regime in which persons were treated as property. Growing free black populations, resulting from the spate of manumissions following the war, raised a new set of problems by creating an anomalous, intermediate status between slavery and freedom requiring legal rationalization. In dialectical fashion, moves toward freedom – whether through gradual emancipation in the north or in individual manumissions in the south – led to the consolidation of the institution for those who remained in bondage. In both cases, white Americans strengthened the hand of government, whether at the federal or state level, in forcing a subject population to labor for their benefit. But, as in other uses of government to promote private interest, the diffusion of power in the federal system tended to disguise its exercise. In the case of slavery, the reliance on local communities to enforce the racial regime and the broad delegation of power over their chattels to individual slaveholders exaggerated this general tendency. Slavery seemed to emerge, almost as if by nature, from the prepolitical domestic sphere, just as the independent republican citizen came forth from his own freehold.

Indian Lands and American Prosperity

Looking back on the history of their first colonial settlements, Americans could easily conclude that the process of westward settlement was inevitable and inexorable. Enlightenment ideas of the progress of civilization through three or four successive stages, from the barbarism of native Americans to the advanced commercial society of the new United States, gave philosophical sanction to this sense of manifest destiny. What was lost from view in this new national mythology was a sense of contingency – the very real possibility of different historical outcomes – and, specifically, of the role of political power in determining those outcomes. Revolutionaries understood that victory was not foreordained, and depended on their ability to forge effective alliances with the French and among the new American states; constitutional reformers had every reason to fear that their fragile union would collapse, opening the way for counter-revolutionary European empires to pick up the pieces. Even when the Constitution was ratified and provision was made for the admission of new states, the ability of the union to project effective authority into frontier regions remained questionable. Britain and Spain would be formidable rivals for ultimate control, respectively of the Great Lakes region and the Mississippi watershed; with their sponsorship, hostile Indian nations might well retard or even reverse the progress of settlement. Settlers who were determined to find markets for their crops did not hesitate to calculate the relative advantages of betraying the revolution and aligning with another power. This could mean, for instance, following the example of Andrew Jackson and other opportunists on the southwestern frontier by taking an oath of allegiance to the King of Spain.

The key variables in the political calculations of frontier settlers were the probability of gaining secure land titles and protection from potential enemies, particularly from Indians threatened with dispossession from ancestral lands. Far from being the dynamic and energetic agent of westward expansion, the poorly armed frontier settler was more likely to be cast in the role of a client who depended on some superior power – *any* superior power – to vindicate his tenuous claims. The myth of the self-reliant pioneer disguised a contradictory reality, for nowhere else in Jeffersonian America was the vaunted independence of the freehold farmer so starkly dependent on the effective exercise of state authority. The freehold, after all, was a land tenure that common law courts recognized and the state was bound to uphold: it did not exist in a state of nature. When illegal squatters banded together in ad hoc political associations, their overriding goal was to gain recognition from some higher authority that could mend their defective land titles.

Most settlers purchased their lands from land speculators whose original titles were more or less doubtful. These speculators, an enterprising cadre of would-be land barons that included virtually every influential politician in the new nation, understood that their private fortunes depended on coopting the power of the state. The problem was that there were so many rival speculations and political factions that could exploit the conflicting claims of competing jurisdictions, state and federal. Some of the most divisive political controversies in the history of the early republic thus grew out of land title controversies. None was more controversial or consequential than the Yazoo speculation, beginning with the sale in 1795 of 35 million acres of Georgia's western land claims (which were themselves highly speculative) by a corrupt state legislature to a syndicate of land speculators. After a new reform-minded legislature rescinded the sale in 1796, land companies that derived their titles from the original purchase turned to the federal courts, insisting on the inviolability of their contracts under the Constitution. The issue was finally decided in favor of the Yazoo speculators by the US Supreme Court in the case of *Fletcher v. Peck* (1810). John Marshall's landmark decision in *Fletcher* may have been crucial to the future development of federal contract law, but it also testified eloquently to the extraordinary power of political insiders to set the course of state policy.

In other states and in the new national domain in the Northwest Territory, governments maintained more effective control over land sales and the process of settlement. Though speculators in many cases still took on the role of middlemen between these governments and ultimate purchasers, provision for accurate survey and the absence of jurisdictional conflicts guaranteed the orderly and swift privatization of public land. State and federal land offices and an expanding court system represented the most visible face of the early American state, buttressed in the most vulnerable frontier regions by military garrisons. Land was never "free" in America, nor could it be brought into market production without the state playing an active, constructive role. The costs of government did not simply constitute a kind of social overhead or tax on the enterprises of private producers. The state also played a more primary, original role in creating the property that settlers could then exploit and in facilitating the "release of energy" that transformed the western landscape. Under the new republican dispensation, Americans believed that they had a natural right to use public power to serve their private purposes. They also believed that they had inviolable rights in the property that governments themselves had brought into existence, rights that could be invoked against government itself. Believing this, Americans could make the state invisible, and so insist that their prosperity came directly from "nature" and their own unaided efforts to realize its great potential value.

Just as the state became invisible to Republicans, they saw no place for the continent's aboriginal inhabitants as they looked to the future. In his First Inaugural Address in March 1801, President Jefferson exulted in the prospect of a open, fertile continent, a "chosen country" that beckoned the industry of the American people, providing them living space "to the thousandth and the thousandth generation."[13] In the same way his Declaration of Independence had "invented a people," transforming provincial Britons into Americans, so his Inaugural Address invented a country, a vast continental domain free from conflicting claims. Demographic trends suggested that Jefferson had some justification for overlooking the Indians. When he was elected there were about 600,000 Indians on all of the land that would eventually become the United States of America, with only a proportion of them living within the new nation's contemporaneous boundaries.

But it was impossible to ignore the Indians during the republic's early years. They might already be vastly outnumbered by white Americans concentrated on the Atlantic seaboard and along the few navigable rivers that penetrated the interior, but Indian nations still controlled the majority of "American" territory. And because Indian country was the site of chronic conflict throughout the revolution, ranging from a few full-scale military encounters to the myriad violent acts of small groups and individuals that gave the American state of nature a distinctly Hobbesian cast, the frontiers of white settlement actually contracted in the decade after American independence.

When the victorious revolutionaries negotiated a favorable peace settlement in Paris, they believed that the balance of power in the west had shifted irrevocably in their favor: without the continuing sponsorship of their British patrons, Indian nations would no longer be able to resist American expansion. Congress's first forays into Indian diplomacy after 1783 constituted critical tests for this assumption. Negotiations with the Iroquois at Fort Stanwix, New York, in 1784 opened with claims by the Congressional commissioners that the Americans had "conquered" all of the territory within the boundaries recognized by the Treaty of Paris. As the Iroquois acceded to the controversial treaty (they had suffered greatly as a result of the devastation caused by General John Sullivan's expedition of 1779), the hope was that the Treaty of Fort Stanwix would signal a new dispensation in Indian diplomacy, and that the western and southern nations would submit gracefully to the demands of the Confederation governments. It was not to be.

The Confederation government could easily proclaim victory over Indian nations that had not really been "defeated" (outside of the Iroquois homeland, the revolution in the west was, at best, a standoff), but it was another thing altogether

to implement such pretensions and reap their anticipated reward. Far from clearing the way for settlement, Congress's
first treaties with the Indians served to galvanize a pan-Indian
resistance, setting in motion a pattern of aggression and re-
prisal that would mark the entire period. Congress's counter-
productive Indian policy underscored its military weakness:
in 1785, in the wake of the postwar demobilization, the western commander, General Josiah Harmar, had fewer than forty
officers and 700 soldiers to deploy throughout the entire Ohio
valley. The army's shortages of manpower and materiel were
chronic throughout the 1780s. At a time when Congress des-
perately needed revenue from public land sales in the Northwest Territory, its inability to secure the western frontier was
potentially disastrous. Concern that the progress of settlement
would be retarded, and perhaps even reversed, contributed
significantly to the general sense of crisis that led to the institution of a more energetic central government under the new
federal Constitution. The irresistible conclusion for expansionists was that fulfillment of their speculative schemes depended
on replacing, not simply abolishing, metropolitan authority.

Under the direction of secretary of war Henry Knox, the
Washington administration retreated from the conquest theory,
recognizing that substantive territorial concessions from the
Indians depended on adhering to traditional, pre-revolutionary diplomatic practices. This more conciliatory stance, combined with a series of military campaigns climaxing in Anthony
Wayne's victory at Fallen Timbers in 1794 and the Treaty of
Greenville in 1795, led to the successful negotiation of a boundary with the Indians of the Ohio country. Similar agreements
were reached in the southwest: Cherokee land cessions at the
Treaty of Holston (1791) were confirmed with additional articles negotiated at Philadelphia in 1794 and 1795, while Creek
cessions at the Treaty of New York (1790) were confirmed
with the Treaty of Coleraine (1796). Though all these settlements led to land acquisitions, federal negotiators showed a
new willingness to take Indian claims seriously: they raised
annuity payments, granted trading privileges, and were care-
ful to keep unscrupulous state agents out of the negotiating

process. The watchword of Federalist Indian diplomacy was gradualism. Henry Knox, and subsequently Timothy Pickering, sought to expand the frontiers of white settlement while "civilizing" the Indian nations and incorporating them into American commercial networks; done slowly and deliberately, both processes abetted one another, and would keep (expensive) frontier warfare to a minimum.

The new federal government also facilitated the expansion of settlement by operating more effectively in the European diplomatic arena. After the revolution, Britain and Spain exploited the vacuum of effective power in the west both by encouraging Indian clients to resist American territorial pretensions and by secret negotiations with discontented white settlers. But Federalists met the diplomatic challenge on both frontiers: in the Jay Treaty of 1794, the British agreed to withdraw from forts in American territory that they had occupied since the revolution; in the Treaty of San Lorenzo in 1795, Spain opened up the navigation of the Mississippi, thus eliminating a major grievance in Kentucky and other western settlements. The Federalist ascendancy in the 1790s is best explained by the prosperity that resulted from these successful exercises of state power. Only by coming to resemble the European powers more closely could the new nation preserve its independence and extend its dominion across the continent.

Federal Indian policy did not change dramatically after Jefferson's election in 1800. But Republicans were much less inclined than their predecessors to acknowledge the role of the state in the new nation's development. Americans eagerly benefited from the vigorous exercise of state power – whether in securing an enslaved laboring population or in expropriating Indian lands – but they liked to think that they owed their prosperity to their own efforts, not to the protection and patronage of any (worldly) higher authority. Anglophiliac Federalists who sought to remodel the central government along British lines considered such pretensions delusional; energetic administration and popular submission to constituted authority could alone sustain the new nation against internal and

external challenges to its vital interests. But Federalists over-
played their hand when they threatened to turn the power of
the federal state against their fellow Americans, as they did
openly in the late 1790s with the Alien and Sedition Acts, and
as western critics of their Indian policy insisted they had always done. In response, Republican oppositionists rallied the
people to reassert their rights and redeem the revolution from
Federalist heresies. Americans had "the strongest government
on earth," Jefferson asserted in his Inaugural Address, because
they governed themselves, not because they relied on the strong
hand of the kind of centralized, metropolitan government they
had rejected in 1776.[14] In Jefferson's formulation, the power
of the state returned to – and was disguised by – its putative
origins, in the power of the sovereign people. This did not
mean, as Federalists were relieved to learn, that Jefferson intended to dismantle the federal state. He had no intention, for
instance, of removing the plank from the platform of Federalist Indian policy that had opened new lands for settlement by
Republican planters and farmers who supported his administration.

Expansionists frequently invoked the image of a natural,
irresistible tide of settlement, temporarily impeded by the artificial political barriers. Yet the very fact that such language
was deployed in order to enlist state support – to sanction
land titles that could be vindicated in its courts, or protect
straggling and often defenseless settlements from Indian reprisals, or facilitate access to distant markets through internal
improvements – belied the premise of this "natural rights"
argument. In the republican political economy, American prosperity was based on the systematic exploitation of extraordinarily fertile new lands for expanding world markets. Thus,
the first order of business was to clear the west of competing
claims, which, being a task that settlers were manifestly in-
capable of achieving by themselves, would require the power
of the federal state. Republican rhetoric "naturalized" this process, exaggerating the agency of the settlers themselves in transforming the wilderness while discounting the critical role of
federal power in preparing the way westward. Theorizing

about the progress from savagery to civilization made the extension of the frontier seem inexorable, diminishing the importance of the specific transactions that made it possible.

The United States was at peace with the European powers during Jefferson's presidency, thus minimizing the leverage Indians could exercise in their negotiations with the Americans. Recognizing his superior bargaining position, Jefferson was content to follow diplomatic precedents established by the Federalists. By the time Jefferson delivered his second inaugural address, Governor William Henry Harrison of the Indiana Territory had negotiated six treaties with the northwestern Indians that built on the framework of Wayne's Greenville Treaty. Nine more treaties, by Harrison and others, followed in the years before the War of 1812. Return Jonathan Meigs, James Wilkinson, and Benjamin Hawkins were the principal negotiators in a series of eleven treaties during Jefferson's administrations with the southern Cherokee, Creek, Choctaw, and Chickasaw nations.

Indians agreed to successive land cessions in order to shore up their unequal and eroding position in market exchanges with whites. In a revealing letter to Harrison in early 1803, Jefferson showed how Indian indebtedness could be turned to the whites' advantage. The administration would "be glad to see the good and influential individuals among" the various Indian nations "run in debt, because we observe that when these debts get beyond what the individuals can pay, they become willing to lop them off by a cession of lands."[15] An economic account of white–Indian relations was particularly attractive to Jefferson because it disguised the role of coercive state power: the marketplace was a neutral site, where free agents met as equals to seek reciprocal benefits; for the philosophically inclined, the market offered the very pattern for natural social relations. From this perspective, the role of the state was secondary and supportive, to guarantee freedom of exchange and to enforce freely made contracts. If exchanges with the Indians led to their retreat from fertile lands that they were unable to exploit effectively, then this was nature's decree – and no one's responsibility. In the meantime, benevo-

lent Jeffersonians would strive to spread the precepts of republican civilization, enabling individual Indians if not entire
communities to survive and prosper.

Jeffersonian philanthropy toward Indians was expressed,
like the Federalist policy it replaced, in the idiom of the civilizing impulse, yet it was supported by a state apparatus far
different from that envisioned by the Federalists. Jefferson ear-
nestly hoped to blend acculturated Indians with white Americans, envisioning a time when they would be "united in one
family."[16] But when natives resisted republican civilization,
forming "unnatural" alliances with corrupt European powers
in order to roll back the frontiers of white settlement, the new
nation would have to make war against its enemies in order to
guarantee its continuing existence.

For Jefferson, self-defense was the only legitimate ground
for war. This was the great justification for the revolution
itself, when Americans met assaults on their rights and interests by a corrupt imperial regime. Jefferson's conception of
the just, defensive war displaced moral responsibility on to
America's adversaries, including Indian nations who sought
secure possession of ancestral lands. His ideas about war in
turn justified his republican conception of a limited government of delegated powers that responded to the will of the
people. The kind of strong central government promoted by
the Federalists would always seek occasions to exercise and
augment its power at the expense of the people's liberties. For
Jefferson, the United States was powerful precisely because it
resorted to force only when the people recognized that their
rights were in jeopardy. The exercise of state power was thus
pushed to the margins of Jefferson's political imagination, as
the means of securing the independence of an enlightened people whose unity was predicated on their adherence to the rule
of law, by mutually beneficial exchanges in a free economy,
and by ties of family and friendship. In eschewing power as an
end in itself, Americans dissolved the historic disjunction between governors and governed, ruling themselves instead in
conformity to natural law and right. But if power was thus
diffused and displaced in republican theory, this simply served

to justify its ubiquitous exercise in republican practice. Throughout the history of the early republic, peace-loving Americans were constantly at war against internal as well external enemies. Nor did they hesitate to turn to government to gain advantage over one another.

Toward a New American System

The Jeffersonian Republican vision enabled Americans to overlook the crucial role of state power in making them prosperous and free. But the republican state could not remain invisible when it was required to act, as it was when the world beyond American borders was thrown into chaos. The stability of the republican political economy was always tenuous. As long as outlets could be found for American produce, most sectors of the union's economy hummed along. Yet Jeffersonian commercial policy did little (and really could do little) to keep access to these markets open. When international crises occurred, as they did in rapid succession from the middle of Jefferson's second term onward, Republican administrations were powerless to shape events. And they were so wedded to a political economy centered on agricultural production and market participation that they could only grudgingly and conditionally accept alternative policy prescriptions devised by their younger colleagues in the Republican party.

The fragile union of interests that the Republicans had facilitated through their neo-mercantilist political economy was threatened when war erupted in Europe after the collapse of the Peace of Amiens in 1805. The cycles of war and peace in the decade and a half following the outbreak of the First War of the French Revolution had been a boon to the United States; American merchants had filled the vacuum caused by the progressive destruction of European merchant fleets to supply both European colonies in the western hemisphere and European nations themselves. But with the formation of the Third Coalition (the alliance of Britain, Prussia, Austria, and Russia) against Napoleon, and the renewal of war, Americans found themselves even more vulnerable to the maritime depredations of both Britain and France than they had been in the 1790s. The stakes of the conflict steadily rose after 1805: within three years, Napoleon had soundly defeated the continental powers of Austria, Prussia, and Russia, while the Royal Navy secured mastery of the seas with Lord Nelson's victory at Trafalgar. With the collapse of the Third Coalition, Britain and France now stood toe to toe in the final phase of their great struggle for Europe's future. This new, anarchic world order made no place for a neutral state, and the United States found themselves, in the words of Congressman George W. Campbell, "placed in a situation equally difficult, critical, and dangerous."[17]

The United States was finally drawn into the European war in 1812. As the War of 1812 wore on, it became obvious that the federal state prescribed by Jeffersonian political economy was poorly prepared for waging war or responding to other challenges presented by emerging international diplomatic and economic order. State governments were able to exercise the limited powers necessary to deliver American agricultural products to world markets, but they could not provide the centralized manufacturing, financial, and transportation services necessary to sustain a national war effort. The American republic survived the War of 1812, barely. In the crucial year of 1814, the government was forced to borrow millions of dollars to maintain its solvency, could not dispatch troops to assist beleaguered coastal cities, and suffered humiliation as the relatively new national capital of Washington was put to the torch by invading British troops. American military successes at Plattsburgh and on Lake Champlain, in concert with British exhaustion after the final defeat of Napoleon, pushed peace negotiations forward, but the Treaty of Ghent ultimately resolved nothing, as it merely restored the status quo ante bellum. And while the concluding victories at Plattsburgh and New Orleans allowed the American populace to remember the war as an American triumph, knowledgeable Republicans were aware of how close to disaster the United States had come. The Republicans who had helped take the United States into war began to formulate plans for the next one.

The rules of war, broadly defined and understood, were utterly transformed from what they had been before the French Revolution began. For the century and a half following the Thirty Years' War, European sovereigns had utilized small, professional armies and emphasized strategies and tactics that avoided destructive set-piece battles, but now the vanguard was Napoleon's *Grande Armée* and the fiscal-military state and bureaucracy which had supported it. In constructing the concept of the "nation" and, in turn, mobilizing the entire nation for war, the successive French revolutionary regimes rewrote the early modern rules of war. Napoleon's organization and centralization of the French state in order to facilitate the conscription and supply of his armies completed the work begun by the Republic, and forced his enemies to respond in kind. As Napoleon's military strategy and tactics would be the subject of open study for years to come, his attempts to turn the European continent into an empire of liberté would have more subtle, and lasting, consequences. While the French Empire and its satellite republics faded into historical memory, the advent of the mass-conscription army, which embodied the life and essence of the nation, persisted as one of the key innovations of the Age of Revolution. The transformation of the sovereign people into a deadly weapon altered forever the scale and scope of warfare, as well as the reach and power of the state into the lives of ordinary citizens. Unlike their French republican brethren, American republicans could never attempt such large-scale centralization efforts, yet their reformulation of the republican political economy and the role of the federal state in it speaks to an awareness of the sea change which had occurred. The United States had to respond in kind to the imperatives of the new age.

Leading Republicans in both the Madison administration and in Congress sought to modify the republican vision of political economy to accommodate the demands of the emerging modern world. State power, once diffuse, would now be more centralized; once hidden behind theories of natural expansion, it would now be deployed more openly. Although

Congress rapidly demobilized the American army to a rump force of only 10,000 men (including officers), it did call for the construction of a series of coastal fortifications. Provisions were made to maintain and strengthen the navy. In order to combat financial difficulties, Congress chartered a new Bank of the United States in 1816. Congressional Republicans, led by South Carolina's John C. Calhoun and Kentucky's Henry Clay, also championed federal spending for internal improvements – lighthouses, roads, canals, turnpikes, and bridges – that would facilitate rapid transportation, communication, and military preparedness. These National Republicans also emphasized how improvements would promote economic development: the strength of the nation would wax with the prosperity of its citizens.

In 1817 Calhoun spearheaded the passage of the Bonus Bill, a measure designed to funnel dividends from the new national bank into internal improvements. Though Madison warmly endorsed the bill's goals, he vetoed the bill for constitutional reasons that will be discussed in the next chapter. Despite this setback, the provisions of the Bonus Bill defined the agenda of a rising generation of National Republicans. These men, including Clay and Calhoun in Congress, as well as current and former administration figures such as Albert Gallatin and Alexander Dallas, felt that the time was right for Jeffersonians to come clean about the role of government. Ideological posturing notwithstanding, good Republicans had never hesitated to use the power of the state to facilitate their various pursuits of happiness. Now that Federalism was vanquished, reformers reasoned, there was no longer any need to worry about the federal government exceeding its delegated powers and seeking to become a despotic, British-style, imperial regime. A more energetic, but thoroughly republican central government alone could ensure the broad diffusion of benefits to each section and state republic while preserving the sovereignty of the union in a dangerous world.

National Republicanism constituted the activist legacy of Jeffersonianism, keyed to a state of national insecurity that justified extraordinary state action. The culmination of this impetus was Henry Clay's American System, an ambitious policy program entailing internal improvements, protection for American manufactures, and efficient central direction of the national economy. The American System sought to reconcile the Republican legacy with the realities of the nineteenth century. Clay envisioned a union that would command respect from foreign powers and prevent future wars. But Clay and his fellow reformers made many Old Republicans nervous; they believed the Jeffersonian rhetoric about limited government, arguing that the whole point of the revolution had been the restraint of state power, not its marshalling. The American System's critics wondered if all the talk about another war was somewhat exaggerated: perhaps the Treaty of Ghent would inaugurate a new epoch of peace. If the promised war never came, would Clay's strong federal state itself become the leading threat to the myriad private pursuits of happiness that were supposed to flourish under a republican regime? The Panic of 1819, which the Second Bank of the United States seemed to exacerbate, and the Missouri controversy, which exposed the vulnerability of the political economy and social order of the slave-based staple economies, were both sobering to more traditional-minded Republicans.

Ensconced in their plantations in the central foothills of Virginia, Madison and Jefferson spent their respective retirements watching events in the wider American republic unfold around them, and they were both troubled and encouraged. Acknowledging that independence in the world economy required national self-sufficiency, Jefferson now – somewhat grudgingly – conceded that Albert Gallatin and Tench Coxe might have been right when they advocated the development of American manufacturing in the early 1810s. In 1816, Jefferson described a new balanced union of interests to Benjamin Austin, noting that "to be independent for the comforts of life we must fabricate them ourselves." This required a subtle reassessment of republican priorities, as "We must now place the manufacturer by the side of the agriculturist."[18] Yet Jefferson refused to affirm this stand publicly, and Madison remained stubbornly agnostic as well. It was not that

Jefferson, Madison, and other Old Republicans disliked manufacturing, or saw a diversified economy as essentially inimical to the maintenance of a republican society. Without the explicit grant of new constitutional authority, however, they remained opposed to the exercise of federal power to achieve these goals.

In the years following the Treaty of Ghent, National Republicans found themselves on the losing side of the debate more often than not. Although nationally-funded internal improvements finally came with the passage of the General Survey Act of 1824, it was already too late to reverse powerful centrifugal tendencies. In keeping with the unstated premises of the Jeffersonian political economy, state power was already being vigorously employed to promote economic enterprise. Yet such development proceeded on a state-by-state basis, and as it did, the prospects for the vitality of the union diminished. The Missouri crisis had raised the specter of a central government that, given the will, could destroy the institution of slavery. The federal government thus might not be a safe repository for the powers that a program of national economic development required; in these circumstances, enterprising Americans turned to their state governments. Yet just as the commercial world offered no guarantees that individual producers and consumers would make good marketplace choices, the structure of the republican union was helpless to prevent individual state republics from making bad choices. The contrasts are both striking and illuminating. While South Carolina expended energy on improving transportation links between the port of Charleston and upcountry cotton districts, New York built the Erie Canal, opening an immense corridor to diversified economic development, and insuring that the produce of the entire Great Lakes Basin would be transhipped through New York City. While northern and midwestern states actively diversified their economies, southern states, quite rationally, ensured that their more profitable staples had cheap access to Atlantic markets. Exercising state power while they railed against it, Jefferson's republican heirs made choices that launched their state-republics on trajectories of economic development that would ultimately and irresistibly clash.

NOTES

1   TJ, *Notes on the State of Virginia*, ed. Wiliam Peden (Chapel Hill, NC, 1954), Query XIX (Manufactures), 164–5.
2   Ibid., 165, 174.
3   Thomas Paine, *Common Sense* (Philadelphia, 1776), reprinted in Merrill Jensen, ed., *Tracts of the American Revolution, 1763–1776* (Indianapolis, 1996), 420.
4   John Adams, *Thoughts on Government* (Boston, 1776), reprinted in Charles S. Hyneman and Donald S. Lutz, eds., *American Political Writing during the Founding Era, 1760–1805*, 2 vols. (Indianapolis, 1983), 1:403.
5   In New England during this period, rates averaged about 20 cents per ton-mile. For the most part, this rendered overland hauls to market of more than twenty miles unprofitable, although there is evidence that entrepreneurial yeomen did travel considerable distances to get the best prices. Winifred B. Rothenburg, "The Market and Massachusetts Farmers, 1750–1855," *Journal of Economic History*, 41 (1981), 295–300.
6   Tench Coxe, *A Statement of the Arts and Manufactures of the United States of America, for the Year 1810* (Philadelphia, 1814), vi.
7   Ibid., viii.
8   Ibid., xxi.
9   Timothy Pitkin, *A Statistical View of the Commerce of the United States of America* (New Haven, 1835), 257–62.
10 Jacob E. Cooke, ed., *The Federalist* (Middletown, Conn., 1961), no. 11 (Hamilton), 68.
11 TJ, *Notes on Virginia*, ed Peden, Query XVIII ("Manners"), 162.
12 TJ to Monroe, 24 Nov. 1801, Merrill D. Peterson, ed., *Thomas Jefferson Writings* (New York, 1984), 1097.
13 TJ, First Inaugural Address, 4 Mar. 1801, ibid., 494.
14 TJ, First Inaugural Address, 4 Mar. 1801, ibid., 493.
15 TJ to William Henry Harrison, 27 Feb. 1803, ibid., 1118.
16 TJ to the Wolf and People of the Mandan Nation, 30 Dec. 1806, ibid., 564.
17 George W. Campbell, Report on Foreign Relations, 22 Nov. 1808, *Annals of Congress*, 10th Congress, 2nd Session, 514.
18 TJ to Benjamin Austin, 9 Jan 1816, Peterson, ed., *Jefferson Writings*, 1371.

4

Federal Republic and Extended Union

"America has a hemisphere to itself. It must have its separate system of interests, which must not be subordinated to those of Europe. The insulated state in which nature has placed the American continent, should so far avail it that no spark of war kindled in the other quarters of the globe should be wafted across the wide oceans which separate us from them."

Jefferson to Baron Alexander von Humboldt, 6 December 1813.[1]

Thomas Jefferson was elected President of the United States during a war crisis which had so divided Americans between the years 1798 and 1800 that many, including Jefferson himself, had seriously imagined the collapse of the American union. Describing American prospects in his first Inaugural Address, he invoked the image of a "rising nation, spread over a wide and fruitful land, traversing all the seas with the rich productions of their industry, engaged in commerce with nations who feel power and forget right." While some commentators have seen a republican Jefferson challenged by the dilemma of how to reconcile the three economic sectors he described – agriculture, industry, and commerce – the most compelling question was how to cope with those "nations who feel power and forget right." In the face of such threats to American republicanism, Jefferson tried to shepherd the growth of a "separate system of interests" that would bind the American republics together, ensuring their security and prosperity.

Jefferson's vision for the future of the nation was premised on fashioning a union of perfect republics. The shape of the world within which the American republics existed made such a union necessary. When they severed the imperial connection with Great Britain and declared their independence, the thirteen American states did not exist in isolation. Political and commercial connections with the rest of the world were unavoidable but dangerous, threatening corruption and dependency. Interstate relations within the union were also fraught with risk. The degree to which the central government could exercise sovereign powers would determine its ability to promote American interests in the Atlantic states system. At the same time, however, the balance of power among the states and the future of their republican governments depended on the structure of the union. Would the United States be a kind of treaty organization, guaranteeing the collective security of its members? Or would the sovereignty of the separate states be completely absorbed in a powerful new national government?

Historians generally distinguish the history of "foreign relations" from the history of political and constitutional development within the union. Jefferson and his contemporaries did not see such a clear distinction. Ideas about foreign relations were inextricably linked with the American experiment in republicanism, within and among the new state-republics. Though Americans withdrew from the British Empire, transforming themselves from subjects of King George III into self-governing citizens, they remained connected to the wider world. The most basic building block of the state republic, the independent household, could not survive or prosper without access to markets for its surpluses at home and abroad. Overseas markets did not open spontaneously: to secure commercial privileges abroad, the American states had to engage in diplomatic relations with the sovereigns of Europe. But American politicians were necessarily concerned with much more than foreign affairs. Negotiations with Indian nations were critically important for the security of frontier regions, access to commercial opportunities, and the acquisition of new lands. The first order of business for the new American republics, however, was to establish a viable political system or union with one another. The following table summarizes some of the most important political agreements in the first half-century of national history.

Major agreements with foreign sovereigns and Indian Nations, 1776–1826

Date	Name of Agreement	Party to Agreement
1776	Declaration of Independence	Continental Congress and states
1777	Articles of Confederation	Continental Congress adopts
1778 Feb.	Treaty of Alliance	France
1778 Feb.	Treaty of Amity and Commerce	France
1778 Sept.	Treaty of Fort Pitt	Delaware nation
1781 Feb.	Articles of Confederation	final state (Maryland) ratifies
1782 Oct.	Treaty of Amity and Commerce	Netherlands
1782 Nov.	Preliminary Treaty of Peace	Great Britain
1783 April	Treaty of Amity and Commerce	Sweden
1783 Sept.	Definitive Treaty of Peace (Treaty of Paris)	Great Britain
1784 Oct.	Treaty of Fort Stanwix	Six Nations (Iroquois)
1785 Jan.	Treaty of lFort McIntosh	Wyandot, Delaware, Chippewa, Ottawa
1785 Sept.	Treaty of Amity and Commerce	Prussia
1785 Nov.	Treaty of Hopewell	Cherokee nation (additional treaties at Hopewell in Jan. 1786 with Choctaw and Chickasaw nations)
1786 June-July	Treaty of Peace and Friendship	Morocco
1790 July	Treaty of New York	Creek nation
1791 July	Treaty of Holston	Cherokee nation
1794 June	Treaty of Philadelphia	Cherokee nation
1794 Nov.	Treaty of Amity and Commerce (Jay Treaty)	Great Britain
1794 Nov.	Treaty of Canandaigua	Six Nations (Iroquois)
1795 Aug.	Treaty of Greenville	Wyandot, Delaware, Shawnee, Ottawa, Chippewa, Potawatomi, Miami; Eel River, Wea, Kickapoo, Piankashaw, Kaskasia
1795 Sept.	Treaty of Peace and Amity	Algiers

Date	Treaty	Party
1795 Oct.	Treaty of Friendship, Limits, and Navigation (Treaty of San Lorenzo)	Spain
1796 June	Treaty of Colerain	Creek Nation
1796 Nov.	Treaty of Peace and Friendship	Tripoli
1797 Aug.	Treaty of Peace and Friendship	Tunis
1799 July	Treaty of Amity and Commerce	Prussia
1800 Sept.	Convention of Môrtefontaine	France
1803 April	Louisiana Treaties	France
	Three treaties cede Louisiana to US. transfer funds to France, and settle outstanding claims.	
1803 June	Treaty of Fort Wayne	Delaware, Shawnee, Potawatomi, Miami, Eel River, Wea, Kickapoo, Piankashaw, Kaskasia
	First of eleven treaties negotiated before war of 1812 by William Henry Harrison as Gov. of Indiana Territory.	
1805 June	Treaty of Peace and Amity	Tripoli
1814 July	Treaty of Greenville	Wyandot, Delaware, Seneca, Shawnee, Miami
1814 Aug.	Treaty of Fort Jackson	Creek nation
1814 Dec.	Treaty of Ghent	Great Britain
	Ends War of 1812	
1815 June-July	Treaty of Peace	Algiers
1819 Feb.	Transcontinental Treaty (Adams-Onis Treaty)	Spain
1823 Dec.	"Monroe Doctrine"	
	Statement by President Monroe and Secy. of State Adams against European intervention in Western Hemisphere	
1824 April	Northwest Coast Convention	Russia
1824 Oct.	Treaty of Peace, Amity, Commerce and Navigation	Colombia

Rather than sharply dividing political relations into foreign and domestic realms, American republicans saw nested sets of relationships rising, like the concentric, crystalline spheres of the Aristotelian cosmos, from the earthly center of the republican household. From local community through states and union to the world of Atlantic commerce, the household's reach extended through many systems of relations, each presenting a different set of challenges and opportunities. Diplomatic relations with foreign powers occupied the outermost circle; relationships between the American states took up their own sphere, differing in shape and degree, but not in kind, from the other sets of political relations. To simply demarcate *foreign* and *domestic* spheres simplifies the complex reality of American politics, taking the existence of the states and their union as givens. In the decades following the Declaration of Independence, contentiousness and competition at every level of politics threatened the republican experiment.

Republican revolutionaries did not distinguish spheres of authority in the modern manner. Instead, they saw all political relations through the prism of natural law. The most influential articulation of natural law for men of Jefferson's age was the law of nations. Treatises by writers such as Hugo Grotius, Samuel Pufendorf, Christian Wolff, and Emmerich de Vattel were particularly useful for revolutionary statesmen as they confronted questions of state. The natural law principles which infused Jefferson's Declaration and undergirded the republican society he longed to create in America also ordered relations between independent states. The challenge for Jefferson and his colleagues was to determine the degree to which the law of nations offered an appropriate framework for organizing a union of republics.

Law of nations writers sought to establish the rules of diplomacy between sovereign states. But their definitions of both *diplomacy* and *sovereignty* were ambiguous and unstable. The realities of eighteenth-century politics defied simple, universally applicable definitions. States of all sorts, from European monarchies and confederacies to the Muslim principalities of the Mediterranean world and American Indian nations, engaged in diplomacy. The principles which guided negotiations in Paris or London were not the same ones which guided negotiations at Albany or Fort Detroit. This does not mean the two systems were not related. Transatlantic empires linked European and American diplomacy; actions at the colonial periphery reverberated at the imperial metropolis, and vice versa. Diplomats everywhere needed to be conscious of the wider world within which their negotiations took place. But the foundations of the different systems of diplomacy were not the same. Despite their adherence to the universal principles of natural law, American revolutionaries recognized that diplomatic negotiations proceeded in various arenas and under different systems of rules.

The definition of *sovereignty*, the capacity of a state to participate on equal terms in the European states system, was also slippery. One of the key intellectual innovations of early modern political thought, the concept of sovereignty had its origins in the works of sixteenth-century French writer Jean Bodin. While Bodin's *The Six Books of the Republic* (1576) delineated the powers which the sovereign held and the boundaries placed on a sovereign's powers, the writings of the Dutch jurist Hugo Grotius, particularly *The Rights of War and Peace* (1625), explored how sovereigns interacted. Grotius identified two realms of sovereign power: private acts affecting individuals were subsumed under his judicial power; public acts included the lawmaking or legislative power, as well as the "making of war and peace and treaties."[2] The acts of waging war, concluding peace, and entering into alliances presumed sovereignty. For Bodin, Grotius, and their contemporaries sovereignty was a principle of natural law, deriving from the law of God. This conceptual framework began to change in the aftermath of the Peace of Westphalia (1648). With the emergence of an increasingly secular states system rooted in great-power diplomacy, political theorists took the existence of contending sovereign states as the given, and from there sought to outline the limits and privileges natural law placed on sovereigns. The Swiss writer Emmerich de Vattel authored the most explicit exposition of these principles in his 1758 work, *The Law of Nations*.

Vattel's *Law of Nations* offered the eighteenth century one of its most concrete and explicit explorations of the nature of sovereignty. For Vattel, sovereignty was "political authority" possessed by the body politic as a whole to "order and direct what is to be done by each" member of society. Sovereignty could be exercised by all, by a few, or by one person. The decision of how a particular nation would be governed belonged to that nation alone; a nation which constituted its own government "without dependence on any foreign power" was a "sovereign state."[3] Vattel's definition of sovereignty did not differ significantly from those of his predecessors. What distinguished his formulation of the law of nations was his clear exposition of the rights of sovereign states participating in a system of states. Sovereign states could regulate commerce by enacting tolls, tariffs, and a whole variety of taxes; they could coin money. At the same time, they were expected to promote commerce with other nations. Sovereignties could defend their essential rights and interests by going to war, but they should also strive to preserve peace. They could send and receive ambassadors to other states and enter into treaties with them. The crucial premise of the diplomatic system codified in the law of nations was its purely voluntary character. No central authority could impose sanctions on a sovereign state that disobeyed the rules; the security of a sovereign's rights depended upon their acceptance by other sovereigns.

When republican revolutionaries turned to the law of nations, they discovered a set of rules that more or less described the world beyond the American union. But the law of nations was less helpful in defining relations among the American republics. Vattel did recognize the advantages of federal alliances such as that established by the Articles of Confederation, noting that "sovereign and independent states may unite themselves together by a perpetual confederacy, without ceasing to be, each individually, a perfect state." These confederated sovereign states "will together constitute a federal republic," in which "their joint deliberations will not impair the sovereignty of each member, though they may, in certain respects, put some restraint on the exercise of it, in virtue of voluntary engagements." But Vattel was unclear whether this federal republic should conduct all diplomatic relations with other sovereignties, or whether its constituent members retained some latent capacity to act independently. If a state ceded its sovereign power to another authority, if its "people passed under the dominion of another," then it was "no longer a state, and can no longer avail itself directly of the law of nations." These subordinate polities might "within themselves" be "governed by their own laws and magistrates," but they could not themselves "make war or contract alliances" or "treat with other nations."[4] Vattel was thus frustratingly ambiguous about the status of confederating states which preserved some indeterminate measure of political independence.

The law of nations was not the only model Americans had at their disposal for conceptualizing their place in the wider world. Before 1776, the American states had been provinces within the British Empire. Legislators, jurists, and political thinkers on both sides of the Atlantic had seen the empire as an extended polity organized under an informal constitution or customary framework of implicitly understood rights and obligations. Under imperial rule, the Anglo-American provinces had enjoyed the freedom and security to construct political societies of freeholders, who were in turn free to pursue their various interests and accumulate the property that secured their independence. The British Empire thus had provided Americans with a model of a system of political relations, which under the dominion of a distant (and therefore weak) metropolis, allowed their polities a degree of sovereignty "within themselves."

The diplomatic system of Europe and the extended polity of the British Empire provided Americans with conceptual frameworks for understanding their place in the world. Vattel taught them that the European world was itself a "republic" of sorts: in theory, each state was an equal member in a society that had fixed rules of behavior. And eighteenth-century thinkers recognized that many of these European states were *empires* or composite states: extended polities of multiple jurisdictions, spanning oceans, and embracing a variety of peoples. Revolutionaries thus were familiar with functioning (or malfunctioning) states systems and the legal principles that supposedly governed their operation. But their revolution was a major crisis for both systems, revealing the radical limitations of both the law of nations and the imperial constitution – if such a thing had ever in fact existed – for the reconstitution of American politics. Would it be necessary to establish a powerful central government in America to secure union without the British imperial connection? Could the states preserve their integrity as "perfect republics" if they delegated sovereign powers to the government of a union sufficiently "energetic" to protect and promote their collective rights and interests in the Atlantic states' system?

By the middle of the eighteenth century a coherent, yet complex, states system centering on the Atlantic Ocean had emerged. Through their own agents, as well as through colonists and local proxies, European empires competed against and allied with one another on the five great continents and on every ocean. When the United States declared independence, Jefferson's Declaration proclaimed it to a "candid world"; Americans knew that their thirteen states were part of an extended Atlantic states system. But their shared history as colonies and partners in rebellion indicated to them their states were part of a distinct system, a separate sphere of relations, what Jefferson was referring to when he wrote in the *Anas* of "a political system of our own, independant of that of Europe."[5] The open question for Jefferson and his generation was how the rules of the two models, the "republic" of Europe and the British Empire, could be modified, adapted, and improved in order to secure American rights and interests in the Atlantic world without jeopardizing their republican experiment.

The Federal Union as a Diplomatic Imperative

When the Treaty of Paris ended the American War for Independence, the future of the thirteen United States as a single, corporate entity was far from certain. Overlapping claims to western lands made many of the states geopolitical rivals. States also competed commercially by imposing discriminatory tariffs and duties. British Canada as well as Spanish Florida and Louisiana threatened the security and prosperity of the American states on the Atlantic as well as the Mississippi. The union was also at risk in the interior from powerful, potentially hostile Indian confederacies, including the Iroquois, Shawnees, Cherokees, and Creeks, particularly when they acted in concert with European imperial powers. Because North America in the revolutionary and post-revolutionary periods was brimming over with geopolitical rivalries, Americans tended to see both intra-state and inter-state relations within the larger diplomatic context of the Atlantic states system as a whole. Not surprisingly, their initial efforts to define the character of the union were couched in the language of the law of nations.

With the guidance of law of nations writers, Americans studied the history of earlier experiments in federal government in order to assess their own prospects. While the revolution still raged, Alexander Hamilton's historical review of such experiments in his *Continentalist* essays led him to conclude that confederations were bound to collapse. The experiences of ancient Greece, the Swiss League, and the Dutch Republic showed that members of confederations were governed by "the plainest principles of human nature": individuals felt more loyalty to their own particular republics or principalities than to their collective government; in order to promote their selfish interests, constituent states promoted "a disposition for abridging the authority of the foederal government."[6] In the summer of 1786, as he prepared for the Annapolis Convention, James Madison reached similar conclusions. Madison's "Notes on Ancient and Modern Confederacies" systematically analyzed the strengths and weaknesses of every confederation, from antiquity through the Dutch Republic and the Holy Roman Empire of the seventeenth and eighteenth centuries. After the Philadelphia convention, Madison and Hamilton, collaborating as "Publius," developed these comparisons at length in *The Federalist*.

While Vattel described natural law ordering relations between sovereign states, Hamilton focused on the manner in which the laws of nature acted on individual men. The fundamental principles which placed all of the European sovereignties in contention with one another would doom a weak American Confederation. "Political societies, in close neighbourhood, must either be strongly united under one government," Hamilton wrote in his *Continentalist* essays, "or there will infallibly exist emulations and quarrels." For this fundamental rule was ordained by "human nature; and we have no reason to think ourselves wiser, or better, than other men": one simply could not expect an individual to pledge allegiance to two sovereign masters at the same time.[7] Madison, and most of the delegates to the Philadelphia convention, seemed to concur. Reporting on the proceedings of the convention to Jefferson, Madison noted that it "was generally agreed that the objects of the Union could not be secured by any system founded on the principle of a confederation of sovereign States."[8] The British imperial constitution may have offered a better model. In *The Federalist*, "Publius" (Hamilton) argued that the Constitution did not provide for the "consolidation of the States into one complete national sovereignty," but only a "partial Union or consolidation" with the state-republics retaining "all the rights of sovereignty which they before had," not "*exclusively* delegated to the United States."[9] Was Hamilton's "partial Union" more like the British empire than Vattel's "federal republic?" Would a state that submitted to such a "dominion" forfeit its sovereignty?

The events of the 1780s revealed both practical and theoretical problems with the organization of the American states under the Confederation. Contention between and within the states led many Americans to question whether a system of equal sovereign states could survive and prosper. Constitutional reformers concluded that the Articles of Confederation were fundamentally flawed and that a stronger central government alone could maintain the union that was so crucial to the preservation of American independence. As we have seen, commerce was the pivot on which American politics turned in the Age of

Jefferson. So it had been in the critical period of the 1780s, when commercial considerations determined relations within, between, and beyond the state-republics. Even before the United States had formally declared independence, American states-men recognized the importance of trade for securing their place in the wider Atlantic states system. Between June and September 1776, John Adams led the Continental Congress in draft-ing a plan of a treaty with France. The "model treaty" would not constitute a conventional political or military alliance, but instead codified the reciprocal commercial rights and privileges to be enjoyed by French and American merchants, strictly de-fined contraband, and set up procedures for the capture and condemnation of prizes during wartime. Americans believed that the benefits of free trade with their states were so obvious as to compel France and other continental powers to recognize the United States and engage in commerce with them, even at the risk of war with Britain. These diplomatic hopes proved unrealistic, as ratification of the Franco-American military alli-ance along with a treaty of commerce in 1778 testifies. Yet the model treaty continued to serve as the basis for the Confedera-tion's diplomacy throughout the 1780s. Commerce pushed Americans into the Atlantic states system, and it remained the source from which future conflicts flowed.

Commercial conflicts also represented the most compelling argument for a more centralized federal union. Sitting in Con-gress in 1784, Jefferson grappled with the dilemmas posed by commerce. If commercial competition divided the states, it could also unite them. "All the world is becoming commer-cial," he wrote George Washington. The sources of this were apparent. "Our citizens have had too full a taste of the com-forts furnished by the arts & manufactures to be debarred the use of them." Thus, as he told John Jay, "Our people are de-cided in the opinion that it is necessary for us to take a share in the occupation of the ocean." The implications of this were obvious: because "we cannot separate ourselves" from the world of Atlantic commerce, full engagement with the diplo-matic machinery of Europe would be necessary. With Ameri-can ships and merchants traversing all corners of the Atlantic, "their property will be violated on the sea" and "in foreign ports," and Americans would face the prospect of insults and imprisonment for "pretended debts, contracts, crimes, contraband" and the like. Diplomacy was the only remedy for such eventualities. Consuls and commercial agents could protect American merchants and mariners operating abroad, commercial compacts negotiated by American ministers would give them a framework within which to work. But ultimately Americans must be prepared to vindicate their rights by military force, particularly naval power. "Our commerce on the ocean and in other countries must be paid for by frequent war." If the majority of Americans were determined to follow through on their choice to become a commercial people, Jefferson recognized that American statesmen would be required to engage in the political, legal, and diplomatic systems of Europe.[10]

As Jefferson and the other members of the Confederation's fledgling diplomatic corps sought to expand the sphere open to American commerce, it became obvious that a Vattelian "federal republic," or confederation that left the sovereignty of its member states intact, was radically insufficient. Only a strong union, a government "partly national, and partly federal," could sustain diplomatic initiatives abroad and contain interstate political and commercial competition at home. During his years as American minister to France, Jefferson constantly found himself combating negative images of American government, economy, and society under the Confederation. In early 1786, he confessed to Archibald Stuart that the "American reputation in Europe is not such as to be flattering to it's citizens." It was both the "nonpaiment of our debts" and "the want of our energy in our government" that Jefferson identified as the key factors which "discourage a connection with us."[11]

After Spain closed the Mississippi River to American navigation in 1784, the Confederation's secretary for foreign affairs, John Jay, entered into negotiations with Spanish minister Don Diego de Gardoqui. Because of the Confederation's weakness within the Atlantic states system, Jay found himself with few options, and acquiesced in the humiliating closure of the river in order to secure commercial concessions. European observers perceived a weak American government that lacked the financial, military, and political wherewithal to be a major player in the commercial life of the Atlantic states system. Although the United States was able to secure commercial treaties with small and medium-sized European powers such as the Netherlands (1782), Sweden (1783), and Prussia (1785), American diplomats such as Jefferson, Adams, and Jay found wresting beneficial commercial accords from the major European powers – Britain, France, and Spain – to be a most difficult endeavor. Hamilton pithily encapsulated the situation in *The Federalist*, noting that the "imbecility of our government even forbids" the European powers "to treat with us," and as a result "our ambassadors abroad are the mere pageants of mimic sovereignty."[12]

The Confederation's weakness handicapped the diplomatic efforts to extend American commerce in other sectors of the Atlantic states system. In the Mediterranean, the nonexistence of an American navy imperilled American commercial prospects. For decades, the Barbary Regencies of North Africa engaged in the systematic capture, plunder, and ransom of any shipping in the Mediterranean that did not pay them an annual tribute. The question of how to respond to the depredations of the "Barbary pirates" became a perennial one for American policy-makers into the early decades of the nineteenth century. As the Confederation's highest-ranking diplomats in the Old World, Jefferson and Adams were called upon to implement Congress's policy of making treaties and paying tribute. Both personally disagreed with the policy. Adams favored an American naval build-up that could effectively police the Mediterranean and protect the American merchant marine; Jefferson preferred an immediate, outright war on all of the Barbary states. Yet both realized that the Confederation government had neither the funds nor the authority to support such aggressive policies. Congress's more conciliatory approach did not produce satisfactory results. Agent Thomas Barclay concluded a treaty of commerce with Morocco, the weakest of the four states, in 1786, but negotiations with Algiers, Tunis, and Tripoli would continue into the 1790s, and did not result in commercial treaties until the new federal government could bring its more substantial resources into play.

Diplomatic relations with American Indian communities followed a similarly tortuous course. Initially, American statesmen argued that the United States gained title to Indian lands through victory in the revolution: all Indians who lived within the boundaries of the United States as recognized by the Treaty of Paris (1783) were a "conquered" people. But it was much easier to formulate than to implement such a claim. Many American Indian communities remained connected to trading partners and potential allies in the European states system: they were powerful enough to resist American pretensions; through alliances with imperial powers they posed a credible challenge to the confederation governments. Negotiators on both the Indian and American sides of the treaty councils perceived that only a United States with a strong central government could offer commercial incentives to rival those offered by the agents of the European empires, or pose a realistic military threat to compel serious negotiation in the first place. Only a strong central government could restrain American settlers from perpetrating acts of violence on the frontier.

The new nation was at risk in every direction. Isolation was not a viable alternative for a commercial, enterprising people. Settlers demanded access to new (Indian) lands; planters, farmers, and merchants sought access to foreign markets on favorable terms. American diplomats were called upon to open avenues for all America's diverse produce and open ports to American shipping. On both sides of the Atlantic, American negotiators found this task to be almost impossible. A frustrated Jefferson captured the general mood in 1786, when he complained about British unwillingness to negotiate a commercial treaty: "Our overtures of commercial arrangement have been treated with a derision which shew their [the British government's] firm persuasion that we shall never unite to suppress their commerce or even to impede it."[13] So, for Jefferson and his contemporaries, a stronger union between the American states became a strategy to combat their weaknesses, both perceived and real, within the Atlantic states system.

In the months preceding the Philadelphia Convention, James Madison concluded that only a strong federal union could preserve republicanism in the separate states and preempt interstate conflict. Without a strong nationalizing force, the American states system would look increasingly like the European states system. In February 1787, Madison observed to Edmund Randolph that "the existing Confederacy is tottering to its foundation," and that some contemplated the adoption of "Monarchy" while other "individuals predict a partition of the States into two or more Confederacies." Madison himself believed the latter was more likely, and without "radical amendment" of the existing Confederation, it was a certainty.[14] A partition of the union seemed a likely outcome if the Philadelphia Convention failed to create a workable restructuring of the confederacy, or if the Constitution that it produced was not ratified.

The federal Constitution of 1787 apparently resolved any ambiguity about the sovereignty of the states under the Confederation by establishing the exclusive authority of the general government over foreign policy, including relations with Indians. At the same time, however, Federalist advocates of ratification sought to assure skeptical voters that their more energetic union would secure the states in their remaining, undelegated rights. Republicanism would flourish in the separate states even while – and because – they ceased to exist as independent polities in the larger world. Madison summarized the Convention's paradoxical achievement in a letter to Jefferson in late October 1787: it was the "unanimous wish of the Convention to preserve the Union of the States," but delegates recognized that the "objects of the Union could not be secured by any system founded on the principle of a confederation of sovereign States." The federal Constitution would not, like the law of nations, operate "on the States," but "operate without their intervention" directly "on the individuals composing them." Antifederalists wondered how the states could possibly survive with this "consolidation" of authority in the central government. Madison acknowledged the legitimacy of such concerns. "The due partition of power, between the General & local Governments," he noted, "was perhaps of all, the most nice and difficult." By establishing the principle of federal supremacy, the new Constitution threatened to collapse the distinctions between the various spheres of authority that, in both Jefferson's and Vattel's formulations, gave republicans the space to govern themselves and perfect the institutions of their separate state-republics. Yet Madison was at this point convinced that escalating interstate conflict and abuses of power by state governments constituted much greater and more immediate threats to American republicanism than did the distant prospect of oppression by any central authority. Under the Constitution, Madison promised, the fact that the "general authority will be derived from subordinate authorities" would militate against either the central sovereignty or the states affecting "mutual projects of usurpation." "The great desideratum in Government," he told Jefferson, "is, so to modify the sovereignty as that it may be sufficiently neutral between different parts of the Society to controul one part from invading the rights of another, and at the same time sufficiently controuled itself, from setting up an interest adverse to that of the entire Society."[15]

Yet the prospects for the "extended Republic of the United States" remained insecure. The concerns Madison had expressed in early 1787 hung in the air as the ratification debates proceeded in late 1787 and early 1788. In *The Federalist*, Madison and Hamilton emphasized the horrible consequences of disunion: disunited states competing for commercial advantage and quarreling over boundaries would be forced to establish standing armies and prepare for war. Not only would the disunited states come to resemble the European states system, with its endemic conflicts, but the European powers themselves would actively involve themselves in American politics. This was not idle talk. Even as Madison worked to ensure the Constitution's ratification in late 1787, one of his correspondents warned him that the western people's "attachment to the American Union will be weakened" if Congress failed to secure the right to navigate the Mississippi.[16] Reconstituting the union was the only way to prevent interstate relations in America from being entangled in European diplomacy.

During the "critical period," reformers effectively argued that the American experiment in republican government was jeopardized by the weakness of the Confederation. Commercial competition and geopolitical rivalries showed that union could not be spontaneous and uncoerced, that the law of nations would not be self-enforcing in the American system of states. "The happy empire of perfect wisdom and perfect virtue" was at best a distant prospect, Hamilton sardonically noted. In the meantime, practical statesmen must "awake from the deceitful dream of a golden age," recognizing that the laws of human nature continued to operate under every form of government, even in republics.[17] But reform entailed its own risks. The transformation of dependent British provinces into independent, self-governing commonwealths depended on the successful management of several sets of political relationships at every horizon beyond the "little republic" of the household. Jettisoning the ideal of a consensual union of states in favor of a "consolidated" national government that could vindicate American rights in the larger Atlantic system jeopardized the very existence of the state-republics that American republicans sought to perfect.

Federalists who advocated ratification of the Constitution sought to insulate American politics from the European states system. In acceding to the new regime, the American republics clearly abdicated their sovereignty within the larger framework of the Atlantic states system to the "federal head." But agreement on this general principle left many questions unanswered, and Antifederalist skeptics did not hesitate to ask them. To what extent would this abdication of sovereignty affect relations between, and within, the states themselves? What guarantees did the new system offer for the rights and liberties of individual citizens and of their separate state-republics? These same questions eventually would divide the Federalists of the late 1780s into the Federalists and Republicans of the 1790s.

Questions of Sovereignty

Proponents of the new Constitution sought to allay the anxieties of their Antifederalist opponents. Hamilton insisted that the Constitution did *not* affect "an intire consolidation of the States into one complete national sovereignty," but that there had been a "division of the sovereign power" granted by the body politic: "all authorities of which the States are not explicitly divested in favour of the Union remain with them in full vigour."[18] This division of sovereignty, Madison explained, was necessary to the proper functioning of the revamped American states system. "In the extended Republic of the United States, the General Government would hold a pretty even balance between the parties of particular States, and be at the same time sufficiently restrained by its dependence on the community, from betraying its general interests."[19] But the sovereignty issue could not be so easily resolved, as Madison himself soon recognized. With the outbreak of the French Revolution and the resulting European wars, events within the Atlantic states system began to transform relations within the American states system. To preserve the new nation's precarious position within the Atlantic system, Federalist administrations pursued policies which Madison, Jefferson, and fellow Republicans believed would destroy the constitutional balance within the federal union.

The new federal government's initial forays into the process of treaty-making put questions about the extent of the sovereign power in the foreground of the national political discussion. When George Washington formed his first administration, the North American continent remained a cockpit of contention within the Atlantic states system. Not surprisingly, the administration's first successful diplomatic negotiations were with the Creek Indians and culminated in the Treaty of New York of 1790. The Creek negotiations prompted one of the earliest discussions of the Constitution's reapportionment of sovereign power.

The Creeks' crucial geopolitical position in the borderland

region between Spanish Florida and the state of Georgia, quickly brought them into the focus of the first Washington administration. Since the close of the revolution, Creek interests had been protected by the deft statecraft of their metís war chief, the Scots-Creek Alexander McGillivray. Exploiting his father's connections with a Scottish mercantile firm and his Creek mother's clan status, McGillivray had played British, Spanish, Creeks, and Georgians off against one another, accumulating wealth and political power for himself and securing the territorial interests of the far-flung Creek Confederacy. Secretary of war Henry Knox recognized McGillivray's powerful position, fashioning a policy of diplomatic engagement with the Creeks in order to avoid warfare, expand commerce, and acquire new lands.

Knox's Creek diplomacy inaugurated a new epoch in American Indian diplomacy, with the federal government retreating from the belligerent and counter-productive conquest theory. In embracing this more prudent course, however, Knox offered a potentially controversial new formulation of the relationship between state and national governments. Knox outlined his policy and the political theorems supporting it in an extended memorandum to President Washington in July 1789. Knox saw that the "critical situation of affairs between the State of Georgia and the Creek Nation" compelled the federal government to address American–Creek relations and, through them, the question of relations with Indians generally. The United States could pursue either a belligerent policy or an attempt to secure its goals through diplomacy. War would be an expensive and risky proposition: the Creeks could field thousands of warriors, and could call on the Spanish in Florida for additional support. Knox preferred a policy of direct and forthright diplomatic negotiation. But this approach was not without its complications. An "amicable negociation" required that commissioners chosen be "invested with full powers to decide all differences respecting boundaries between the State of Georgia and the Creek Indians." Knox defined "full powers" capaciously, as the commissioners were to be "unconstrained by treaties said to exist between the said parties otherwise than the same may be reciprocally acknowledged." Knox had in mind the controversial Treaties of Galphinton (1785) and Shoulderbone (1786), which Georgia accepted as law, but which were negotiated with only two of nearly a hundred Creek villages. Knox's position was that the federal government now not only had the sole power to negotiated diplomatic accords, but also had the power to abrogate or validate treaties made by the sovereign states under the Articles of Confederation.[20]

Knox's repudiation of conquest theory pointed to a reapportionment of sovereignty among federal government, states, and Indian nations. He called on Congress for a "declarative Law" that would assert that the "Indian tribes possess the right of the soil of all lands within their limits respectively and that they are not to be divested thereof but in consequence of fair and bona fide purchases, made under the authority, or with the express approbation of the United States." Though Knox understood that such legislation might jeopardize delicate balances in the federal system, he insisted that "no individual State could with propriety complain of invasion of its territorial rights." Knox's premise was that "the independent nations and tribes of indians ought to be considered as foreign nations, not as the subjects of any particular state." It followed that the "general Sovereignty," meaning the federal government, "must possess the right of making all treaties on the execution or violation of which depend peace or war." Knox proceeded to show how the government could affect a "noble liberal and disinterested administration of indian affairs" through the postponement of purchases of Indian lands and the formation of "Colonies" in the west with military garrisons which could restrain and regulate white settlement. The Treaty of New York (August 1790), the final negotiation of which Knox oversaw personally, gave the Creeks some of their lands back and secured commercial privileges for Alexander McGillivray in an American port. It was the first thread in the fabric of the relatively humane Federalist Indian policy of diplomatic engagement, "benevolence," and gradual "civilization."[21]

Jefferson would come to disagree with many of the implications of Knox's Indian diplomacy. Yet Jefferson's initial reaction to Knox's diplomatic initiatives blended general approval with a measure of bewilderment about the appropriate protocols of Indian diplomacy. For the time being at least, there was no viable alternative to conceding de facto sovereignty to the Indian nations. In the New York negotiations Alexander McGillivray could thus claim the right to determine which Americans traded inside the Creek Nation. Jefferson acknowledged that the Creeks had the "right to give us their peace, and to withhold their commerce, to place it under what monopolies or regulations they please." Furthermore, an explicit agreement on this point would be in the interest of the United States, as "we gain some advantage in substituting citizens of the U.S." in place of "both British and Spaniards" as the principal agents of commerce with the Creek Nation. Viewing the Atlantic geopolitical dynamic as a whole, Jefferson saw that a treaty clause that possibly compromised the rights and interests of particular states might nonetheless serve a more inclusive national interest.[22]

At the same time, Jefferson was troubled by the implications of Knox's policy for American federalism. He wondered in his memorandum what role the American government would play in maintaining the Creeks' monopolistic commercial practices. Any treaty clause that dealt with questions of commerce was fraught with danger, for a "treaty made by the President with the concurrence of two thirds of the Senate, is a law of the land, and a law of superior order, because it not only repeals past laws, but cannot itself be repealed by future ones." Any international agreement, including treaties with Indians, could thus make law within the American states system. A treaty might "expressly stipulate" that "no person be permitted to trade in the Creek country, without a licence from the President," giving the executive extraordinary discretion over the regulation of American commerce and preempting both federal and state legislatures. While Jefferson felt that in fact "no law will be violated" under the Creek treaty, more suspicious colleagues were not so easily reassured. An alarmed New

York newspaper essayist, who sarcastically took the name "Anti Republican," charged that the treaty constituted an assault on Georgia's sovereignty: the federal government was "slicing from a state one of its counties" simply "because Mr. McG——— took a fancy to it." This was a dangerous precedent, Anti Republican concluded, for it "plainly indicates, that if the governors think it necessary, they may not only treat away part, but the whole of the state of Georgia, and so of any other state that might prove refractory." The essay went on to raise fears that the administration would dispatch a "standing army" to enforce the treaty; in response "those Georgia people may declare the treaty unconstitutional."[23] Anti Republican anticipated concerns about the abuse of the federal treaty power that would figure prominently in Republican rhetoric over the next decade. As Federalists deployed the machinery of the new federal state to protect American interests in the larger Atlantic system, oppositionists feared for the future of the state-republics that the union was supposed to secure.

Throughout the 1790s, debates about how the federal government should conduct diplomacy in the Atlantic states system often turned into questions about the structure of the federal union. This was the case in 1793, as Revolutionary France went to war with nearly all of Europe in the aftermath of the execution of Louis XVI. When the French National Convention dispatched a minister, Edmond Genêt, to the United States, the Washington administration was forced to decide whether to receive him and thus recognize the French Republic. Washington's cabinet was divided on the matter, with secretary of state Jefferson arguing for recognition and secretary of the treasury Hamilton arguing against. Revolutionary change in France raised controversial questions in the law of nations, most notably whether the Franco-American treaties of 1778 remained in effect after Louis's death. Did the French nation continue to exercise its sovereignty through the new republican regime? A related issue also polarized the cabinet. Jefferson and Hamilton agreed that the United States should steer clear of the European wars, whatever the language of the French treaty, but they divided over how this neutrality should be constitutionally determined and promulgated. Hamilton believed that a decision on neutrality hinged on the interpretation of a treaty, and therefore fell solely to the executive. Jefferson thought Congress should play the decisive role, "as the Executive cannot decide the question of war on the affirmative side, neither ought it to do so on the negative side."[24] Washington decided on a compromise of sorts, recognizing Genêt and the treaties but unilaterally issuing the Proclamation of Neutrality on 22 April 1793.

Debate over the Proclamation simmered throughout the summer of 1793. It was largely a debate about means, not ends. Both Federalists and Republicans saw an Atlantic states system erupting into war and concluded that it was in the interest of the United States to remain neutral. But Republicans worried that the administration's responses to the transformation of the European system would transform the carefully balanced structures of the American states system. Conflicting partisan perspectives were fully elaborated in a polemical exchange between Hamilton (writing as "Pacificus") and Madison ("Helvedius"). Hamilton insisted that the ability to declare neutrality was part of the President's executive powers. "The legislative department is not the *organ* of intercourse between the United States and foreign nations," he asserted, "it is charged neither with *making* nor *interpreting* treaties." Because the neutrality proclamation simply stated and clarified, but did not in itself effect any change in the nation's situation, it fell well within the power of the President to execute the laws.[25] Madison disagreed fundamentally, echoing earlier opposition to Knox's broad construction of the executive's power to conclude Indian treaties. Pacificus's thinly-veiled agenda was to use plausible arguments about the interpretation of treaties to justify a dangerous concentration of power in the executive branch. Madison invoked Vattel and other authorities to demonstrate that the power to make war, peace, and treaties, and therefore to declare the nation's neutrality was a *legislative*, not an executive, power. The clear language of the Constitution left no doubt about where the disputed power lay. Because of far-reaching implications of the treaty power, any ambiguity on this point was intolerable. "A treaty is not an execution of laws," Madison insisted, but "is, on the contrary, to have itself the force of a *law*," for indeed, the Constitution made any treaty "the supreme law of the land." As a result, treaties "have sometimes the effect of changing not only the external laws of the society, but operate also on the internal code."[26] Here was the ultimate source of Republican fears about the course of Federalist diplomacy. An enterprising president and his minions could corrupt the Senate, depriving the legislature of its legitimate role in conducting foreign policy. Once the executive gained the upper hand, he could then make law, altering the delicate constitutional balance the Convention had struggled to establish and endangering the residual sovereignty of the state-republics. The machinery which would keep the spheres of the republican political cosmos separate and distinct was in danger.

These were the concerns that shaped the Republican response to the Jay Treaty two years later. The commercial treaty that John Jay negotiated with Britain in 1794 and 1795 became a subject of national controversy when it was ratified by the Senate and made public. To secure commercial reciprocity (equal trade restrictions on both sides) with Great Britain itself, Jay had allowed trade with the British West Indies to remain closed; he had also abandoned the principle of "free ships, free goods," acceding to the British "Rule of 1756," which stipulated that a trade not open to a neutral in peacetime could not be opened in time of war. The Jay Treaty also failed to stop either the British practice of seizing contraband from neutral ships or the impressment of sailors from American ships. Republican critics concluded that the administration had betrayed the principles of the model treaty of 1776 by accepting limitations on American sovereignty and limiting the commercial choices available to American producers.

Historians have exaggerated Jefferson's Anglophobia and love for Revolutionary France in explaining his opposition to the Jay Treaty. Jefferson was most disturbed by the prospect that the treaty would alter power relationships within both

the Atlantic and American states systems. The treaty's aban-
donment of neutral rights, a key principle in Jefferson's understanding of the law of nations, was particularly upsetting.
From the Republican perspective, American independence and
sovereignty in the Atlantic system were inextricably linked.
Favoring the commerce of one nation over another could reduce American producers to dependency; the sovereignty of
dependent states and their ability to assert their rights under
the law of nations was radically, perhaps fatally, compromised.

At the same time, the Jay Treaty promised to alter the shape
of the relations between sovereignties within the American
states system. Writing to Madison in late 1795, Jefferson cast
the problem in the starkest terms: the Federalists' campaign
for the treaty was "the boldest act they have ever ventured to
undermine the constitution" and thus destroy the union. "For
it is certainly an attempt of a party which finds they have lost
their majority in one branch of the legislature to make a law
by the aid of the other branch, and of the executive, under
color of a treaty, which shall bind up the hands of the adverse
branch from ever restraining the commerce of the patron-
nation."[27] This was the same specter Madison had raised in
the "Helvidius" essays. The quest of particular interests for
commercial advantage in the Atlantic trading system jeopardized the structure of the American union. If the administration party could use diplomacy to subvert the federal legislative
process, how could the state-republics be safe from unconstitutional encroachments?

American Republicans were not alone in their alarm at the
apparent tendency of administration policy. The French Directory saw the ratification of Jay's "English Treaty" as a sign of a
rapprochement between Britain and its former colonies, thus
revealing the hollowness of American claims to neutrality.
French privateers, as well as what remained of the French Navy,
began to interdict American merchantmen, mostly in the West
Indies, ostensibly to search for contraband. Conciliatory initiatives by American minister James Monroe failed to end France's
attacks on American shipping. In 1797, as domestic political
frustration over the situation grew, President John Adams dis-

patched Charles Cotesworth Pinckney, John Marshall, and Elbridge Gerry to France for further negotiations. The peace mission ended in failure with the famous XYZ Affair, when French agents refused to begin talks until a bribe was paid. News of the XYZ Affair enraged public opinion in the United States and led Federalists to clamor for war. As Franco-American relations deteriorated during the ensuing "Quasi-War" of 1798–1800, an undeclared naval war largely fought in the Caribbean, the Adams administration put the nation on a war footing: building a new navy, making preparations to raise an army, and moving to stifle internal dissent. These last measures convinced Republicans that the fears they had been harboring for the past few years were all too justified.

Republicans were convinced that their opponents meant to exploit the war crisis to transform the federal Constitution. During the summer of 1798, the Federalists pushed the controversial Alien and Sedition Acts through Congress by narrow votes: the new legislation tightened naturalization requirements, made it easier for the federal government to deport resident aliens, and defined sedition so broadly as to make any criticism of the administration a crime.

The threat posed by the Alien and Sedition Acts was similar in kind to the earlier crises. In order to achieve ends within the realm of extra-state diplomacy, the Federalists were engaging in actions that fundamentally altered the rules of the American system. What made the crisis of 1798 different was that the assault on republicanism was so much larger in scope. Both the executive and legislative power had fallen into the hands of forces inimical to the republican experiment. With the Sedition Act, there was simply no protected space within which the perfect republic could be preserved. As in 1787, the metes and bounds of the American state system had to be clarified if they were going to be preserved at all.

As the machinery of government was directed against Republican newspaper editors and political operatives, Jefferson and Madison moved into action, drafting protest resolutions that were subsequently adopted by the Kentucky and Virginia legislatures respectively. Returning to what they claimed were the first principles of the federal charter, Jefferson and Madison argued that the Constitution was a *compact* among sovereign states. The states were not dissolved by joining the union, but retained the right to self-preservation as specified by the first law of nature. The "several states" were "not united on the principle of unlimited submission to their government," Jefferson wrote in his original draft of the Kentucky Resolutions, but were rather joined "by a compact under the style and title of Constitution for the U.S. and amendments thereto." The states had only delegated to the general government "certain definite powers, reserving each state to itself, the residuary mass of right to their own self-government."[28] Though Madison's language was less strident, his Virginia Resolutions made the same point: "the powers of the federal government" resulted "from the compact to which the states are parties."[29] Compact theory gave the states the sovereign power they needed to preserve their character as perfect republics.

Many historians have focused on the politically expedient, opportunistic character of Republican compact theory. But the doctrine of the Virginia and Kentucky Resolutions had a respectable enough pedigree, traceable to Antifederalist criticisms of the Constitution – and Federalist efforts to allay their opponents' anxieties. Compact theory grew logically out of a decade of increasingly polarized debate about the nature of the American union and the status of its component state-republics. Had Republicans wished merely to challenge the constitutionality of the Alien and Sedition Acts, they did not have to rethink the whole structure of the union. Republican John Dawson thus concluded (as would subsequent generations of legal scholars) that the Sedition Act was unconstitutional because it violated the First Amendment.[30] By 1798, however, Republicans were no longer satisfied with a narrowly circumscribed debate about the constitutionality of specific administration measures. They were instead convinced that fundamental questions about both the nature of the federal union and the conduct of foreign relations hung in the balance. Federalists had been willing, even eager, to allow events within the realm of European and Atlantic diplomacy to alter the constitutionally prescribed distribution of sovereign powers within the American system. If the states did not retain a necessary measure of sovereignty, there would be no room within which citizens could fashion their perfect republics, and the whole republican experiment would fail.

Extended Union

The experiences of the 1790s shaped Jefferson's policies as his party took power in the federal executive and legislature following the 1800 election. The intense party battles over the Proclamation of Neutrality, the Jay Treaty, and the Quasi-War confirmed Republican fears of the dangers of becoming entangled in European politics. Federalist efforts to promote particular American interests in the Atlantic states system had nearly undermined the sovereignty of states within the American union, as well as the balance between federal and state power that underlay the Madisonian "extended republic." If the independence of the state-republics was compromised, Jeffersonians feared, the republican experiment would fail. Jefferson's response to the Federalist ascendancy was an aggressive assertion of state sovereignty. While the Republican administrations slowly backed away from the extreme implications of the "Principles of '98," they remained sensitive to the distinctive, divergent interests of each state-republic.

The 1790s had thus revealed how dangerous the politics of the Atlantic system could be for the American states and their union. But withdrawal from the larger world was never an option. Republicans knew that the American republics could not survive and prosper without overseas trade. Jefferson and his followers sought to resolve this conundrum by ensuring that national commercial policy would secure and harmonize diverse interests across the continent. The pursuit of commerce would be made a national concern. The costs and benefits of Atlantic commerce would be borne by all Americans. Peace would be made with the Indians on the northwest and southwest borderlands; the navigation of the Mississippi, as well as the other rivers that ran through the Floridas, would be secured; and, most importantly, the rights of neutral American navigators on the Atlantic "frontier" would be ensured by enforcing a progressive interpretation of neutral rights. Success on all these fronts would vindicate the Jeffersonian conception of an extended, de-centered union of free state-republics.

The idea of a union without a dominant metropolis had always been a bedrock principle of Jefferson's republicanism. By contrast, the Jeffersonian rationale for territorial expansion emerged as a *defensive* response to changing circumstances in a period of international instability. During the Louisiana crisis of 1802–3, Republicans faced the same situation confronted by their Federalist predecessors: diplomatic conflict in Europe threatened to engulf and destroy the American union. Shortly after the Convention of Môrtefontaine (1800) ended the Quasi-War with France, Napoleon's government signed the secret Treaty of San Ildefonso with Spain. This treaty provided for the retrocession of Louisiana, which had been French territory before 1763. When the terms of the treaty became public in 1802, Americans worried how a French presence on the Mississippi would affect the geopolitical dynamic of North America. These fears were exacerbated when the Spanish colonial government at New Orleans suspended the Americans' right of deposit, thus effectively closing the Mississippi to American commerce. President Jefferson and secretary of state Madison dispatched instructions to the American minister to France, Robert R. Livingston, to explore the possibility of purchasing New Orleans. Napoleon proved surprisingly receptive: the imminent collapse of the short-lived Peace of Amiens (1802) and the destruction of General LeClerc's army on Saint Domingue forced him to abandon his dream of an American empire. Napoleon offered Livingston not only New Orleans but all of Louisiana. As special envoy James Monroe arrived in France to assist the negotiations, Livingston accepted Napoleon's offer.

The Louisiana Purchase may have been a diplomatic triumph, but it raised troubling questions for Republicans in the administration and in Congress. The strict constructionist Jefferson wondered if implementation of the Purchase required a constitutional amendment. Simply incorporating Louisiana would make the union's "written Constitution" a "blank paper by construction," he wrote Virginia Congressman Wilson Cary Nicholas. He had not forgotten Hamilton's cavalier disregard for constitutional limitations. If the treaty-making power was "boundless," then "we have no Constitution." Since the Louisiana Treaty altered the bounds of the United States so fundamentally, it would be best to "set an example against broad construction, by appealing for new power to the people." Yet Jefferson, fearing that Napoleon might change his mind if the Senate failed to act quickly – "if we give the least opening, they will declare the treaty void" – was persuaded to keep his constitutional misgivings to himself.[31]

The Louisiana question was debated during the autumn of 1803 in both the House and the Senate. Congressional Republicans argued against a constitutional amendment, insisting that the treaty power was sufficient to incorporate Louisiana into the union. Federalist Samuel Purviance of North Carolina stated the case bluntly: "it would be better to have the ceded territory on any terms than not to have it at all."[32] But other Federalists, relishing the opportunity to invoke strict constructionist arguments against Jefferson, wondered how "this new, immense, unbounded world" possibly could be "incorporated in this Union" without "altering the Constitution."[33] The treaty-making power did not include the right to grant citizenship to French subjects, according to New York congressman Gaylord Griswold, or to extend privileges to the port of New Orleans not enjoyed by other American ports, or to add such extensive territory to the union that "the rights of the present citizens of the United States would be swallowed up and lost."[34] But Republicans in 1803 were impervious to the kinds of arguments they had used as oppositionists in the 1790s. On October 20, the treaty was ratified by a comfortable margin (24–7) in the Republican-dominated Senate.

The Louisiana debate forced Republicans to articulate and

refine their vision of an expanding union of free republics. A vision of an extended union coalesced gradually in the writings and speeches of the Jeffersonians. In justifying the acquisition of Louisiana, Vermont congressman James Elliott turned to the principles of the law of nations, thus affirming the construction of the union as a compact of sovereignties, and opening the door to a union that could expand limitlessly. As Elliott saw it, the "American people, in forming their Constitution, had an eye to that law of nations," and "with a view to this law the treaty-making power was constructed," thus making it possible to acquire new territory. The "Constitution is a compact between the American people," Elliott asserted, forming "a federal system, novel in its nature," in which the "States as such were equal." There was no reason whatsoever that the American union could not expand. "If we cannot find, in the peculiar principles of our form of Government, and in the virtue and intelligence of our citizens, a sufficient security against the dangers from a widely extended territory, in vain we shall seek it elsewhere."[35] As Virginia's John Randolph explained, if "so widely extended a country cannot subsist under a Republican Government," then the United States "have already exceeded the limits which visionary speculatists have supposed capable of free Government." Both Randolph and Elliott suggested that the American constitutional compact was potentially boundless: "there is no magical quality in a degree of latitude or longitude, a river or a mountain."[36]

Jefferson also believed an expanding union would ensure the future of the American republics. As he explained to John Breckinridge, the environs of New Orleans would be "immediately a territorial government, and soon a State." The territory west of the Mississippi would be given to the Indians "in exchange for their present country," and the sale of these vacated lands would "make this acquisition [of Louisiana] the means of filling up the eastern side, instead of drawing off its population." Extension could continue, for "when we shall be full on this side, we may lay off a range of States on the western bank from the head to the mouth, and so, range after range, advancing compactly as we multiply." Opponents of the Louisiana Treaty predicted that it inevitably would lead to a division of the union into eastern and western confederacies. The prospect did not trouble Jefferson. "If it should become the great interest" of new western states "to separate . . . why should the Atlantic States dread it?" Whether they belonged to one union or many, all Americans would be citizens of perfect republics, bound together by common principles. "The future inhabitants of the Atlantic and Mississippi States" would also share a common national identity: wherever they chose to live, they all "will be our sons."[37]

In extending the American states system, Jeffersonian Republicans hoped to remove European powers from the neighborhood of the American republics and so minimize dangerous entanglements in the Old World's never-ending conflicts. When Jefferson and his contemporaries – Federalists and Republicans alike – imagined the future of the American union, the European presence in North America continent was the most unpredictable factor. Samuel Purviance warned that once the French were ensconced in Louisiana, they "would soon stride across the Mississippi, and every encroachment which conquest or cunning could effect might be expected." In lieu of an open invasion, the French would engage local proxies to do their dirty work: "the tomahawk of the savage and the knife of the negro would confederate in the[ir] league."[38] The extension of the American states system at the expense of the European powers opened a space within which Americans could create new state-republics while securing the republican character of the original states.

Security on the western borderlands was only one part of the Jeffersonian strategy to sustain a republican union. Because every state had overseas commercial interests of one kind or another, the rights of American merchantmen to ply the Atlantic and Caribbean became a leading concern of Republican policy. States with interests in commerce and manufacturing needed protection and support as much as staple-producing states. When they were the opposition party, Republicans railed against commercial accords such as the Jay Treaty that systematically favored one region at the expense of others. Jefferson and his allies now sought to implement more even-handed commercial policies that would benefit all sectors of the economy – and regions of the country – equally.

The key principle of Jeffersonian commercial diplomacy was the protection of neutral rights. Republican administrations insisted that under the "modern" law of nations, neutral nations had the right to trade with each other and with belligerents, subject only to explicit, well-defined limitations that flowed from the actual conduct of war itself. Other violations of American neutral rights were construed as attacks on the new nation's sovereignty and independence. The prosperity and security of the American union depended on continuing access to overseas markets. Just as Jeffersonian expansionism in Louisiana and the Floridas reflected the need to promote economic development in the south and west, the crusade for neutral rights at sea stemmed from the recognition that the economic vitality of every part of the country – and particularly of the northeast, where the carrying trade was most important – depended on protecting American ships on the Atlantic.

Though the vision of a worldwide regime of free trade remained within the realm of fantasy, the Peace of Amiens (1802) briefly removed American merchantmen from harm's way. The Convention of Môrtefontaine kept French ports open to American shipping, while American commerce with the British Empire flourished under a loose construction of the Jay Treaty. For the time being, the British government accepted the principle of the "broken voyage," as set forth by the Admiralty Court in the *Polly* case (1800): American traders could import products of the British West Indies into American ports for subsequent exportation to Britain. American merchants thus found themselves trading with France, Britain, most of continental Europe, and the Mediterranean. The steady growth of overseas trade during Jefferson's first administration was, like the acquisition of Louisiana, more the result of the actions of other powers than of American diplomatic initiatives. American diplomats found that they could do little when the vital interests of the great powers were at stake, most conspicuously when they failed to curb the Royal Navy's practice of impressing seamen. The administration understood the limits of American power. The goal of its diplomacy was to exploit the balance of power when it could, to gain the support of as many European powers as possible for its expansive interpretation of neutral rights.

American attempts to secure neutral rights became more urgent as the Peace of Amiens collapsed between 1803 and 1805 and war between Britain and France resumed. Once again in a fight for their lives against Napoleon, British policy-makers would no longer tolerate any neutral trade with France or its colonies. With the *Essex* decision (1805), the British Admiralty Court rejected the broken voyage doctrine and also reinstated the moribund "Rule of '56," thus banning neutral trade with the French Empire that in peacetime had been technically illegal, according to French mercantilist regulations. Under this draconian interpretation of the law of nations, vast numbers of American merchantmen were captured as prizes by the Royal Navy. As American trade was strangled, the Jefferson administration recognized the threat to the new nation's independence in the Atlantic system, and by extension to the balance of interests that was so vital to the security and prosperity of the union. Republican diplomacy sought to address both threats. The vindication of neutral rights would secure American sovereignty while balancing the divergent interests of an extended and expanding union.

In the wake of the *Essex* decision, Jefferson authorized James Monroe and William Pinkney to negotiate a new commercial treaty with Britain. Monroe and Pinkney's negotiations with their British counterparts, Lords Auckland and Holland, produced an agreement which would have extended the provisions of the recently-expired Jay Treaty for another decade, thus pledging the American government to forgo the implementation of any non-importation laws, but which failed to address the vexing issue of impressment. Jefferson found the treaty unacceptable and refused to present it to the Senate. Secretary of state Madison offered an elaborate official explanation to Monroe and Pinkney, underscoring the administration's objections to nearly every article of the proposed pact. The treaty compromised American sovereignty by preempting future commercial sanctions against Britain: prospective costs to the nation as a whole were much greater than immediate benefits to commercial interests.

The rejection of the Monroe-Pinkney Treaty reflected the Republicans' determination to preserve American sovereignty and independence in the Atlantic states system while securing the vital interests of all parts of the union. The deepening European conflict made these goals unattainable, particularly after Russia's capitulation to Napoleon at the Peace of Tilsit (June 1807). Now suzerain of Europe, Napoleon devised a "continental system" of trade that would strangle the British into submission: according to his Berlin and Milan Decrees (November 1806 and December 1807), any ship touching at a British port was subject to seizure. Standing alone in opposition to Napoleon's imperial ambitions, Britain retaliated with a series of Orders in Council interdicting trade with French-controlled Europe. American shipping was thus subject to assault from both belligerents: henceforth neutrals would have no "rights." The Chesapeake Affair of June 1807 heralded the new era of total war. Just beyond the three-mile territorial limit at Norfolk Roads, the British frigate *Leopard* fired on the *USS Chesapeake*, killing three American sailors in the course of impressing four others for service in the Royal Navy. Pro-war sentiment spread rapidly to all parts of the union, as patriotic Americans recollected their revolutionary fervor. But the United States was poorly prepared to make war on anyone, much less on both of the world's superpowers.

Jefferson concluded that "during the present paroxysm of the insanity of Europe," there was little hope of protecting American overseas trade, and therefore it was thought "wisest to break off all intercourse with her."[39] Every American ship that approached Europe risked capture. A desperate Jefferson thus urged Congress to enact an embargo on American foreign commerce, which he signed into law on 22 December 1807. The Embargo represented a measured, prudent, and temporary response to an international crisis, not

a long-term policy of disengagement from the Atlantic system. In keeping the American merchant marine in port in early
1808, Jefferson spared the navigating states hundreds of thousands of dollars in losses of cargo and bottoms. From the administration's perspective, the Embargo could be seen as an
attempt to preserve the American commercial apparatus, and
thus to protect the interests of the northeastern states. But this
was not how it looked to those who were most immediately
and seriously affected.

Enforcement of the various embargo acts generated discontent and resistance, particularly in the commercial northeast.
As Congress contemplated prolonging the Embargo into a second year, the backlash revealed fundamental sectional differences over commercial policy that threatened to destroy the
union. The administration was hard pressed to enforce its will
on a recalcitrant population. The minuscule American navy
could not possibly interdict every merchantman approaching
the American coast, and the initial embargo permitted the
coasting trade – commerce between American ports – which
provided a substantial opening for smuggling. Communities
located near national frontiers also found the temptation to
smuggle, by land or by sea, irresistible. Popular resistance to
the Embargo was abetted by official remonstrances. New England Congressmen introduced numerous local resolutions tes-
tifying to the hardships caused by the Embargo. Northeastern
mercantile interests were not convinced by the administration's
claims that the Embargo was a temporary measure, designed
to protect them. It was either a pathetically ineffective effort
to coerce the great powers or, for those of a more paranoid
disposition, "a permanent measure" designed to "put down
commerce and set up manufactures."[40] Rather than see the
Embargo as the attempt to protect regional and national interests that Jefferson had intended, northeasterners saw a thinly
veiled attempt to destroy their interests. The chief effect of the
Embargo was to give the Federalists a new lease on life as a
national opposition party, checking and reversing Republican
gains in the opposition party's traditional northeastern strongholds.

When Madison took office in 1809, Congress repealed part of the Embargo, leaving the Non-intercourse Act, which prohibited trade with Britain and France only, in its place. At first, the new policy seemed promising, as the British minister to the United States, David Erskine, offered to repeal the hated Orders in Council. But Erskine's offer was repudiated by prime minister George Canning. For lack of any better alternative, the Madison administration continued to resort to commercial sanctions. Macon's Bill No. 2, passed by Congress in 1810, promised to lift non-intercourse for the first state, Britain or France, to repeal its restrictions. An unofficial and ambiguous overture from Napoleon intimated that he might rescind the Berlin and Milan Decrees. Whether he had done so remained unclear in 1811, but French seizures of American vessels did decrease. Madison attempted to use these tentative concessions to cajole the British into repealing their Orders in Council. By the time the new Castlereagh ministry finally decided on repeal, on 16 June 1812, it was too late. Unaware that relief was in sight, Congress declared war on 18 June.

Jefferson and Madison had vainly sought to avert war through commercial diplomacy. Interlocking commitments to free and unfettered commerce, neutral rights, and the new nation's equal standing in the community of nations left them little room to maneuver. In a revolutionary world where the law of nations had collapsed, American independence could be vindicated only through war, as it had been in the American revolution. The policies which led the Madison administration into the War of 1812 were a product of the Jeffersonian construction of an extended union that was inextricably implicated in the Atlantic system. Madison sought to protect American shipping from capture while responding to the pleas of mercantile interests desperate to engage in overseas commerce. Madison and his Republican allies in Congress hoped the policy of non-intercourse would be a happy medium: the United States would resume trade with any or either of the belligerents which rescinded its own objectionable commercial regulations. But non-intercourse, by encouraging the warring powers to bid for American favor, simply guaranteed that the United States would be sucked into the vortex of the European conflict. Madison's quixotic campaign for the recognition of neutral rights and national sovereignty, based on his understanding of the modern law of nations, was bound to fail in an age when belligerent powers had long since abandoned any pretense of recognizing legal restraints. The implications of this failure were profound, for it subverted the distinction between American and Atlantic spheres that had been a bulwark of Jeffersonian policy. Because Republicans tied neutral rights with national independence, the United States were forced to go to war against Great Britain in 1812. Indeed, under the anarchic conditions of world war, making war constituted the only remaining way to assert and secure sovereignty.

But the United States did not go to war united, as dissident votes on the declaration of war made clear. Madison hoped to secure the vital interests of all parts of the union: the failure to vindicate the new nation's rights would undermine its future position as an independent power and destroy its commerce. A large number of Americans were not persuaded by Madison's logic. Western and southern "War Hawks" rallied behind the administration, but the important mid-Atlantic states of New York and Pennsylvania remained divided throughout the war, and New England remained intransigent: the Federalist governors of Massachusetts, Rhode Island, and Connecticut refused to send their militias beyond their borders; Boston's leading banking and mercantile houses refused to lend funds to the cash-strapped federal government (which, thanks to republican strict constitutionalists, struggled to finance the war without the benefit of a national bank). As during the Embargo, northeastern commercial interests rejected Republican neo-mercantilism; they were skeptical about the possibility of all regions sharing equally in the costs and benefits of union. Instead, they saw a coercive central government pursuing policies that were destructive to their most vital interests, thus setting – or, more accurately, reinforcing – a pattern of intersectional suspicion and conflict that would dominate the early history of American federalism. War and the political economy of the federal republic were a difficult fit. In preparing for full-scale mobilization, the federal government was obliged to take any appropriate measures, including the requisition of troops and supplies and the borrowing of large sums of money at any available terms. The premise of national unity was hard to sustain in a political system that encouraged Americans to pursue and defend their distinctive interests. Under the circumstances, the willingness of so many Americans to make sacrifices for the common cause, despite the administration's failures to articulate a clear and compelling set of war aims or to manage the war effort effectively, testified to widespread patriotic sentiment.

Americans had various, sometimes conflicting notions of why they were fighting this second war of independence. Visionary republicans hoped that the war would lead to the expansion of the union, both by eliminating effective Indian resistance to new settlement and by driving the British out of Canada. The annexation of Canada, a long-standing goal of American expansionists, could be seen as a logical sequel to the Louisiana Purchase: purchase and conquest (as an incident of war) were equally valid ways to acquire territory under the law of nations. Expansion to the north would provide still more space for establishing new state-republics and extending the commerce and guaranteeing the security of the existing republics. Yet this was not the administration's main objective in invading Canada. Instead, Madison sought to force concessions from the British respecting the maritime rights issues which had led to war in the first place. Madison's immediate goals thus worked at cross-purposes with the Jeffersonian vision of an extended union, insulated from the European balance of power. Conquering Canadian territory in order to make the Atlantic safe for American commerce drew the United States into the European war, once again making North America an arena for rivalries among the great powers – as it had been throughout colonial history. Invading Canada collapsed the boundary between the spheres of Atlantic and American state relations. The union came perilously close to flying apart, as dissident New Englanders seemed inexorably drawn back into the orbit of British influence. The conclusion of the Treaty of Ghent in late 1814 and the end of the war came none too soon for an exhausted United States.

Jeffersonian Republicans modified their vision of the structure of the American union, as well as their ideals about how it should engage with the larger world, in the years between the "Revolution of 1800" and the Treaty of Ghent. The partisan conflicts surrounding the Quasi-War showed Republicans how contingencies within the Atlantic states system, as well as the apparatus of the federal government, could be used to undermine the republican experiment. Jefferson and his allies did not forget these lessons as they fashioned a strategy of commercial diplomacy that was supposed to balance the interests of different parts of the union. As unforeseen circumstances led to the acquisition of new territory, Republicans began to envision the possibility of a dynamically expanding union that depended on consent and not coercion. They imagined that Americans could both participate in the progress of world civilization, enjoying the prosperity that the Atlantic trade had long afforded them, and at the same time be insulated from the diplomatic entanglements that chronically jeopardized their republican experiment. In the American system, equal, perfect republics would be sovereign in their respective spheres but would merge into a single sovereignty when dealing with the larger world. The administration's incompetent conduct of the War of 1812 demonstrated the radical limitations and contradictions of that vision. But, somehow, the United States survived. And the mere fact of its survival was all the proof many patriotic Americans needed of the success of their republican experiment and its manifest destiny to change the world.

"An Example of a Free System"

With the conclusion of the War of 1812, the shape of world in which the American republican experiment had been born had irrevocably changed. Understandably, contemporaries were slow to recognize this changed state of affairs. The Atlantic states system was, apparently, restored to its status quo prior to 1793, before the French Revolution unleashed its furies. With a brief interlude during the "Hundred Days" (when Napoleon returned from his first exile in Elba in March 1815 to terrorize his enemies yet once more, before his final defeat at Waterloo), the Congress of Vienna spent the year following the French emperor's abdication in April 1814 resetting the balance between the Great Powers that had characterized the century and a half following the Peace of Westphalia (1648). The Bourbons were reinstalled in France, and the Holy Roman Empire was reborn as the Germanic Confederation. In North America, little seemed outwardly different. American statesmen looked eastward across the Atlantic and saw a system of contending powers whose next war would yet again, inevitably, involve their fragile union of republics. Britain still held Canada and its West Indian colonies, and the Spanish remained in Florida, as well as the lands west of the Sabine River. Yet the United States had survived a second war for their independence. From the Republicans' perspective, the best news was that the Federalist opposition, disgraced by the Hartford Convention (1814) and its flirtation with disunion, was rapidly fading from the national scene. When another Virginia Republican, James Monroe, succeeded Madison as President in early 1817, the status of the union seemed as secure as it had ever been since 1776.

Republicans drew different lessons from the War of 1812. A rising generation of National Republicans, led by Henry Clay, John C. Calhoun, and John Quincy Adams, continued to embrace the Jeffersonian conception of an expanding union of self-governing republics. But, now that the Federalist threat had been suppressed, they saw no reason why a more energetic federal government should not take the lead in strengthening the union so that it would be better prepared for the next war. In 1817, Calhoun and Clay authored and secured passage of the Bonus Bill, a measure which provided for federal funding of internal improvements, such as roads and canals, that would facilitate military preparedness and economic development. Although they professed fealty to the "Principles of '98," these young nationalists envisioned a federal compact that, to suspicious Old Republicans at least, looked more Hamiltonian than Jeffersonian.

The attempt by the rising generation to adjust the American states system to the new world order met with an unexpected rebuke when Madison vetoed the Bonus Bill the day before he left office in March 1817. Madison argued that the Bonus Bill was unconstitutional: national sponsorship of improvements fell outside Congress's enumerated powers, and that the bill's construction of the "common defense and general welfare" clause was far too expansive. Under such a broad construction of the "general welfare" clause, future Congresses would likely embrace "every object and act within the purview of a legislative trust"; ultimately, the constitutions and laws of the states "in all cases not specifically exempted" would "be superseded by laws of Congress." Echoing Antifederalist concerns about the dangers of "consolidation" during the ratification debates, Madison warned that the federal balance was at risk. It was his bedrock principle that "the permanent success of the Constitution depends on a definite partition of powers between the General and State Governments." If the American people – or, more accurately, the peoples of the American states – thought it was necessary to delegate new powers to the federal government (and both Jefferson and Madison agreed that it was), the federal Constitution should be amended accordingly.[41]

Madison's veto testified to his belief that the American union retained the character of a Vattelian "federal republic," founded in a compact of semi-sovereign, state-republics, and that its survival and prosperity depended upon the equality and internal inviolability of its constituent members. He shared the concerns of National Republicans with the manifest weaknesses of the union, but balked at their solutions. A few months after his veto message, Madison explained his thinking to John Adams. Reflecting on a passage in Condorcet which advocated "the idea of Government 'in one centre,'" Madison could not help but note that the concept "seems now every where to be exploded." The constitutions of the separate states and of the United States as a whole "had placed the powers of Government in different depositories," showing that the division of sovereign powers was the best "means of controlling the impulse and sympathy of the passions, and affording to reason better opportunities of asserting its prerogatives." Madison had never abandoned the principles of constitutional construction he first advocated in the late 1780s and elaborated as a Republican oppositionist in the 1790s. A union of perfect republics could be achieved through the proper construction of the *system* within which such republics existed. This was the ultimate lesson of the law of nations: because no state existed in perfect isolation, the challenge for civilized men was to organize a system of states. It was "the great question now to be decided, and it is one in which humanity is more deeply interested than in any political experiment yet made." Under the federal Constitution, the never-ending conflicts of the European balance of power (which the law of nations had demonstrably failed to control or refine) were exchanged for a system where "checks and balances sufficient for the purposes of order, justice, and the general good" were "created by a proper division and distribution of power among different bodies, differently constituted , but all deriving their existence from the elective principle, and bound by a responsible tenure of trusts." Madison continued to believe that such a system could work in America. "The experiment is favored by the extent of our Country, which prevents the contagion of evil passions; and by the combination of the federal with the local systems of Government, which multiplies the divisions of power, and the mutual checks by which it is to be kept within its proper limits and direction."[42]

Jefferson was less optimistic than his fellow Republican in the efficacy of constitutional machinery. If Madison sought to sustain a middle course between National Republicans and their Old Republican critics, Jefferson was drawn increasingly into the Old Republican, states' rights camp. The powers of the federal government had to be carefully confined by a strict construction of the federal Constitution so that the state-republics would attain the progressive improvement that true self-government made possible. Jefferson's solicitude for Missouri's autonomy as a self-constituted republic explains his hostility to efforts by congressional "restrictionists" to halt the spread of slavery into the new state. When the legislature of the Missouri Territory petitioned for statehood in late 1819, a substantial number of northern Congressmen objected to the proposed state constitution, which permitted slavery. After months of negotiations, a majority of the Congress agreed to admit Missouri as a slave state and the Maine District of Massachusetts as a free state, and to prohibit future slave states from being created out of territory north of 36 degrees 30 minutes of latitude. For Jefferson and many other southerners, the so-called "Missouri Compromise" was ominous, not simply because of its limitations on, and implied rejection of, African-American slavery, but for the limits it placed on the state-republics to write their own constitutions and govern themselves. They were convinced that restrictionists meant to destroy the union.

Claims of state sovereignty resonated with Republican memories of 1798, and evoked the Vattlelian "federal republic" of "perfect states." These conceptions permeated the debates over the Missouri question, as Congressmen cited the law of nations and invoked the "compact" again and again. Virginia Senator James Barbour painted the picture in the starkest and plainest terms. The question was whether the "people of Missouri" would be permitted "the right of self-government"': the efforts of the restrictionists were simply an "attempt to control the people of Missouri in the exercise of the great privilege of making their own government."[43] Georgian John Elliott reminded his fellow senators that the Constitution guaranteed "every State in this Union a republican form of government," and that to restrict any part of the act of state self-creation impinged on that right. The specter of corrupted union and ultimate disunion was in the air. "The strength of this Union must depend upon the sameness of the political institutions, and the equality of the rights which are secured to the States that compose it." To disturb this "sameness" was tempting fate; "impose this restriction, sir, and it will lead to others." The nearly inevitable consequence of such a course was disunion, as "any Union which can subsist under such circumstances will be scarcely worth maintaining."[44]

Of course, northerners who advocated restriction saw matters differently. Connecticut's Samuel Dana agreed that the decision to "admit a new associate in the empire" was a momentous one.[45] Restrictionists conceived of a national compact that included not only the Constitution, but the Northwest Ordinance of 1787 and the Declaration of Independence. Pennsylvanian Jonathan Roberts thus extolled that "immortal ordinance and its elder sister," through which "all the States declared, before the Supreme Judge of the world, that slavery was a violation of His truth, and admitted the binding obligation to remedy the wrong, when possible."[46] The antislavery clause of the Northwest Ordinance, reaffirmed by the First Congress, as well as the rhetoric of rights and equality that permeated the Declaration, bound Americans to do all they could to limit slavery and provide for its eventual extinction.

Restrictionists disclaimed any intention of attacking slavery where it was already established. Congress had not attempted, and would not attempt, to alter the status of slavery in the former Southwest Territory, David Morrill of New Hampshire asserted, because "this territory was detached from States where slavery was tolerated at the time of the Constitution," and these states, "as sovereigns of the soil," had the right to preserve the institution in those territories. "We mean to keep that compact," Morrill asserted. But Missouri was "a part of the Louisiana purchase," it had been "bought with the common fund," and therefore "the common interest must be consulted." Simply put, Congress had "a sovereign power over its territories," and it was well within the power of Congress to set conditions on the admission of states from territory over which it held sovereignty.[47] The needs of the whole union had to be consulted. Samuel Dana invoked this principle as he argued against the expansive boundaries of the new state, noting that "reference ought to be had to the whole extent of the country, and to the relations of its different sections."[48] This principle of balancing the interests of various sections to serve the common good had been the hallmark of Jefferson's and Madison's policies. But was it possible to define the common good in a union of such unequal states, some slave and some free?

While Jefferson must have been vexed to read his Declaration and *Notes on Virginia* quoted by the restrictionists in the Congressional debates, what was likely more troubling was how unworkable the union was proving to be. Could a conception of a union consisting of perfect and perfectly equal state-republics be reconciled with a republican federal head that calculated and balanced the union's diverse interests as it engaged the wider world?

Since 1798, the cornerstone of Jeffersonian Republicanism was a conception of the federal union as a compact among sovereign states. Not merely a political expedient, compact theory had solid roots in eighteenth-century ideas about politics and diplomacy. Yet the identification of compact theory as such became explicit only over time. In the 1790s and the early decades of the nineteenth century, Jefferson and his allies were forced to confront and develop the implications of ideas they had first broached in the political discussions of the 1770s and 1780s. But it was impossible to abandon the concept of the "extended republic" Madison had put forth in 1787. Madison himself never did. Although he was well aware that the line between federal republic and federal dominion was a fine one, he firmly believed, as he told Lafayette in 1820, that "a Government like ours has so many safety-valves giving vent to overheated passions, that it carries within itself a relief against the infirmities from which the best of human Institutions cannot be exempt." Even with the ongoing crisis in Missouri, Madison looked toward the future with hope. "Free States seem indeed to be propagated in Europe, as rapidly as new States are on this side of the Atlantic." Madison believed that the United States could provide a model for these young republics, with the American union "giving an example of a free system."[49]

But Jefferson was not so sure. The Missouri crisis reminded him how vulnerable the state-republics were to federal interference. Jefferson and other Republican ideologues thus became increasingly skeptical about the very possibility of a federal republic, a republic of republics capable of defining and pursuing their common interests. Compiling the *Anas* in 1818, Jefferson read compact theory back into the history of the founding, describing the Articles of Confederation as "treaty of alliance" between "separate independencies," and the Constitution of 1787 as merely a "further bond of union." Jefferson reaffirmed this, because, like Madison, he saw the federal union as an organization of a system of states. But the point of this system was not to be a "Beacon" or an "example" for the wider world, but to maintain the existence of "a political system of our own, independant of that of Europe," and in doing so to secure a union of republics that would preserve the liberties of free men.[50]

NOTES

1 TJ to Joseph C. Cabell, 6 Dec. 1813, Andrew A. Lipscomb and Albert Ellery Bergh, eds., *The Writings of Thomas Jefferson*, 20 vols. (Washington, DC, 1903–4), 14:22.

2 Hugo Grotius, *The Rights of War and Peace* (Amsterdam, 1646), trans. A. C. Campbell (1901; Westport, Conn., 1993), book I, ch. 3, sect. vi, at 61.

3 Emmerich de Vattel, *The Law of Nations; or the Principles of the Law of Nature, Applied to the Conduct and Affairs of Nations and Sovereigns* (Geneva, 1758), trans. Joseph Chitty (Philadelphia, 1844), book I, ch. 1, sects. 3–4, at 2.

4 Ibid., book I, ch. 1, sects. 10–11, at 3–3a.

5 Jefferson, "Anas," in Lipscomb and Bergh, eds., *Writings of Jefferson*, 1:267.

6 Alexander Hamilton, "Continentalist, No. II," Harold C. Syett and Jacob Cooke, eds., *The Papers of Alexander Hamilton*, 27 vols. (New York, 1961–87), 2:654–7.

7 "Continentalist, No. III," ibid., 2:660–5.

8 Madison to TJ, 24 Oct. 1787, J. C. A. Stagg et al., eds., *The Papers of James Madison: Congressional Series*, 17 vols. (Chicago and Charlottesville, 1959–91), 10:207.

9   Jacob E. Cooke, ed., *The Federalist* (Middletown, Conn., 1961), no. 32 (Hamilton), 199–200.

10 TJ to George Washington, 15 Mar. 1784; TJ to John Jay, 23 Aug. 1785, Julian Boyd et al., eds., *The Papers of Thomas Jefferson*, 27 vols. to date (Princeton, NJ, 1950–), 7:26, 8:427.

11 TJ to Archibald Stuart, 25 Jan. 1786, ibid., 9:217–18.

12 Cooke, ed., *The Federalist*, no. 15 (Hamilton), 92.

13 TJ to John Page, 4 May 1786, Boyd et al., eds., *Papers of Jefferson*, 9:446.

14 Madison to Edmund Randolph, 25 Feb. 1787, Stagg et al., eds., *Papers of Madison*, 9:299–300.

15 Madison to TJ, 24 Oct. 1787, ibid., 10:205–20.

16 Caleb Wallace to Madison, 12 Nov. 1787, ibid., 10:249–51.

17 Cooke, ed., *The Federalist*, no. 6 (Hamilton), 55.

18 Ibid., no 32 (Hamilton), 199, 203.

19 Madison to TJ, 24 Oct. 1787, Stagg et al., eds., *Papers of Madison*, 10:214.

20 Knox to Washington, 7 July 1789, W. W. Abbot et al., eds., *Papers of Washington: Presidential Series*, 8 vols. to date (Charlottesville, 1987–), 3:134–41.

21 Ibid.

22 TJ, "Opinion on McGillivray's Monopoly,: 29 July 1790, Boyd et al., eds., *Papers of Jefferson*, 17:288–9.

23 "Anti-Republican," *New York Daily Gazette*, 17 Aug. 1790, 2–3.

24 TJ to Madison, 24 Mar. 1793, Boyd et al., eds., *Papers of Jefferson*, 25:442.

25 "Pacificus" (Hamilton), no. 1, 29 June 1793, Syrett and Cooke, eds., *Papers of Hamilton*, 15:37.

26 "Helvidius" (Madison), no. 1, 24 Aug. 1793, Stagg et al., eds., *Papers of Madison*, 15:69.

27 TJ to Madison, 21 Sept. 1795, ibid., 16:88–9.

28 Draft enclosed in TJ to Madison, 17 Nov. 1798, ibid., 17:175–81.

29 Madison, "Virginia Resolutions," 21 Dec. 1798, ibid., 17:185–91.

30 Circular Letter from John Dawson to Madison, 19 July 1798, ibid., 17:165–6.

31 TJ to Wilson Cary Nicholas, 7 Sept. 1803, Lipscomb and Bergh, eds., *Writings of Jefferson*, 10:419, 420, 418.

32 Samuel Purviance speech, 25 Oct. 1803, *Annals of the Congress of the United States, 1789–1824*, 42 vols. (Washington, DC, 1834–56), 8th Congress, 1st session, 443.

33 Samuel White speech, 2 Nov. 1803, ibid., 33.

34 Gaylord Griswold speech, 25 Oct. 1803, ibid., 432–4.

35 James Elliott speech, 25 Oct. 1803, ibid., 448, 450.

36 James Elliott speech, 25 Oct. 1803, ibid., 450.

37 TJ to John Breckinridge, 12 Aug. 1803, Lipscomb and Bergh, eds.,

Jefferson Writings, 10:410, 409.

38 Samuel Purviance speech, 25 Oct. 1803, *Annals of Congress*, 8th Congress, 1st session, 443–4.

39 TJ to John Armstrong, 2 May 1808, Lipscomb and Bergh, eds., *Jefferson Writings*, 12:43.

40 Sen. James Hillhouse (Conn.) speech, 21 Nov. 1808, *Annals of Congress*, 10th Congress, 2nd session, 26–7.

41 Madison, "Veto Message," 3 Mar. 1817, Gaillard Hunt, ed., *The Writings of James Madison*, 9 vols. (New York, 1900–10), 8:386–8.

42 Madison to John Adams, 22 May 1817, ibid., 8:390–2.

43 James Barbour speech, 14 Jan. 1820, *Annals of Congress*, 16th Congress, 1st session, 103–4.

44 James Elliott speech, 17 Jan. 1820, ibid., 129–35.

45 Samuel Dana speech, 14 Jan. 1820, ibid., 117.

46 Jonathan Roberts speech, 17 Jan. 1820, ibid., 121–2.

47 David Morrill speech, 17 Jan. 1820, ibid., 146.

48 Samuel Dana speech, 14 Jan. 1820, ibid., 118.

49 Madison to Lafayette, 25 Nov. 1820, Hunt, ed., *Madison Writings*, 9:35–8.

50 Jefferson, "Anas," in Lipscomb and Bergh, eds., *Writings of Jefferson*, 1:267.

Further Reading

The literature on Jefferson (hereafter TJ) and his times is vast and rich. For a superb history of his changing reputation see Merrill D. Peterson, *The Jefferson Image in the American Mind* (New York, 1960). Peter S. Onuf reviews historical writing since the publication of Peterson's landmark study, focusing particularly on the controversial question of race, in "The Scholars' Jefferson," *William and Mary Quarterly*, 3rd ser., 50 (1993), 671–99. More recent work is discussed in Jan Ellen Lewis and Peter S. Onuf, "American Synecdoche: Thomas Jefferson as Image, Icon, Character, and Self," *American Historical Review*, 103 (1998), 125–36. For a sampling of recent scholarly perspectives on TJ see the essays collected in Onuf, ed., *Jeffersonian Legacies* (Charlottesville, 1993) and in Lewis and Onuf, eds., *Sally Hemings and Thomas Jefferson: History, Memory, and Civic Culture* (Charlottesville, 1999).

The definitive TJ biography is Dumas Malone's *Jefferson and His Time*, 6 vols. (Boston, 1948–81). Good single-volume studies include Noble Cunningham, Jr., *In Pursuit of Reason: The Life of Thomas Jefferson* (Baton Rouge, La., 1987); Andrew Burstein, *The Inner Jefferson: Portrait of a Grieving Optimist* (Charlottesville, 1995); and Joseph J. Ellis, *American Sphinx: The Character of Thomas Jefferson* (New York, 1997).

The character of TJ's "republicanism" has been the subject of heated debate. Opposing views are staked out most clearly in Lance Banning, *The Jeffersonian Persuasion: Evolution of a Party Ideology* (Ithaca, NY, 1978), who situates TJ in a "classical" republican tradition, and in the work of Joyce Appleby, who depicts TJ as a forward-looking "liberal" in *Capitalism and a New Social Order: The Republican Vision of the 1790s* (New York, 1984) and in essays in her *Liberalism and Republicanism in the Historical Imagination* (Cambridge, Mass., 1992). Political theorist Michael Zuckert emphasizes TJ's indebtedness to the natural rights tradition in *Natural Rights and the New Republicanism* (Princeton, 1994); see also Jean M. Yarbrough, *American Virtues: Thomas Jefferson on the Character of a Free People* (Lawrence, Kans., 1998). In *Jefferson's Empire: The Language of American Nationhood* (Charlottesville, 2000) Peter Onuf argues that TJ's idealized conception of the pre-revolutionary British Empire shaped his republican vision.

Scholars have focused extraordinary attention on the Declaration of Independence. The classic study is Carl L. Becker's *The Declaration of Independence: A Study in the History of Political Ideas* (New York, 1922). Other important works include Garry Wills's controversial *Inventing America: Jefferson's Declaration of Independence* (New York, 1978), which discounts John Locke's influence on TJ, and Jay Fliegelman's *Declaring Independence: Jefferson, Natural Language, and the Culture of Performance* (Stanford, Calif., 1993), a provocative study of TJ's rhetoric and its sources. The story of the Declaration's drafting is definitively recounted in Pauline Maier, *American Scripture: Making the Declaration of Independence* (New York, 1997). At first, TJ's authorship of the Declaration was not widely known or celebrated, as Robert M. S. McDonald shows in his "Jefferson & America: Episodes in Image Formation" (PhD. diss., University of North Carolina, 1998).

The best short survey of the history of the early republic is Norman K. Risjord's *Jefferson's America* (Madison, Wis., 1991). Marshall Smelser's *The Democratic Republic, 1801–1815* (New York, 1968) is the best introduction to the history of the Virginia Dynasty. But see also Henry Adams's classic *History of the United States During the Administrations of*

Thomas Jefferson and James Madison, 9 vols. (New York, 1891–6). The years of Federalist ascendancy preceding Jefferson's election are covered in great and illuminating detail in Stanley Elkins and Eric McKitrick, *The Age of Federalism* (New York, 1993). Important studies of Federalism provide a valuable counterpoint to our study of Republicanism. See particularly David Hackett Fischer, *The Revolution of American Conservatism: The Federalist Party in the Era of Jeffersonian America* (New York, 1964); Linda K. Kerber, *Federalists in Dissent: Imagery and Ideology in Jeffersonian America* (Ithaca, NY, 1970); James M. Banner, Jr., *To the Hartford Convention: The Federalists and the Origins of Party Politics in Massachusetts, 1789–1815* (New York, 1970); and the stimulating essays collected in Doron S. Ben-Atar and Barbara Oberg, eds., *Federalists Reconsidered* (Charlottesville, 1998).

The election results depicted in the maps at the end of the introduction were taken from Robert A. Diamond, ed., *Congressional Quarterly's Guide to US Elections* (Washington, 1975).

Chapter 1: The Republican Revolution

"The Revolution of 1800"

Historians have quarreled endlessly about how "revolutionary" TJ's "Revolution of 1800" really was. The most vigorous argument in the affirmative is Daniel Sisson, *The American Revolution of 1800* (New York, 1974). The "revolution" was most notable for its peaceful character, as Richard Hofstadter suggested in his influential *The Idea of a Party System: The Rise of Legitimate Opposition in the United States, 1780–1840* (Berkeley, Calif., 1969).

Important work on the "first party system" includes Joseph Charles, *The Origins of the American Party System: Three Essays* (Chapel Hill, NC, 1956); William Nisbet Chambers, *Political Parties in a New Nation* (New York, 1963); and Paul Goodman, "The First American Party System," in William

Nisbet Chambers and Walter Dean Burnham, eds., *The American Party Systems: Stages of Political Development* (New York, 1967), 56–89. The emergence of the "republican synthesis" in the 1960s and 1970s shifted scholarly attention away from institution-building to ideology and psychology. The best political history of the period in the republican mode is Richard Buel, Jr., *Securing the Revolution: Ideology in American Politics, 1789–1815* (Ithaca, NY, 1972). The most influential study of Republican ideology is Lance Banning's *The Jeffersonian Persuasion: Evolution of a Party Ideology* (Ithaca, NY, 1978).

As they focused on ideological appeal and popular response, scholars tended to underestimate the fragility of the union, and therefore the possibility of violence. For a valuable corrective, emphasizing the contingency of events and the anxieties of the protagonists, see James Roger Sharp, *American Politics in the Early Republic: The New Nation in Crisis* (New Haven, 1993). Joanne B. Freeman's brilliant *Affairs of Honor: Political Combat and Character in the Early American Republic* (New Haven, 2001) persuasively argues that the election itself was a massive "affair of honor," with the reputations of politicians as well as the survival of the union at issue.

The period of political and constitutional crisis leading up to TJ's election is further illuminated by James Morton Smith, *Freedom's Fetters: The Alien and Sedition Laws and American Civil Liberties* (Ithaca, NY, 1956), Alexander DeConde, *The Quasi-War: The Politics and Diplomacy of the Undeclared War with France, 1797–1801* (New York, 1966), and Stephen Kurtz, *The Presidency of John Adams: The Collapse of Federalism, 1795–1800* (Philadelphia, 1957). For a good explanation of the Jefferson–Burr deadlock in the Electoral College, see Tadahisa Kuroda, *The Origins of the Twelfth Amendment: The Electoral College in the Early Republic, 1787–1804* (Westport, Conn, 1994). The central role of the partisan press in the transformation of "public opinion" is comprehensively treated in Donald H. Stewart, *The Opposition Press of the Federalist Period* (Albany, NY, 1969) and Mark Augustus Smith, "Crisis, Unity, and Partisanship: The Road to the Sedition Act" (Ph.D. diss., University of Virginia,

1998). Jeffrey L. Pasley pursues the history of political editors over a longer period, demonstrating their crucial role for political party development. See his excellent *"The Tyranny of Printers": The Rise of Newspaper Politics in the Early American Republic* (Charlottesville, 2001).

TJ's First Inaugural Address offered a compelling definition of American national identity. This theme – and much of the discussion in the first section of this chapter – is anticipated and elaborated in Peter S. Onuf, *Jefferson's Empire: The Language of American Nationhood* (Charlottesville, 2000), 80–108. The best study of American nationalism is David Waldstreicher, *In the Midst of Perpetual Fetes: The Making of American Nationalism, 1776–1820* (Chapel Hill, NC, 1997). See also David M. Potter's important essay, "The Historian's Use of Nationalism and Vice Versa," in Don E. Fehrenbacher, ed., *History and Society: Essays of David M. Potter* (New York, 1973), 60–108; Paul C. Nagel, *This Sacred Trust: American Nationality, 1798–1898* (New York, 1971); and Wilbur Zelinsky, *Nation into State: The Shifting Symbolic Foundations of American Nationalism* (Chapel Hill, NC, 1988).

Republicans created problems for themselves in the 1790s when they began to criticize George Washington, "the father of his country." Washington remained an iconic figure for Federalists throughout this period, though Republicans joined in his apotheosis after his death in 1799. Important studies of Washington's symbolic role in American national consciousness include Garry Wills, *Cincinnatus: George Washington and the Enlightenment* (New York, 1984) and Paul Longmore, *The Invention of George Washington* (Berkeley, Calif.,1988). The crucial contemporaneous text is Mason Locke Weems, *The Life of Washington*, ed. Peter S. Onuf (Armonk, NY, 1996). Weems reprinted Washington's Farewell Address, in which the retiring president warned of the baneful effects of disunion. See Felix Gilbert, *To the Farewell Address: Ideas of Early American Foreign Policy* (Princeton, NJ, 1961).

The Republican Appeal

For a good introduction to the rise of Republicanism in Virginia and neighboring states see Norman K. Risjord, *Chesapeake Politics,1781–1800* (New York, 1978) and his *The Old Republicans: Southern Conservatism in the Age of Jefferson* (New York, 1965). The literature on the American revolution in Virginia is reviewed in Herbert Sloan and Onuf, "Politics, Culture, and the Revolution in Virginia," *Virginia Magazine of History and Biography*, 91 (1983), 259–84. For a vigorous, neo-progressive account, emphasizing the revolution's social dimensions, see Woody Holton, *Forced Founders: Indians, Debtors, Slaves, and the Making of the American Revolution in Virginia* (Chapel Hill, NC, 1999). Lance Banning's *The Sacred Fire of Liberty: James Madison and the Founding of the Federal Republic* (Ithaca, NY, 1995), offers illuminating perspectives on Virginia and national politics through the early 1790s, including an excellent account of the Richmond ratifying convention. We are indebted to Herbert E. Sloan's *Principle and Interest: Thomas Jefferson and the Problem of Debt* (New York, 1995) for insightful perspectives on the political economy – and psychology – of Virginia planters. Constantine Gutzman traces Virginians' thinking about their place in the union over a more extended period in "Old Dominion, New Republic: Making Virginia Republican, 1776–1840" (Ph.D. diss., University of Virginia, 1999). Republican fears of a revival of metropolitan power under the aegis of Federalism are elaborated in Lance Banning, *The Jeffersonian Persuasion: Evolution of a Party Ideology* (Ithaca, NY, 1978). For a political biography of the leading Republican polemicist see Robert E. Shalhope, *John Taylor of Caroline: Pastoral Republican* (Columbia, SC, 1980).

The Virginians' setbacks in the national political arena are gleefully recounted in Stanley Elkins and Eric McKitrick, *The Age of Federalism* (New York, 1993). Sloan's *Principle and Interest* includes good discussions of Jefferson's growing misgivings about Hamilton's financial plan and of his own role in the famous "Dinner Table Bargain" of 1790, trading federal assumption of state revolutionary debts for siting the new national capital in what would become Washington, DC. For further discussion of the capital location issue see Kenneth R. Bowling, *The Creation of Washington, DC: The Idea and Location of the American Capital* (Fairfax, Va., 1991).

Republicanism in the South and West

Thomas Perkins Abernethy provides a comprehensive history of *The South in the New Nation, 1789–1819* (Baton Rouge, La., 1961). For a good general introduction to civil conflict in the region, see Ronald Hoffman, "The 'Disaffected' in the Revolutionary South," in Alfred F. Young, *The American Revolution: Explorations in the History of American Radicalism* (DeKalb, Ill., 1976), 273–316; and the essays collected in Ronald Hoffman, Thad W. Tate, and Peter J. Albert, eds., *An Uncivil War: The Southern Backcountry during the American Revolution* (Charlottesville, 1985).

A spate of fine recent studies, including Joyce E. Chaplin, *An Anxious Pursuit: Agricultural Innovation and Modernity in the Lower South, 1730–1815* (Chapel Hill, NC, 1993) and Rachel N. Klein, *The Unification of a Slave State: the Rise of the Planter Class in the South Carolina Backcountry, 1760–1808* (Chapel Hill, NC, 1990), emphasizes the importance of sectional tensions in South Carolina. On slavery in Carolina see Robert Olwell, *Masters, Slaves, and Subjects: The Culture of Power in the South Carolina Low Country, 1740–1790* (Ithaca, NY, 1998), and Peter Coclanis, *The Shadow of a Dream: Economic Life and Death in the South Carolina Low Country* (New York, 1989). The best history of the revolution in the state is Jerome J. Nadelhaft, *The Disorders of War: The Revolution in South Carolina* (Orono, Maine, 1981). On the ratification of the Constitution see Robert M. Weir, "South Carolina: Slavery and the Structure of the Union," in Michael Allen Gillespie and Michael Lienesch, eds., *Ratifying the Constitution* (Lawrence, Kans., 1989), 201–34. James Haw's double biography of *John and Edward Rutledge of South Carolina* (Athens, Ga., 1997) outlines the state's early political history.

For a brilliant account of subsequent developments, see William W. Freehling, *Prelude to Civil War: The Nullification Controversy in South Carolina, 1816–1836* (New York, 1965).

Kenneth Coleman's *American Revolution in Georgia, 1763–1789* (Athens, Ga., 1958) is the standard account. The rapid ratification of the Constitution there is discussed in Edward J. Cashin, "Georgia: Searching for Security," in Gillespie and Lienesch, eds., *Ratifying the Constitution*, 93–116. For a fascinating account of the Yazoo controversy see Peter Magrath, *Yazoo: Law and Politics in the New Republic: The Case of Fletcher v. Peck* (Providence, RI, 1966). Risjord reviews North Carolina developments in his *Chesapeake Politics*. For North Carolina's belated ratification, see Michael Lienesch, "North Carolina: Preserving Rights," in *Ratifying the Constitution*, 343–67.

The most influential monograph on the history of the early west is Frederick Jackson Turner, *The Frontier in American History* (New York, 1920). Separatist tendencies were pronounced throughout the region, particularly south of the Ohio River. Andrew R. L. Cayton provides an able analysis of separatism in "'When Shall We Cease to Have Judases?' The Blount Conspiracy and the Limits of the 'Extended Republic,'" in Ronald Hoffman and Peter J. Albert, eds., *Launching the 'Extended Republic': The Federalist Era* (Charlottesville, 1996), 156–89; see also Cayton's suggestive "'Separate Interests' and the Nation-State: The Washington Administration and the Origins of Regionalism in the Trans-Appalachian West," *Journal of American History*, 79 (1992), 39–67. On new state movements generally see Peter S. Onuf, "Territories and Statehood," in Jack P. Greene, ed., *Encyclopedia of American Political History*, 3 vols. (New York, 1984), 3:1283–1304; Onuf, *The Origins of the Federal Republic: Jurisdictional Conflicts in the United States, 1775–1787* (Philadelphia, 1983); and Onuf, *Statehood and Union: A History of the Northwest Ordinance* (Bloomington, Ind., 1987). On Kentucky statehood see Patricia Watlington, *The Partisan Spirit: Kentucky Politics, 1779–1792* (New York, 1972) and Joan Wells Coward, *Kentucky in the New Republic: The Process of Constitution*

Making (Lexington, Ky., 1979). For an excellent social history of the state see Stephen Aron, *How the West Was Lost: The Transformation of Kentucky from Daniel Boone to Henry Clay* (Baltimore, Md., 1996). On Tennessee, see the classic account by Abernethy, *From Frontier to Plantation in Tennessee: A Study in Frontier Democracy* (Chapel Hill, NC, 1932). Robert Remini's magisterial *Andrew Jackson and the Course of American Empire, 1767–1821* (New York, 1944), the first volume in his three-volume biography, serves as an excellent introduction to Tennessee's turbulent politics in the early period. For a broader context, see Thomas D. Clark and John D. W. Guice, *Frontiers in Conflict: The Old Southwest, 1795–1830* (Albuquerque, N.Mex., 1989). Diplomatic developments played a central role in the region's history: see, particularly, Arthur Preston Whitaker, *The Spanish-American Frontier, 1783–1795: The Westward Movement and the Spanish Retreat in the Mississippi Valley* (Boston, 1927) and idem, *The Mississippi Question, 1795–1803: A Study in Trade, Politics, and Diplomacy* (New York, 1934). For the recurrence of the separatist threat during TJ's second administration, see Thomas Perkins Abernethy, *The Burr Conspiracy* (New York, 1954).

On the early history of the Old Northwest see John D. Barnhart's, *Valley of Democracy: The Frontier versus the Plantation in the Ohio Valley, 1775–1818* (Bloomington, Ind., 1953), which emphasizes the crucial significance of slavery for social and political development. Cayton and Onuf review more recent literature on the Old Northwest, providing a more skeptical account of the region's frontier history, in *The Midwest and the Nation: Rethinking the History of an American Region* (Bloomington, 1990). Cayton's fine history of early Ohio politics, *The Frontier Republic: Ideology and Politics in the Ohio Country, 1780–1825* (Kent, Ohio, 1986) has recently been supplemented by Donald J. Ratcliffe's authoritative *Party Spirit in a Frontier Republic: Democratic Politics in Ohio, 1793–1821* (Columbus, 1998). For a general history of the state, see R. Douglas Hurt, *The Ohio Frontier: Crucible of the Old Northwest, 1720–1830* (Bloomington, Ind., 1996).

Republicanism in the North and East

The best political history of the two most important middle colonies is Alan Tully, *Ideals, Interests, and Institutions in Colonial New York and Pennsylvania* (Baltimore, Md., 1994). On party conflict in the revolutionary and early national periods see Robert Brunhouse, *The Counter-Revolution in Pennsylvania, 1776–1790* (Philadelphia, 1942), and Richard Alan Ryerson, "Republican Theory and Partisan Reality in Revolutionary Pennsylvania: Toward a New View of the Constitutionalist Party," in Ronald Hoffman and Peter J. Albert, eds., *Sovereign States in an Age of Uncertainty* (Charlottesville, 1981), 95–133. Eric Foner offers an engaging portrait of the revolutionary radical who helped prepare the way for Republican mobilization in Pennsylvania in *Tom Paine and Revolutionary America* (New York, 1976). On the rise of Republicanism in Philadelphia, see Roland M. Baumann, "Philadelphia's Manufacturers and the Excise Taxes of 1794: The Forging of the Jeffersonian Coalition," *Pennsylvania Magazine of History and Biography*, 106 (1982), 509–30; and Kim T. Philips, "William Duane, Philadelphia's Democratic Republicans, and the Origins of Modern Politics," *Pennsylvania Magazine of History and Biography*, 101 (1977), 365–87. The east–west split was fundamental to Pennsylvania politics, as Thomas P. Slaughter shows in *The Whiskey Rebellion: Frontier Epilogue to the American Revolution* (New York, 1986), the best study of this crucial episode in state and national history.

Patricia U. Bonomi's *A Factious People: Politics and Society in Colonial New York* (New York, 1971) is the standard account of political conflict in that colony. For a good history of the revolution there, emphasizing political mobilization, see Edward Countryman, *A People in Revolution: The American Revolution and Political Society in New York, 1760–1790* (Baltimore, Md., 1981). Linda Grant De Pauw provides a comprehensive account of the ratification of the Constitution in *The Eleventh Pillar: New York State and the Federal Constitution* (Ithaca, NY, 1966). The leading study of Republicanism – in any of the states – is Alfred F. Young, *The Demo-cratic Republicans of New York: The Origins, 1763–1797* (Chapel Hill, NC, 1967). For an informative biography of the dominant political figure in New York, see John P. Kaminski, *George Clinton: Yeoman Politician of the New Republic* (Madison, Wis., 1993). The literature on New York City in the early republic is increasingly rich. Leading studies include: Sean Wilentz, *Chants Democratic: New York City and the Rise of the American Working Class, 1788–1850* (New York, 1984); and Paul Gilje, *The Road to Mobocracy: Popular Dis-order in New York City, 1763–1834* (Chapel Hil, NC, 1987). For a superb history of an upstate community that illuminates the early development of party competition, see Alan Taylor, *William Cooper's Town: Power and Persuasion on the Fron-tier of the Early Republic* (New York, 1996).

On the political history of revolutionary Massachusetts, see Richard D. Brown, *Revolutionary Politics in Massachusetts: The Boston Committees of Correspondence and the Towns, 1772–1774* (Cambridge, 1970); Stephen E. Patterson, *Politi-cal Parties in Revolutionary Massachusetts* (Madison, Wis., 1973); and Gregory H. Nobles, *Divisions Throughout the Whole: Politics and Society in Hampshire County, Massachu-setts, 1740–1775* (New York, 1983). Robert A. Gross's excel-lent history of revolutionary Concord, *The Minutemen and Their World* (New York, 1976), shows how the war trans-formed one Massachusetts community. For a comprehensive history of subsequent developments see Ronald P. Formisano, *The Transformation of Political Culture: Massachusetts Par-ties, 1790s–1840s* (New York, 1984). The best account of the Jeffersonians is Paul Goodman, *The Democratic-Republicans of Massachusetts: Politics in a Young Republic* (Cambridge, 1964). For the Federalists see Stephen E. Patterson, "The Roots of Massachusetts Federalism: Conservative Politics and Po-litical Culture before 1787," in Hoffman and Albert, eds., *Sovereign States in an Age of Uncertainty*, 31–61; and James M. Banner, Jr., *To the Hartford Convention: The Federalists and the Origins of Party Politics in Massachusetts, 1789–1815* (New York, 1970). George Athan Billias offers a good portrait of one of the leading Massachusetts Republicans in *Elbridge Gerry of Massachusetts: Founding Father and Republican Statesman* (New York, 1976). The rise of Republicanism on Massachusetts's eastern frontier is ably chronicled by Alan Taylor in *Liberty Men and Great Proprietors: The Revolutionary Settlement on the Maine Frontier, 1760–1820* (Chapel Hill, NC, 1990). Republican politicians were enterprising opportunists, Taylor shows, with little interest in challenging the existing social order.

Chapter 2: Little Republics

In this chapter we draw heavily on exciting new work in various related fields, particularly on the history of family and gender relations and on the construction of individual and collective identities. The common ground for the best work is an empirically grounded but theoretically sophisticated cultural history. Our debts to Jan Ellen Lewis (on contemporaneous conceptions of family, society, and polity), Joanne Freeman (on the early national political culture), David Waldstreicher (on the public sphere and national identity) and Richard Bushman (on elite and middle-class cultural aspirations and behavior) will be particularly conspicuous.

Republican Fathers

The best treatment of TJ's retirement years is Dumas Malone, *The Sage of Monticello*, vol. 6 of his *Jefferson and His Time*, 6 vols. (Boston, 1948–81); see pp. 233–82, 365–425, on the founding of the University. On the importance of education to the founding generation see Richard D. Brown, *The Strength of a People: The Idea of an Informed Citizenry in America, 1650–1870* (Chapel Hill, NC, 1996), esp. 49–118; Lorraine Smith Pangle and Thomas L. Pangle, *The Learning of Liberty: The Educational Ideas of the American Founders* (Lawrence, Kans., 1993); and the essays collected in James Gilreath, ed., *Thomas Jefferson and the Education of a Citizen* (Washington, DC, 1999). For a good brief discussion of TJ's educational ideas see Joseph Kett, "Education," in Merrill D. Peterson, ed., *Thomas Jefferson: A Reference Biography* (New York, 1986), 233–51. Merrill Peterson recounts the history of the Revisal of the Laws, including the Bill for the Diffusion of Knowledge, in his *Thomas Jefferson and the New Nation: A Biography* (New York, 1970), 97–165.

For the history of education in this period see Lawrence A. Cremin, *American Education: The National Experience, 1783–1876* (New York, 1980), and Carl F. Kaestle, *Pillars of the Republic: Common Schools and American Society, 1780–1860* (New York, 1983). Joseph F. Kett provides a broad perspective on the ethos of self-improvement in the early republic in his *The Pursuit of Knowledge Under Difficulties: From Self-improvement to Adult Education in America, 1750–1990* (Stanford, Calif., 1994). For the proposals of Benjamin Rush and other reformers see Frederick Rudolph, ed., *Essays on Education in the Early Republic* (Cambridge, Mass., 1965).

TJ's "ward republics" have attracted much attention from historians and political theorists. The most provocative and influential account is in theorist Richard K. Matthews's, *The Radical Politics of Thomas Jefferson: A Revisionist View* (Lawrence, Kans., 1984), esp. 77–95. Our interpretation has also been influenced by William J. K. Antholis, "Liberal Democratic Theory and the Transformation of Sovereignty" (Ph.D. diss., Yale University, 1993), esp. chapter 4 ("Thomas Jefferson and the American Dissolution of Sovereignty"). For further discussion see Peter S. Onuf, *Jefferson's Empire: The Language of American Nationhood* (Charlottesville, 2000), 117–21.

Joyce Appleby emphasizes TJ's appeal to farmers and other enterprising Americans in *Capitalism and a New Social Order: The Republican Vision of the 1790s* (New York, 1984) and in important essays collected in *Liberalism and Republicanism in the Historical Imagination* (Cambridge, Mass., 1992). She shows how the new ethos of "hope" was reflected in the life histories of post-revolutionary Americans in *Inheriting the Revolution: The First Generation of Americans* (Cambridge, Mass., 2000). Exponents of the "republican synthesis" have focused less on enterprisers' hopes and more on agrarian anxieties about threats to the virtue and independence of freeholding farmers; see particularly, Drew R. McCoy, *The Elusive Republic: Political Economy in Jeffersonian America* (Chapel Hill, NC, 1980). Though Appleby's "liberal" view of early American political economy is now ascendant, the republican interpretation has had a more profound impact on our understanding of gender, as we indicate below. Literary and cultural historians have been most helpful on patriarchy and generational relations. See particularly Jay Fliegelman, *Prodigals and Pilgrims: The American Revolution against Patriarchal Authority* (Cambridge, UK, 1982) and Melvin Yazawa, *From Colonies to Commonwealth: Familial Ideology and the Beginnings of the American Republic* (Baltimore, Md., 1985). For an insightful account of TJ's thinking about paternal authority see Harold Hellenbrand, *The Unfinished Revolution: Education and Politics in the Thought of Thomas Jefferson* (Newark, Del., 1990).

Population data is drawn from *Historical Statistics of the United States*. The literature on colonial New England demographic and social history is too voluminous to be discussed extensively here. For a good synthesis see James A. Henretta and Gregory H. Nobles, *Evolution and Revolution: American Society, 1600–1820* (Lexington, Mass., 1987); on the shortage of land, see Kenneth Lockridge, "Land, Population, and the Evolution of New England Society, 1630–1790," *Past and Present*, 39 (1968), 62–80. On responses to market penetration see the sources cited. For discussion of the social impact of the Revolution, see Gordon S. Wood, *The Radicalism of the American Revolution* (New York, 1992) esp. 243–70, and Wood, "Interests and Disinterestedness in the Making of the Constitution," in Richard Beeman et al., *Beyond Confederation: Origins of the Constitution and American National Identity* (Chapel Hill, NC, 1987), 69–109. On the progress of western settlement see Malcolm J. Rohrbough's two studies, *The Land Office Business: The Settlement and Administration of American Public Lands, 1789–1837* (New York, 1968) and *The Trans-Appalachian Frontier: People, Societies, and Institutions* (New York, 1978); and Andrew R. L. Cayton and

Peter S. Onuf, *The Midwest and the Nation: Rethinking the History of an American Region* (Bloomington, Ind., 1990).

Wives and Mothers: Fathers and Sons

For the history of women in revolutionary and early republican America, see Linda K. Kerber, *Women of the Republic: Intellect and Ideology in Revolutionary America* (Chapel Hill, NC, 1980). Several of the essays collected in Ronald Hoffman and Peter J. Albert, eds., *Women in the Age of the American Revolution* (Charlottesville, 1989), discuss property transmission and family structure. The development of family law over the nineteenth century, as Michael Grossberg shows in *Governing the Hearth: Law and Family in Nineteenth Century America* (Chapel Hill, NC, 1985), mitigated patriarchal authority and expanded the ambit of women's rights. Rosemarie Zagarri argues that revolutionary natural rights doctrine provided the conceptual foundation for women's rights in "The Rights of Man and Woman in Post-revolutionary America," *William and Mary Quarterly*, 55 (1998), 203–20.

Contemporaneous understandings of population growth are discussed in James H. Cassedy, *Demography in Early America: Beginnings of the Statistical Mind, 1600–1800* (Cambridge, Mass., 1969); see particularly chapter VII ("Virgin Land, Teeming Women"). See also. McCoy, *The Elusive Republic*, for a good discussion of Franklin's demography; see also McCoy, "Jefferson and Madison on Malthus: Population Growth in Jeffersonian Political Economy," *Virginia Magazine of History and Biography*, 88 (1980), 259–76. The best introduction to population theory in the early republic is James Russell Gibson, "Americans Versus Malthus: The Population Debate in the Early Republic" (Ph.D. diss., Clark University, 1982). For Spanish concerns about Anglo-American population growth see David J. Weber, *The Spanish Frontier in North America* (New Haven, 1992). James E. Lewis, Jr., discusses the implications of rapid westward settlement for American foreign policy in *The American Union and the Problem of Neighborhood: The United States and the Collapse of the Span-*

ish Empire, 1783–1829 (Chapel Hill, NC, 1998). On frontier settlers and guns, see the superb new study by Michael A. Bellesiles, *Arming America: The Origins of a National Gun Culture* (New York, 2000), esp. chapters 7–8.

On the spread of white population into Indian country and its justifications see the classic studies by Albert K. Weinberg, *Manifest Destiny: A Study in Nationalist Expansionism in American History* (Baltimore, Md., 1935) and Roy Harvey Pearce, *The Savages of America: A Study of the Indian and the Idea of Civilization* (Baltimore, Md., 1953). On TJ and the Indians see Bernard W. Sheehan, *Seeds of Extinction: Jeffersonian Philanthropy and the American Indian* (Chapel Hill, NC, 1973), Anthony F. C. Wallace, *Jefferson and the Indians: The Tragic Fate of the First Americans* (Cambridge, Mass., 1999), and Onuf, *Jefferson's Empire*, chapter 1. For a provocative reading of TJ's Notes, focusing on his anthropology, see James W. Ceaser, *Reconstructing America: The Symbol of America in Modern Thought* (New Haven, 1997), 19–53.

Our discussion of family, gender, and politics throughout this chapter relies heavily on the work of Jan Ellen Lewis, including "'The Blessings of Domestic Society': Thomas Jefferson's Family and the Transformation of American Politics," in Peter S. Onuf, ed., *Jeffersonian Legacies* (Charlottesville, 1993),109–46, and *The Pursuit of Happiness: Family and Values in Jefferson's Virginia* (New York, 1983). On "republican mothers," see Kerber, *Women of the Republic*, and on "republican wives," see Lewis, "The Republican Wife: Virtue and Seduction in the Early Republic," *William and Mary Quarterly*, 44 (1987), 689–721. Kerber and Lewis both illuminate the character of "female patriotism." The "deputy husband" theme is elaborated in Laurel Thatcher Ulrich, *Good Wives: Image and Reality in the Lives of Women in Northern New England, 1650–1750* (New York, 1982); for the experience of New England women in the early republic, see Ulrich's superb case study, *A Midwife's Tale: The Life of Martha Ballard, Based on Her Diary, 1785–1812* (New York, 1990). Cathy N. Davidson provides an excellent introduction to Judith

Sargent Murray, Susanna Rowson, and other female writers of the early republic in *Revolution and the Word: The Rise of the Novel in America* (New York, 1986); she also devotes an interesting chapter to William Wells Brown's *Power of Sympathy*.

For a balanced appraisal of TJ's indebtedness to Scottish moral philosophy see Jean M. Yarbrough, *American Virtues: Thomas Jefferson on the Character of a Free People* (Lawrence, Kans., 1998). Ari Helo's "Thomas Jefferson's Republicanism and the Problem of Slavery" (Ph.D. diss., Tampere University, 1999) includes an extended commentary on TJ's letter to Thomas Law as well as the best available discussion of Lord Kames's influence on his thinking. Our discussion of men's "capacity for feminine feeling" relies heavily on the work of Jan Lewis, cited above.

The concept of "virtue," supposedly central to the "classical republican" ethos has generated a vast literature. The most thorough account is Richard Vetterli and Gary Bryner, *In Search of the Republic: Public Virtue and the Roots of American Government* (Totowa, NJ, 1987). For an excellent discussion of Madison's speech to the Virginia Convention, see Lance Banning, "Some Second Thoughts on Virtue and the Course of Revolutionary Thinking," in Terence Ball and J. G. A. Pocock, eds., *Conceptual Change and the Constitution* (Lawrence, Kans., 1988), 194–212. On the feminization of virtue see the influential essay by Ruth Bloch, "The Gendered Meanings of Virtue in Revolutionary America," *Signs*, 13 (1987), 37–58.

The emergence of sentimentalism in literary culture is charted in works by Fliegelman and Davidson cited above. Gordon Wood's *Radicalism of the American Revolution* underscores the importance of sentimental sensibility for revolutionary republicans. The most ambitious effort to reinterpret national beginnings in sentimental terms is Andrew Burstein's *Sentimental Democracy: The Evolution of America's Romantic Self-Image* (New York, 1998).

Burstein's *The Inner Jefferson: Portrait of a Grieving Optimist* (Charlottesville, 1995) offers a compelling portrait of TJ as a sentimentalist. For further insight into TJ's family life see Jack McLaughlin, *Jefferson and Monticello: The Biography of a Builder* (New York, 1988); Elizabeth Langhorne, *Monticello: A Family Story* (Chapel Hill, NC, 1989); and Jan Ellen Lewis, "The White Jeffersons," in Jan Ellen Lewis and Peter S. Onuf, eds., *Sally Hemings and Thomas Jefferson: History, Memory, and Civic Culture* (Charlottesville, 1999), 127–60. For a sensitive account of contemporaneous Virginian responses to high mortality rates, see Lewis, *Pursuit of Happiness*, chapter 3 ("Death"). For a study of attitudes toward death in New England see David E. Stannard, *The Puritan Way of Death: A Study in Religion, Culture, and Social Change* (New York, 1977). See also David Hackett Fischer, *Growing Old in America*, expanded edn. (New York, 1978).

On the importance of "generations" for TJ see Herbert E. Sloan, "'The Earth Belongs in Usufruct to the Living,'" in Onuf, ed., *Jeffersonian Legacies*, 281–315, and *Principle and Interest: Thomas Jefferson and the Problem of Debt* (New York, 1995). See also Michael Grossberg, "Citizens and Families: A Jeffersonian Vision of Domestic relations and Generational Change," and Holly Brewer, "Beyond Education: Thomas Jefferson's 'Republican' Revision of the Laws Regarding Children," in Gilreath, ed., *Jefferson and the Education of a Citizen*, 3–27, 48–62; and Peter S. Onuf, "Liberty to Learn," in *Thomas Jefferson: Genius of Liberty* (New York, 2000), 138–43. Brewer's important essay, "Entailing Aristocracy in Colonial Virginia: 'Ancient Feudal Restraints' and Revolutionary Reform," *William and Mary Quarterly*, 54 (1997), 307–46, provides the essential context for understanding TJ's campaign against "aristocracy."

On the new regime in labor relations see Sharon V. Salinger, "Artisans, Journeymen, and the Transformation of Labor in Late Eighteenth-Century Philadelphia," *William and Mary Quarterly*, 40 (1983), 62–84. Gordon Wood discusses these broad developments in his account of the transition from "Monarchical" to "Republican" and then "Democratic" society in his *Radicalism of the Revolution*. The literature on early American political economy is reviewed in the next section.

Bonds of Brotherhood: The Associational Impulse

On the Declaration of Independence and family values, see Jay Fliegelman, *Declaring Independence: Jefferson, Natural Language, and the Culture of Performance* (Stanford, Calif., 1993) and *Prodigals and Pilgrims*. For a provocative psychological reading of independence see Winthrop D. Jordan, "Familial Politics: Thomas Paine and the Killing of the King, 1776," *Journal of American History*, 60 (1973–4), 294–308. Our discussion of honor culture is taken from the important new work of Joanne B. Freeman on the new nation's political culture. See her "Dueling as Politics: Reinterpreting the Burr-Hamilton Duel," *William and Mary Quarterly*, 53 (1996), 289–318; "Slander, Poison, Whispers, and Fame: Jefferson's 'Anas' and Political Gossip in the Early Republic," *Journal of the Early Republic*, 15 (1995), 25–57; and *Affairs of Honor: Political Combat and Character in the Early American Republic* (forthcoming, New Haven, 2001).

The most influential study of revolutionary print culture is Michael Warner, *Letters of the Republic: Publication and the Public Sphere in Eighteenth-Century America* (Cambridge, Mass., 1990). Richard D. Brown's *Knowledge is Power: The Diffusion of Information in Early America, 1700–1865* (New York, 1989) provides a good introduction to the communications media and contexts. On "the American republic of letters" see Robert A. Ferguson, *The American Enlightenment, 1750–1820* (Cambridge, Mass., 1997); Ferguson, *Law and Letters in American Culture* (Cambridge, Mass., 1984); Thomas Gustafson, *Representative Words: Politics, Literature, and the American Language, 1776–1865* (New York, 1992); and Burstein, *Sentimental Democracy*. On the political press see the superb new study by Jeffrey L. Pasley, *"The Tyranny of Printers": The Rise of Newspaper Politics in the Early American Republic* (Charlottesville, 2001); Pasley provides a valuable account of the career of William Duane, editor of the Philadelphia *Aurora*. A generous sampling of Duane's journalism has been collected in Richard N. Rosenfeld, *American Aurora: A Democratic-Republican Returns: The Suppressed*

History of our Nation's Beginnings and the Heroic Newspaper That Tried to Report It (New York, 1997). For a content analysis of the political press in the 1790s see Mark Augustus Smith, "Crisis, Unity, and Partisanship: The Road to the Sedition Act" (Ph.D. diss., University of Virginia, 1998).

We are indebted to David Waldstreicher, *In the Midst of Perpetual Fetes: The Making of American Nationalism, 1776–1820* (Chapel Hill, NC, 1997) for our understanding of construction of American national identity. Other studies of the political culture of nationalism include Len Travers, *Celebrating the Fourth: Independence Day and the Rites of Nationalism in the Early Republic* (Amherst, Mass., 1997) and Simon Newman, *Parades and Politics of the Street: Festive Culture in the Early American Republic* (Philadelphia, 1997). Much of this work has been inspired by Benedict Anderson, *Imagined Communities: Reflections on the Origin and Spread of Nationalism*, revised edn. (London and New York, 1991). The ideological divisions and political rhetoric of the 1790s are discussed in chapter 1 above.

The classic discussion of the associational impulse in America is Alexis de Tocqueville, *Democracy in America*, trans. Phillips Bradley, 2 vols. (New York, 1945). For a review of the literature, see John S. Gilkeson, "Voluntary Associations," in Jack P. Greene, ed., *Encyclopedia of American Political History: Studies of the Principal Movements and Ideas*, 3 vols. (New York, 1984), 3:1348–61. On voluntarism in this period, see Richard D. Brown, "The Emergence of Urban Society in Rural Massachusetts, 1760–1820," *Journal of American History*, 61 (1974–5), 29–51, and "The Emergence of Voluntary Associations in Massachusetts, 1760–1830," *Journal of Voluntary Action Research*, 2 (1973), 64–73. Albrecht Koschnik's study of civic life in Philadelphia, "Voluntary Associations, Political Culture, and the Public Sphere in Philadelphia, 1780–1830" (Ph.D. diss., University of Virginia, 2000) is the most ambitious attempt to date to contextualize associational activity in the early republic. See also Sam Bass Warner, *The Private City: Philadelphia in Three Periods of Its Growth* (Philadelphia, 1968). The literature for the later period, following

Tocqueville's lead, is much richer. See, for influential examples, Mary P. Ryan, *Cradle of the Middle Class: The Family in Oneida County, New York, 1790–1865* (New York, 1981), and *Civic Wars: Democracy and Public Life in the American City during the Nineteenth Century* (Berkeley, Calif., 1997). On the history of colonial cities see Carl Bridenbaugh, *Cities in Revolt: Urban Life in America, 1743–1776* (New York, 1955) and Gary B. Nash, *The Urban Crucible: Social Change, Political Consciousness, and the Origins of the American Revolution* (Cambridge, Mass., 1979); for civic and institutional development see also David J. Rothman, *The Discovery of the Asylum: Social Order and Disorder in the New Republic* (New York, 1971). Stephen C. Bullock's excellent new study, *Revolutionary Brotherhood: Freemasonry and the Transformation of the American Social Order* (Chapel Hill, NC, 1996), shows the importance of fraternal ties.

Andrew R. L. Cayton and Peter S. Onuf discuss social and cultural developments in the Old Northwest in *The Midwest and the Nation: Rethinking the History of an American Region* (Bloomington, Ind., 1990). For a good survey of American religious history see Sydney E. Ahlstrom, *A Religious History of the American People* (New Haven, 1972), esp. 385–509, and, for a provocative recent study, see Jon Butler, *Awash in a Sea of Faith: Christianizing the American People* (Cambridge, Mass., 1990). On disestablishment see Thomas J. Curry, *The First Freedoms: Church and State in America to the Passage of the First Amendment* (New York, 1986), and Stephen Botein, "Religious Dimensions of the Early American State" in Beeman et al., *Beyond Confederation*, 315–30. For the effects of voluntarism see Nathan O. Hatch, *The Democratization of American Christianity* (New Haven, 1989).

On the "expatriation" theme see John Phillip Reid, *The Authority of Rights*, vol. 1 of *Constitutional History of the American Revolution*, 4 vols. (Madison, Wis., 1986–93), 118–20. For Jefferson on this theme see H. Trevor Colbourn, *The Lamp of Experience: Whig History and the Intellectual Origins of the American Revolution* (Chapel Hill, NC, 1965); Charles A. Miller, *Jefferson and Nature: An Interpretation*

(Baltimore, Md., 1988). The most important study of revolutionary political thought, Bernard Bailyn's *The Ideological Origins of the American Revolution* (Cambridge, Mass., 1967), shows how provincial Anglo-Americans discovered their own "virtue." See also Jack P. Greene, *The Intellectual Construction of America: Exceptionalism and Identity from 1492 to 1800* (Chapel Hill, NC, 1993), and the essays collected in *Imperatives, Behaviors, and Identities: Essays in Early American Cultural History* (Charlottesville, 1992), most notably, "Search for Identity: An Interpretation of the Meaning of Selected patterns of Social Response in Eighteenth-Century America," 143–73. On Jefferson's provincialism see Onuf, *Jefferson's Empire*.

On the new national history see Lester H. Cohen, *The Revolutionary Histories: Contemporary Narratives of the American Revolution* (Ithaca, NY, 1980) and Freeman, *Affairs of Honor*, epilogue. See also Michael Kammen, *A Season of Youth: The American Revolution and the Historical Imagination* (New York, 1978). Kenneth A. Silverman's *A Cultural History of the American Revolution* (New York, 1976) is a good introduction to its subject. For the subsequent development of American culture see Lawrence J. Friedman, *Inventors of the Promised Land* (New York, 1975) and, on the appeal of the "genteel" and "respectable" culture emanating from the metropolis, Richard L. Bushman, *The Refinement of America: Persons, Houses, Cities* (New York, 1992). For an unsympathetic account of Noah Webster's cultural politics, see Richard M. Rollins, *The Long Journey of Noah Webster* (Philadelphia, 1980). Ambitious Americans continued to cultivate classical learning long after independence, as Kevin Brooks Sheets shows in "Et Tu, America? The Rise and Fall of Latin in Schools, Society, and the Culture of the Educated Man" (Ph.D. diss., University of Virginia, 2000).

On early American writers see Davidson, *Revolution and the Word*, and Michael T. Gilmore, "The Literature of the Revolutionary and Early National Periods," in Sacvan Bercovitch, ed., *The Cambridge History of American Literature*, vol. 1 (New York, 1994), 539–693. For Cooper, see Alan

Taylor's prize-winning *William Cooper's Town: Power and Persuasion on the Frontier of the Early American Republic*, 406–27; on Brown, see Steven Watts, *The Romance of Real Life : Charles Brockden Brown and the Origins of American Culture* (Baltimore, Md., 1994); and on the Connecticut Wits, see William C. Dowling, *Poetry and Ideology in Revolutionary Connecticut* (Athens, Ga., 1990). On TJ, see Lee Quinby, "Thomas Jefferson: The Virtue of Aesthetics and the Aesthetics of Virtue," *American Historical Review*, 87 (1982), 337–56. See also Leo Marx, *The Machine in the Garden: Technology and the Pastoral Ideal* (New York, 1964); Miller, *Jefferson and Nature*, and Pamela Regis, *Describing Early America: Bartram, Crèvecoeur, and the Rhetoric of Natural History* (DeKalb, Ill., 1992).

Max Weber's classic work on the culture of capitalism is *The Protestant Ethic and the Spirit of Capitalism*, trans. Talcott Parsons (1920; New York, 1958). On capitalist culture in colonial America see Stephen Innes, *Creating the Commonwealth: The Economic Culture of Puritan New England* (New York, 1995). Also see the essays collected in Thomas L. Haskell and Richard F. Teichgraeber III, *The Culture of the Market : Historical Essays* (New York, 1993). Steven Watts argues that the War of 1812 played a key role in consolidation of "liberal," capitalist culture in *The Republic Reborn: War and the Making of Liberal America* (Baltimore, Md., 1987). Anxious reformers identified excessive consumption of alcohol as the leading symptom of social disorder in the republic. See William J. Rorabaugh, *The Alcoholic Republic: An American Tradition* (New York, 1979). Richard Bushman shows the importance of Protestant religiosity to the culture of respectability in his *Refinement of America*. On the cultural imperatives of self-fashioning see John F. Kasson, *Rudeness and Civility: Manners in Nineteenth-Century Urban America* (New York, 1990).

On disestablishment in Virginia see Merrill D. Peterson and Robert C. Vaughan, eds., *The Virginia Statute for Religious Freedom: Its Evolution and Consequences* (New York, 1988). The best introduction to Jefferson's religious life is Eugene

Sheridan's introduction to *Jefferson's Extracts from the Bible: "The Philosophy of Jesus" and "The Life and Morals of Jesus,"* ed. Dickinson W. Adams, *The Papers of Thomas Jefferson*, 2nd ser. (Princeton, NJ, 1983); see also, Paul Conkin, "The Religious Pilgrimage of Thomas Jefferson," in Onuf, ed., *Jeffersonian Legacies*, 19–49, and Charles W. Sanford, *The Religious Life of Thomas Jefferson* (Charlottesville, 1984). Our discussion of TJ's attitude toward politics and family life relies heavily on Lewis, "'The Blessings of Domestic Society'."

Chapter 3: Pursuits of Happiness

Jeffersonian political economy is the subject of a rich, often contentious literature, to which our own analysis is indebted. Drew McCoy's *The Elusive Republic: Political Economy in Jeffersonian America* (Chapel Hill, NC, 1980) explores the connections between Republican economic thought and early American foreign policy. McCoy's influential book, including a superb account of the "four-stage theory" of human history developed by Scottish social theorists, has had a profound impact on contemporary historiography. But his argument that "classical republican" concerns about the loss of virtue and the inevitability of the republic's decline inspired TJ and Madison to promote westward expansion has been challenged (see Appleby's works, cited at the beginning of this essay, and Onuf, "Liberty, Development, and Union: Visions of the West in the 1780s," *William and Mary Quarterly*, 43 (1986),179–213). The most comprehensive – and sympathetic – treatment of Republican political economy is John R. Nelson, Jr., *Liberty and Property: Political Economy and Policymaking in the New Nation, 1789–1812* (Baltimore, Md., 1987). Other critics of Jeffersonian political economy include Forrest McDonald, whose *Alexander Hamilton: A Biography* (New York, 1979), offers an admiring account of the Hamiltonian alternative. Herbert Sloan, whose *Principle and Interest: Thomas Jefferson and the Problem of Debt* (New York, 1995) amply documents the limits of TJ's understanding of economics, even-handedly suggests that Hamilton also had his limits. The verdict on

Hamiltonian finance is mixed at best, as Sloan shows in "Hamilton's Second Thoughts: Federalist Finance Revisited" in Doron S. Ben-Atar and Barbara B. Oberg, eds., *Federalists Reconsidered* (Charlottesville, 1998), 61–76 For the mature reflections of one of the leading protagonists of the "republican synthesis" on the significance of clashing economic visions for party development see Lance Banning, "Political Economy and the Creation of the Federal Republic," in David T. Konig, ed., *Devising Liberty: The Conditions of Freedom in the Early American Republic* (Stanford, Calif., 1995), 11–49.

Jeffersonian commercial policy has been particularly controversial. The best study of TJ's thinking on foreign trade in the years before he drafted his famous "Report on the Privileges and Restrictions on the Commerce of the United States in Foreign Countries" (16 Dec. 1793) is Merrill Peterson's "Jefferson and Commercial Policy, 1783–1793," *William and Mary Quarterly*, 22 (1965), 584–610. TJ's fealty to free trade principles is persuasively challenged by John E. Crowley, *The Privileges of Independence: Neomercantilism and the American Revolution* (Baltimore, Md., 1993). The most blistering attacks on Republican foreign and commercial policy are Robert W. Tucker and David C. Hendrickson, *Empire of Liberty: The Statecraft of Thomas Jefferson* (New York, 1990) and Doron S. Ben-Atar, *The Origins of Jeffersonian Commercial Diplomacy* (New York, 1993). For a more sympathetic account, emphasizing the intractability of a hostile international environment, see Peter S. Onuf and Nicholas G. Onuf, *Federal Union, Modern World: The Law of Nations in an Age of Revolutions, 1776–1814* (Madison, Wis., 1993). The literature on foreign policy is discussed at greater length in the concluding part of this essay.

American Commonwealths

However farsighted – or reactionary – TJ's political economy may have been, it had little direct impact on the lives of most Americans. Law and government played a much more critical role at the state level. The classic studies of the Commonwealth tradition of activist state governments are Oscar Handlin and Mary Flug Handlin, *Commonwealth: A Study of the Role of Government in the American Economy: Massachusetts, 1774–1861* (Cambridge, Mass., 1947) and Louis Hartz, *Economic Policy and Democratic Thought: Pennsylvania, 1776–1800* (Cambridge, Mass., 1948). An excellent addition to this literature is L. Ray Gunn, *The Decline of Authority: Public Economic Policy and Political Develooment in New York State, 1800–1860* (Ithaca, NY, 1988). See also the stimulating essays in James Willard Hurst, *Law and the Conditions of Freedom in the Nineteenth Century United States* (Madison, Wis., 1956). Lawrence M. Friedman offers a useful overview of state activity in his *American Law: An Introduction*, rev. and updated edn. (New York, 1998).

On the locations of state and federal capitals see Rosemarie Zagarri, *The Politics of Size: Representation in the United States, 1776–1850* (Ithaca, NY, 1987); Rubil Morales, "Monuments, Markets, and Manners: The Making of the City of Washington, 1783–1837" (Ph.D. diss., Rutgers University, 1999). Kenneth R. Bowling, *The Creation of Washington, DC: The Idea and Location of the American Capital* (Fairfax, Va., 1991). On fears of monopoly and the uses of the corporate form, see Pauline Maier, "The Revolutionary Origins of American Corporation," *William and Mary Quarterly*, 50 (1993), 51–84. On banking see Bray Hammond, *Banks and Politics in America: From the Revolution to the Civil War* (Princeton, NJ, 1957).

Agriculture and Improvement

Our interpretation of the history of the early American economy relies heavily on Curtis P. Nettels, *The Emergence of a National Economy, 1775–1815* (New York, 1962) and, for the colonial and revolutionary periods, John J. McCusker and Russell Menard, *The Economy of British America, 1607–1789* (Chapel Hill, NC, 1985). For long-term developments see Douglass C. North, *The Economic Growth of the United*

States, 1790–1860 (1961; New York, 1966) and Stuart Bruckey, *The Roots of American Economic Growth, 1607–1861* (1965; New York, 1968). The classic histories of agriculture in the period are Percy Wells Bidwell and John I. Falconer, *History of Agriculture in the Northern United States, 1620–1860* (Washington, DC, 1925) and Lewis Cecil Gray, *History of Agriculture in the Southern United States to 1860*, 2 vols. (Washington, DC, 1933). On responses to the spread of markets see Jack P. Greene, *Pursuits of Happiness: The Social Development of Early Modern British Colonies and the Formation of American Culture* (Chapel Hill, NC, 1988); Daniel Vickers, "Competency and Competition: Economic Culture in Early America," *William and Mary Quarterly*, 47 (1990), 3–29; Allan Kulikoff, *The Agrarian Origins of American Capitalism* (Charlottesville, 1992); and Richard Lyman Bushman, "Markets and Composite Farms in Early America," *William and Mary Quarterly*, 55 (1998), 351–98. For a generous representation of the best new thinking on the political economy of the early republic, see Paul A. Gilje, ed., *Wages of Independence: Capitalism in the Early American Republic* (Madison, Wis., 1997).

We are indebted to John L. Larson's many essays on the political economy and constitutional implications of internal improvements. See particularly his "'Bind the Republic Together': National Union and the Struggle for a System of Internal Improvements," *Journal of American History*, 74 (1987), 363–87; "Jefferson's Union and the Problem of Internal Improvements," in Peter S. Onuf, ed., *Jeffersonian Legacies* (Charlottesville, 1993), 340–69, which includes a fine discussion of Madison's Bonus Bill Veto; and "'Wisdom Enough to Improve Them': Government, Liberty, and Inland Waterways in the Rising American Empire," in Ronald Hoffman and Peter J. Albert, eds., *Launching the 'Extended Republic': The Federalist Era* (Charlottesville, 1996), 223–48. We eagerly await the forthcoming publication of Larson's monograph on this important subject. To illuminate the contrasts between two different state development regimes, compare Lacy K. Ford's account of South Carolina in *Origins of*

Southern Radicalism: The South Carolina Upcountry, 1800–1860 (New York, 1988) with that of New York in Carol Sherriff, *The Artificial River: The Erie Canal and the Paradox of Progress, 1817–1862* (New York, 1996) and Evan Cornog, *The Birth of Empire: DeWitt Clinton and the American Experience, 1769–1828* (New York, 1998).

For TJ's interest in internal improvements see Joseph H. Harrison, Jr., "Sic et non: Thomas Jefferson and Internal Improvement," *Journal of the Early Republic*, 7 (1987), 335–49. For more on Gallatin, see Nelson's *Liberty and Property*, 100–33. Tench Coxe is the subject of an excellent biography by Jacob E. Cooke, *Tench Coxe and the Early Republic* (Chapel Hill, NC, 1978); on Coxe's Statement of the Arts and Manufactures see the discussion at 498–502. The impact of constitutional debates on improvements on the subsequent history of federalism is reviewed in Richard E. Ellis's *The Union at Risk: Jacksonian Democracy, States' Rights, and the Nullification Crisis* (New York, 1987). On state promotion of canals see Carter Goodrich, *Government Control of Canals and Railroads, 1800–1890* (New York, 1960) and the "Commonwealth" studies cited above.

The Politics of Development

For a discussion of the importance of political economic issues to the ratification controversy see Cathy D. Matson and Peter S. Onuf, *A Union of Interests: Political and Economic Thought in Revolutionary America* (Lawrence, Kans., 1990). The most comprehensive history of trade policy is Vernon G. Setser, *The Commercial Reciprocity Policy of the United States* (Philadelphia, 1937). For an elaboration of our interpretation of TJ and commerce, see Peter S. Onuf, *Jefferson's Empire: The Language of American Nationhood* (Charlottesville, 2000), 70–5, 85–93. The literature on TJ's commercial policy is reviewed at the beginning of this section; on foreign policy generally, see the next section.

Slavery, Commerce, and the State

All studies of the early American economy emphasize the centrality of slave-produced export staples. The scholarship on slavery in the early republic is burgeoning. For a fine synthesis, with extensive citations to recent work, see Ira Berlin, *Many Thousands Gone: The First Two Centuries of Slavery in North America* (Cambridge, Mass., 1998), esp. 217–357. See also the essays collected in Berlin and Ronald Hoffman, eds., *Slavery and Freedom in the Age of the American Revolution* (Charlottesville, 1983). The leading study of slavery as an ideological problem is David Brion Davis, *The Problem of Slavery in the Age of Revolution, 1779–1823* (Ithaca, NY, 1975); see also Jan Ellen Lewis's insightful essay "The Problem of Slavery in Southern Discourse," in David Thomas Konig, ed., *Devising Liberty: Preserving and Creating Freedom in the New American Republic* (Stanford, Calif., 1995), 265–97.

On slavery in Virginia see also Robert McColley, *Slavery and Jeffersonian Virginia*, 2nd edn. (Urbana, Ill., 1973); Douglas R. Egerton, *Gabriel's Rebellion: The Virginia Slave Conspiracies of 1800 and 1802* (Chapel Hill, NC, 1993); and James Sidbury, *Plowshares into Swords: Race, Rebellion, and Identity in Gabriel's Virginia, 1730–1810* (New York, 1997). For provocative essays on TJ and slavery and on slavery and the Constitution see Paul Finkelman, *Slavery and the Founders: Race and Liberty in the Age of Jefferson* (Armonk, NY, 1996). The best study of TJ and his slaves is Lucia C. Stanton, "'Those Who Labor for My Happiness': Thomas Jefferson and his Slaves," in Onuf, ed., *Jeffersonian Legacies*, 147–80. For scholarly responses to TJ's liaison with his slave Sally Hemings see Jan Ellen Lewis and Peter S. Onuf, eds., *Sally Hemings and Thomas Jefferson: History, Memory, and Civic Culture* (Charlottesville, 1999). Our interpretation of TJ's thinking on the problem of slavery is further elaborated in Onuf, *Jefferson's Empire*, 147–88. The spread of the plantation regime is well discussed in Berlin, *Many Thousands Gone*, and in the literature on the southern states in the first section of this essay. For the Carolinians' Atlantic orientation see Joyce E. Chaplin, *An*

Anxious Pursuit: Agricultural Innovation and Modernity in the Lower South, 1730–1815 (Chapel Hill, NC, 1993).

Indian Lands and American Prosperity

The history of the westward expansion of white settlement is comprehensively surveyed in Malcolm J. Rohrbough, *The Trans-Appalachian Frontier: People, Societies, and Institutions, 1775–1850* (New York, 1978). See also Francis S. Philbrick, *The Rise of the West, 1754–1830* (New York, 1965). The best study of land speculation and jurisdictional controversies in the revolutionary period is Thomas Perkins Abernethy, *Western Lands and the American Revolution* (New York, 1937) and Jack M. Sosin, *The Revolutionary Frontier, 1763–1783* (New York, 1967). The political dimensions of land claims and acquisition are discussed at the national level in Malcolm J. Rohrbough, *The Land Office Business: The Settlements and Administration of American Public Lands, 1789–1837* (New York, 1968), as well as in Peter S. Onuf, *The Origins of the Federal Republic: Jurisdictional Conflicts in the United States, 1775–1787* (Philadelphia, 1983), and Onuf, *Statehood and Union: A History of the Northwest Ordinance* (Bloomington, Ind., 1987). The role of land speculation is discussed specifically in Jeffrey P. Brown and Andrew R. L. Cayton, eds., *The Pursuit of Public Power: Political Culture in Ohio, 1787–1861* (Kent, Ohio, 1994). Urbanization was crucial to the progress of frontier development, as Richard Wade shows in *The Urban Frontier: The Rise of Western Cities* (Cambridge, Mass., 1959). The lived experiences of those effected by the successive regimes of speculation and development are discussed in two fine recent works, John Mack Faragher, *Daniel Boone: The Life and Legend of an American Pioneer* (New York, 1992) and Elizabeth A. Perkins, *Border Life: Experience and Memory in the Revolutionary Ohio Valley* (Chapel Hill, NC, 1998). That such concerns were not simply trans-Appalachian ones is reflected in Alan Taylor's *William Cooper's Town:* Power and Persuasion on the Frontier of the Early Republic (New York, 1996) and *Liberty Men and Great Proprietors: The Revolutionary Settlement on the Maine Frontier, 1760–1820* (Chapel Hill, NC, 1990), as well as Michael A. Bellesiles, *Revolutionary Outlaws: Ethan Allen and the Struggle for Independence on the Early American Frontier* (Charlottesville, 1993).

The subject of Indian–white relations during the revolutionary and early national periods has spawned an extensive literature in recent years. The work about which the historiography turns is Richard White, *The Middle Ground: Indians, Empires, and* Republics in the Great Lakes Region, 1650–1815 (Cambridge, Mass., 1991). Other major studies include Colin G. Calloway, *Crown and Calumet: British–Indian Relations, 1783–1815* (Norman, Okla., 1987); Daniel K. Richter and James H. Merrell, eds., *Beyond the Covenant Chain: The Iroquois and Their Neighbors in Indian North America, 1600–1800* (Syracuse, NY, 1987); Gregory Evans Dowd, *A Spirited Resistance: The North American Indian Struggle for Unity, 1745–1815* (Baltimore, Md., 1992); Calloway, *The American Revolution in Indian Country: Crisis and Diversity in Native American Communities* (Cambridge, Mass., 1995); and Eric Hinderaker, *Elusive Empires: Constructing Colonialism in the Ohio Valley, 1673–1800* (Cambridge, Mass., 1997). For further discussion of the history and culture of Indian diplomacy in the early republic, see the next section.

Toward a New American System

The changes in the economy and society of the United States following the War of 1812 are outlined in Charles Sellers's provocative but sometimes problematic *The Market Revolution: Jacksonian America, 1815–1846* (New York, 1991). Sellers highlights the nationalism of the young National Republicans in the postwar period, particularly in chapters 2 and 3. A more thorough discussion of the lineaments of Henry Clay's nationalism and desire to fund a national system of internal improvements can be found in Maurice G. Baxter, *Henry Clay and the American System* (Lexington, Ky., 1995).

On Clay generally see Robert V. Remini, *Henry Clay: States-man for the Union* (New York, 1991). Merrill Peterson's *The Great Triumvirate: Webster, Clay, and Calhoun* (New York, 1987) includes a good account of John C. Calhoun's early nationalism, as well as the relationship between Calhoun and Clay.

That the period after 1815 saw the rise of a recognizably modern world is the great theme of Paul Johnson, *The Birth of the Modern: World Society, 1815–1830* (New York, 1991). In *Europe Under Napoleon, 1799–1815* (London, 1996), Michael Broers argues that the modern nineteenth century had its origins in the Napoleonic period, and specifically in Napoleon's Europe-wide systems of administrative reorganization and conscription.

Chapter 4: Federal Republic and Extended Union

This chapter combines one of the most dynamic areas of recent historical investigation – early American constitutional history and the history of the federal union – with a field that has suffered from a dearth of scholarship of late – early American diplomatic history. Key to our understanding of the constitutionalism of this period are works which emphasize and explore the contingent nature of the American federal union. We draw heavily on Jack P. Greene, *Peripheries and Center: Constitutional Development in the Extended Polities of the British Empire and the United States, 1607–1788* (Athens, Ga., 1986); Peter S. Onuf, *Origins of the Federal Republic: Jurisdictional Controversies in the United States, 1775–1787* (Philadelphia, 1983); and Cathy D. Matson and Peter S. Onuf, *A Union of Interests: Political and Economic Thought in Revolutionary America* (Lawrence, Kans., 1990). Further insight on the question of the federal union can be found in the essays in Terence Ball and J. G. A. Pocock, eds., *Conceptual Change and the Constitution* (Lawrence, Kans., 1988), particularly Pocock's "States, Republics, and Empires: The American Founding in Early Modern Perspective," at 55–77; and in Peter B. Knupfer, *The Union as It Is: Constitutional Union-*

ism and Sectional Compromise (Chapel Hill, NC, 1991). For discussion of the Jeffersonian Republicans' conceptions of the union, see Peter S. Onuf, *Jefferson's Empire: The Language of American Nationhood* (Charlottesville, 2000) and Lance Banning, *The Sacred Fire of Liberty: James Madison and the Founding of the Federal Republic* (Ithaca, NY, 1995).

Reginald Horsman's *The Diplomacy of the New Republic, 1776–1815* (Arlington Heights, Ill., 1985) offers a good brief treatment of early American diplomatic history. For more detailed accounts see Lawrence S. Kaplan, *Colonies into Nation: American Diplomacy, 1763–1801* (New York, 1972) and Bradford Perkins, *The Creation of a Republican Empire, 1776–1865*, vol. 1 of *The Cambridge History of American Foreign Relations* (New York, 1993). The starting point for all historians of early American diplomatic history remains the magisterial and influential corpus of Samuel Flagg Bemis. Generally, one should consult *A Diplomatic History of the United States*, 4th edn. (New York, 1955). Also covering this entire period is Bemis's *John Quincy Adams and the Foundations of American Foreign Policy* (1949; Westport, Conn., 1981). Other older works also remain useful, including Felix Gilbert, *The Beginnings of American Foreign Policy: To the Farewell Address* (New York, 1961) and Paul A. Varg, *Foreign Policies of the Founding Fathers* (East Lansing, Mich., 1963). We are particularly indebted to the classic studies of Gerald Stourzh, *Benjamin Franklin and American Foreign Policy*, 2nd edn. (1954; Chicago, 1969), and *Alexander Hamilton and Republican Government* (Stanford, Calif., 1970).

The debate over the Republicans' motives and methods in shaping foreign policy – and Jefferson's in particular – has been quite acrimonious. Much of the disagreement centers around the question of whether Jefferson was, in political scientists' parlance, an "idealist" or a "realist." The argument that Jefferson, while motivated by the ideals of natural law and republicans, fashioned foreign policy in a realistic manner, has been made recently by Lawrence S. Kaplan, in *"Entangling Alliances with None": American Foreign Policy in the Age of Jefferson* (Kent, Ohio, 1987), and more briefly by

Walter LaFeber in his essay, "Jefferson and an American Foreign Policy," in Peter S. Onuf, ed., *Jeffersonian Legacies* (Charlottesville, 1993), 370–91. The most recent and thorough critical analyses of Jefferson as an idealist are Robert W. Tucker and David C. Hendrickson, *Empire of Liberty: The Statecraft of Thomas Jefferson* (Oxford, 1990) and Doron S. Ben-Atar, *The Origins of Jeffersonian Commercial Policy and Diplomacy* (New York, 1993).

Our discussion of the origins of early American thinking about diplomacy is rooted in a understanding that the founders were heavily influenced by Enlightenment writers who discussed the question of sovereignty and who explored the interactions of sovereigns within the literature of the law of nations. Our starting point is Peter S. Onuf and Nicholas G. Onuf, *Federal Union, Modern World: The Law of Nations in an Age of Revolutions, 1776–1814* (Madison, Wis., 1993), which begins with a treatment of Emmerich de Vattel's influence, at 1–29. The best account of the role of the law of nations on the thinking of the founders is Andrew C. Lenner, *The Federal Principle in American Law and Politics, 1790–1833* (Madison, Wis., 2000).

The emergence of the concept of sovereignty and of the law of nations are key themes in the history of political thought. The most relevant study for our purposes is Richard Tuck, *The Rights of War and Peace: Political Thought and the International Order from Grotius to Kant* (New York, 1999). On the development of early modern political thought, see J. G. A. Pocock, *The Machiavellian Moment: Florentine Political Thought and the Atlantic Republican Tradition* (Princeton, NJ, 1975); Quentin Skinner, *The Foundations of Modern Political Thought*, 2 vols. (Cambridge, UK, 1978); and Tuck, *Natural Rights Theories: Their Origins and Development* (Cambridge, 1979). See also the essays collected in in J. H. Burns and Mark Goldie, eds., *The Cambridge History of Political Thought, 1450–1700* (Cambridge, 1991) and David Wootton, ed., *Republicanism, Liberty, and Commercial Society, 1649–1776* (Stanford, Calif., 1994).

The Federal Union as a Diplomatic Imperative

The best study of the diplomatic context of the American Revolution is Jonathan R. Dull's *A Diplomatic History of the American Revolution* (New Haven, 1985). Samuel Flagg Bemis, *The Diplomacy of the American Revolution* (1957; Westport, Conn., 1983) also remains valuable. On the French Alliance see William C. Stinchcombe, *The American Revolution and the French Alliance* (Syracuse, NY, 1969) and the essays in Ronald Hoffman and Peter J. Albert, eds., *Diplomacy and Revolution: The Franco-American Alliance of 1778* (Charlottesville, 1981). The negotiations leading to the Treaty of Paris are described in intricate detail in Richard B. Morris, *The Peacemakers: The Great Powers and American Independence* (New York, 1965), which should be supplemented by the essays in Hoffman and Albert, eds., *Peace and the Peacemakers: The Treaty of 1783* (Charlottesville, 1985). Of great value, both descriptively and analytically, is James H. Hutson, *John Adams and the Diplomacy of the American Revolution* (Lexington, Kentucky, 1980). For Thomas Jefferson's career as a diplomat, and his mission to France, see Lawrence S. Kaplan, *Jefferson and France: An Essay on Politics and Political Ideas* (New Haven, 1967).

On the diplomatic challenges faced by the Confederation see Frederick W. Marks, III, *Independence on Trial: Foreign Affairs and the Making of the Constitution* (Baton Rouge, La., 1973). Histories of congressional politics help explain the course of American diplomacy. See Merrill Jensen, *The New Nation: A History of the United States During the Confederation, 1781–1789* (New York, 1950); Forrest McDonald, *E Pluribus Unum: The Formation of the American Republic, 1776–1790* (1965; Indianapolis, 1979); and, most notably, Jack N. Rakove, *The Beginnings of National Politics: An Interpretive History of the Continental Congress* (New York, 1979). That the union was at risk in 1787 is discussed in Matson and Onuf, *Union of Interests*. James Madison's changing view of the union is summarized in Lacy K. Ford, Jr., "Inventing the Concurrent Majority: Madison, Calhoun, and the

Problem of Majoritarianism in American Political Thought," in *Journal of Southern History*, 60 (1994), 19–58, while his opinions on foreign policy are discussed in Drew R. McCoy, "Republicanism and American Foreign Policy: James Madison and the Political Economy of Commercial Discrimination, 1789 to 1794," in *William and Mary Quarterly*, 3rd ser., 31 (1974), 633–46.

American diplomatic and cultural relations with North Africa are explored in Robert J. Allison, *The Crescent Obscured: The United States and the Muslim World, 1776–1815* (New York, 1995).

Questions of Sovereignty

The general literature on Indian–white relations is discussed in the previous section. The most recent history of the history of the Creek Indians is Claudio Saunt, *A New Order of Things: Property, Power, and the Transformation of the Creek Indians, 1733–1816* (New York, 1999). Other important works include Kathryn E. Holland Braund, *Deerskins and Duffels: The Creek Indian Trade with Anglo-America, 1685–1815* (Lincoln, Neb., 1993); J. Leitch Wright, Jr., *Creeks and Seminoles: The Destruction and Regeneration of the Muscogulge People* (Lincoln, Neb., 1986) and William S. Coker and Thomas D. Watson, *Indian Traders of the Southeastern Spanish Borderlands : Panton, Leslie & Company and John Forbes & Company, 1783–1847* (Gainesville, Fla., 1986). A provocative discussion of Creek history can be found in Joel W. Martin, *Sacred Revolt: The Muskogees' Struggle for a New World* (Boston, 1991). The major personality in the annals of Creek diplomacy, Alexander McGillivray, is the subject of John Walton Caughey, *McGillivray of the Creeks* (Norman, Okla., 1938); on McGillivray's father see Edward J. Cashin, *Lachlan McGillivray, Indian Trader: The Shaping of the Southern Colonial Frontier* (Athens, Ga., 1992). The events of the Treaty of New York are summarized in J. Leitch Wright, "Creek-American Treaty of 1790: Alexander McGillivray and the Diplomacy of the Old Southwest," *Georgia Historical Quarterly*, 51 (1967), 379–400.

Henry Knox's Indian policy is analyzed in a excellent essay by Bernard W. Sheehan, "The Indian Problem in the Northwest: From Conquest to Philanthropy," in Hoffman and Albert, eds., *Launching the "Extended Republic:" The Federalist Era* (Charlottesville, 1996), 190–222, which builds on Sheehan's earlier analysis of attitudes and governments policies towards American Indians in *Seeds of Extinction: Jeffersonian Philanthropy and the American Indian* (Chapel Hill, NC, 1973). Jefferson's Indian policy is further analyzed in Onuf, *Jefferson's Empire*, 18–52. The most recent contribution to this discussion, which Sheehan began, is Anthony F. C. Wallace, *Jefferson and the Indians: The Tragic Fate of the First Americans* (Cambridge, Mass., 1999). More general discussions of the Indian in the American consciousness can be found in Philip J. Deloria, *Playing Indian* (New Haven, 1998) and Robert F. Berkhofer, Jr.'s, classic *The White Man's Indian: Images of the American Indian from Columbus to the Present* (New York, 1978).

Indian treaty-making is analyzed as a system in Dorothy V. Jones, *License for Empire: Colonialism by Treaty in Early America* (Chicago, 1982); Francis Jennings, ed., *The History and Culture of Iroquois Diplomacy: An Interdisciplinary Guide to the Treaties of the Six Nations and Their League* (Syracuse, NY, 1985); and Francis Paul Prucha, *American Indian Treaties: The History of a Political Anomaly* (Berkeley, Calif., 1994). For an excellent study of the culture of Indian diplomacy in a specific location see James H. Merrell's *Into the American Woods: Negotiators on the Pennsylvania Frontier* (New York, 1999).

Our discussion of concerns about the treaty-making power in the Constitution is indebted to Jack N. Rakove's insightful "Solving a Constitutional Puzzle: The Treatymaking Clause as a Case Study," in *Perspectives in American History*, new ser., 1 (1984), 233–81, which illuminates the difficulties in interpreting the clause that have stemmed from its problematic and obscure origins.

There are many accounts of the diplomatic affairs of the 1790s. Jerald A.Combs, *The Jay Treaty: Political Battleground of the Founding Fathers* (Berkeley, Calif., 1970) is valuable, as are Harry Ammon, *The Genet Mission* (New York, 1973) and Alexander DeConde, *Entangling Alliance: Politics and Diplomacy Under George Washington* (Durham, NC, 1958). Samuel Flagg Bemis's two monumental studies, *Jay's Treaty: A Study in Commerce and Diplomacy* (New Haven, 1962) and *Pinckney's Treaty: America's Advantage from Europe's Distress, 1783–1800* (New Haven, 1960) offer a wonderful starting point for students of the two treaties. George A. Phelps, *George Washington and American Constitutionalism* (Lawrence, Kans., 1993) and Stanley Elkins and Eric McKitrick, *The Age of Federalism* (New York, 1993) offer a broader perspective on the period's diplomacy.

The best accounts of the events surrounding the Quasi-War with France are Alexander DeConde, *The Quasi-War: The Politics and Diplomacy of the Undeclared War with France, 1797–1801* (New York, 1966) ; William C. Stinchcombe, *The XYZ Affair* (Westport, Conn., 1980); and Albert H. Bowman, *The Struggle for Neutrality: Franco-American Diplomacy During the Federalist Era* (Knoxville, Tenn., 1974). On the Adams presidency generally see Ralph A. Brown, *The Presidency of John Adams* (Lawrence, Kans., 1975) and Stephen Kurtz, *The Presidency of John Adams: The Collapse of Federalism, 1795–1800* (Philadelphia, 1957). For an affecting portrait of Adams in retirement see Joseph Ellis, *Passionate Sage: The Character and Legacy of John Adams* (New York, 1993).

Extended Union

The diplomacy of the Jefferson administrations is discussed in a number of works. For the Louisiana Purchase, see Alexander DeConde, *This Affair of Louisiana* (New York, 1976), as well as the account found in George Dangerfield's biography of Robert Livingston, *Chancellor Robert Livingston of New York, 1746–1813* (New York, 1960). Also valuable, both for the Louisiana Purchase and subsequent diplomacy, is the narrative in Harry Ammon's biography of Monroe, *James Monroe: The Quest for National Identity* (New York, 1971 and Charlottesville, 1990). American diplomacy with Great Britain is ably discussed in Bradford Perkins, *The First Rapprochement: England and the United States, 1795–1805* (Philadelphia, 1955) and *Prologue to War: England and the United States, 1805–1812* (Berkeley, Calif., 1961), while relations with France following the Louisiana treaty are handled in Clifford L. Egan, *Neither Peace nor War: Franco-American Relations, 1803–1812* (Baton Rouge, La., 1983). An important interpretation of the Jefferson administration's response to the international crisis of the Napoleonic wars that led to the embargo is Burton Spivak, *Jefferson's English Crisis: Commerce, Embargo, and the Republican Revolution* (Charlottesville, 1979).

An excellent account of the origins, progress, and effects of the War of 1812, with an eye to the policy goals of the Republican administrations, is J. C. A. Stagg, *Mr. Madison's War: Politics, Diplomacy, and Warfare in the Early American Republic, 1783–1830* (Princeton, NJ, 1983). Also valuable are Donald R. Hickey, *The War of 1812: A Forgotten Conflict* (Urbana, Ill., 1989) and classic accounts by Reginald Horsman, *The Causes of the War of 1812* (Philadelphia, 1962) and *The War of 1812* (New York, 1969). Federalist resistance to Republican war measures is recounted in James M. Banner, Jr., *To the Hartford Convention: The Federalists and the Origins of Party Politics in Massachusetts* (New York, 1970). The question of whether the War of 1812 was motivated by the desire to facilitate westward expansion is a controversial one, begun by Julius W. Pratt in *The Expansionists of 1812* (New York, 1925). A recent discussion of the issue, brought about by the discovery of new evidence, can be found in J. C. A. Stagg, "Between Black Rock and a Hard Place: Peter B . Porter's Plan for an American Invasion of Canada in 1812," *Journal of the Early Republic*,19 (1999), 385–422. The peace negotiations leading to the Treaty of Ghent are narrated in Fred L. Engleman, *The Peace of Christmas Eve* (New York, 1962).

"An Example of a Free System"

The postwar period – the "Era of Good Feelings" – has its own body of historiography, which grows at the same steady rate as that of the Age of Jefferson. However, the diplomatic history of the period has generally been overlooked. A notable exception to this trend, which expertly links questions of diplomacy and union, is James E. Lewis, Jr., *American Union and the Problem of Neighborhood: The United States and the Collapse of the Spanish Empire* (Chapel Hill, NC, 1998). Lewis's idea have influenced our discussion of the events of this period. Other useful discussions of American diplomatic history during this period can be found in Ernest R. May, *The Making of the Monroe Doctrine* (Cambridge, Mass., 1975); Bradford Perkins, *Castlereagh and Adams: England and the United States, 1812–1823* (Berkeley, Calif., 1964) and Bemis's *John Quincy Adams and American Foreign Policy*.

Good surveys of the political history of the postwar period include Harry Watson, *Liberty and Power: The Politics of Jacksonian America* (New York, 1990); George Dangerfield, *The Awakening of American Nationalism, 1815–1828* (New York, 1965); Merrill Peterson, *The Great Triumvirate: Webster, Clay, and Calhoun* (New York, 1987); and Robert V. Remini, *The Life of Andrew Jackson* (New York, 1988). For Madison's veto of the Bonus Bill, see John L. Larson, "Jefferson's Union and the Problem of Internal Improvements," in Peter S. Onuf, ed., *Jeffersonian Legacies* (Charlottesville, 1993), 340–69. For a discussion of the politics of internal improvements, see Maurice G. Baxter, *Henry Clay and the American System* (Lexington, Ky., 1995).

The most thorough discussion of the Missouri debates and compromises is Glover Moore, *The Missouri Controversy, 1819–1821* (Lexington, Ky., 1953). Jefferson's response to Missouri is discussed in Onuf, *Jefferson's Empire*, 109–46, as well as in John Chester Miller, *The Wolf by the Ears: Thomas Jefferson and Slavery* (New York, 1977), 221–33. Madison's thinking during his retirement is expertly handled in Drew R. McCoy, *The Last of the Fathers: James Madison and the Republican Legacy* (New York, 1989).

Index

MIL